MICROSOFT®

WINDOWS 8

Nita Rutkosky
Pierce College at Puyallup,
Puyallup, Washington

Denise Seguin
Fanshawe College,
London, Ontario

Audrey Roggenkamp
Pierce College at Puyallup,
Puyallup, Washington

Ian Rutkosky
Pierce College at Puyallup,
Puyallup, Washington

Paradigm
PUBLISHING

St. Paul

Contents

Managing Editor	Christine Hurney
Director of Production	Timothy W. Larson
Production Editor	Sarah Kearin
Cover and Text Designer	Leslie Anderson
Copy Editor	Sid Korpi, Proof Positive Editing
Design and Production Specialists	Jack Ross and Sara Schmidt Boldon
Testers	Desiree Carvel; Ann E. Mills, Ivy Tech Community
	College of Indiana, Indianapolis, IN; Brienna McWade
Indexer	Terry Casey
VP & Director of Digital Projects	Chuck Bratton
Digital Project Manager	Tom Modl

Windows® SECTION 1
Exploring Windows 8

Skills

- Navigate the Windows 8 Start screen
- Navigate the Windows 8 desktop
- Perform actions using the mouse, such as point, click, double-click, and drag
- Start and close a program
- Open and close a window
- Shut down Windows 8
- Move a window
- Minimize, maximize, and restore a window
- Stack and cascade windows
- Use the snap feature to position windows on the desktop
- Change the date and time
- Use components of a dialog box
- Adjust the volume using the Speaker slider bar
- Customize the Taskbar
- Use the Help and Support feature
- Turn on the display of file extensions

Projects Overview

Your department at Worldwide Enterprises has received new computers with the Windows 8 operating system. You will explore the Windows 8 Start screen and desktop; open, close, and manipulate windows; open a program; customize the Taskbar; explore the online help for Windows 8; and turn on the display of file extensions.

Activity 1.1

Exploring the Windows 8 Start Sceen

When you turn on your computer, the Windows 8 operating system loads and the Windows 8 Start screen displays on your monitor. The Windows 8 Start screen contains tiles you can use to open programs or access features within Windows 8. By default, the Windows 8 Start screen displays tiles for the most commonly used applications and features. Display all of the applications installed on your computer by right-clicking a blank area of the Start screen and then clicking the All apps icon that displays in the lower right corner of the screen. Windows 8 includes a Charm bar containing five buttons you can use to perform tasks such as searching apps, sharing apps, and shutting down the computer. Display the Charm bar by hovering the mouse over the upper or lower right corner of the screen.

Project

Tutorial 1.1
Exploring the Windows 8 Start Screen

Your department has received new computers with Windows 8 installed. You decide to take some time to explore the Windows 8 Start sceen to familiarize yourself with this new operating system.

1 Complete the step(s) needed to display the Windows 8 Start screen.

Check with your instructor to determine the specific step(s) required to display the Windows 8 Start screen on your computer. If you are at school, you may need a user name and password to log on to the computer system. When Windows 8 starts, you will see a Start screen similar to the one shown in Figure 1.1. Your Start screen may contain additional tiles or have a different background than the one shown in Figure 1.1.

2 Move your mouse and notice how the corresponding pointer moves in the Windows 8 Start screen.

The *mouse* is a device that controls the pointer that identifies your location on the screen. Move the mouse on your desk (preferably on a mouse pad) and the pointer moves on the screen. For information on mouse terms, refer to Table 1.1 and for information on mouse icons, refer to Table 1.2.

FIGURE 1.1 Windows 8 Start Screen

current user

tiles

Click this tile to display the Windows 8 desktop.

scroll bar

zoom out

TABLE 1.1 Mouse Terms and Actions

Term	Action
point	Position the mouse pointer on the desired item.
click	Quickly tap the left button on the mouse once.
right-click	Quickly tap the right button on the mouse once.
double-click	Tap the left mouse button twice in quick succession.
drag	Press and hold down the left mouse button, move the mouse pointer to a specific location, and then release the mouse button.

TABLE 1.2 Mouse Icons

Icon	Description
I	The mouse appears as an I-beam pointer in a program screen in which you enter text (such as Microsoft Word) and also in text boxes. You can use the I-beam pointer to move the insertion point or select text.
↖	The mouse pointer appears as an arrow pointing up and to the left (called the *arrow pointer*) on the Windows desktop and also in other program title bars, menu bars, and toolbars.
↘↗ ↕↔	The mouse pointer becomes a double-headed arrow (either pointing left and right, up and down, or diagonally) when performing certain functions, such as changing the size of a window.
✛	Select an object in a program, such as a picture or image, and the mouse pointer displays with a four-headed arrow attached. Use this four-headed arrow pointer to move the object left, right, up, or down.
↖	When you position the mouse pointer inside selected text in a document (such as a Microsoft Word document) and then drag the selected text to a new location in the document, the pointer displays with a gray box attached, indicating that you are moving the text.
↖○	When a request is being processed or a program is being loaded, the mouse pointer may display with a moving circle icon beside it. The moving circle means "please wait." When the process is completed, the moving circle disappears.
☝	When you position the mouse pointer on certain icons or hyperlinks, it turns into a hand with a pointing index finger. This image indicates that clicking the icon or hyperlink will display additional information.

(3) Click the Desktop tile in the Start screen.

> The desktop is the main screen in Windows 8. Different tools and applications can be opened on the desktop, similar to how different tools, documents, and items can be placed on a desk.

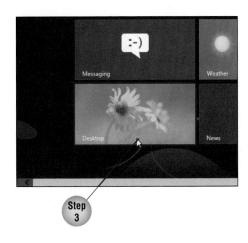

Step 3

continues

4 Position the mouse in the upper right corner of the desktop screen until the Charm bar displays.

> The Charm bar contains five buttons you can use to access different features and tools in Windows 8.

5 With the Charm bar displayed, click the Start button to return to the Start screen.

> Alternatively, you can return to the Start screen by positioning the mouse pointer in the lower left corner of the desktop until a Start screen thumbnail displays and then clicking the left mouse button.

6 Right-click in a blank area of the Start screen and then click the All apps icon that appears in the lower right corner of the screen.

> The Windows 8 Start screen displays the most commonly used applications and features. Display all applications (grouped in categories) in the Start screen if you cannot find a desired application.

7 Click the Calculator tile that displays in the *Windows Accessories* section.

> Clicking the Calculator tile causes the Calculator tool to open and display on the desktop.

8 Close the Calculator by clicking the Close button ⊠ that displays in the upper right corner of the program.

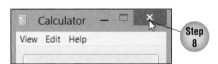

9 Complete Steps 4 and 5 to return to the Start screen.

10 Click the Internet Explorer tile.

> Certain applications, such as Internet Explorer, can be opened in the Start screen as well as on the desktop. Applications opened in the Start screen have been optimized to be used on touch devices.

11 Close Internet Explorer by positioning the mouse pointer at the top of the screen until the pointer turns into a hand, holding down the left mouse button, dragging the mouse pointer to the bottom of the screen, and then releasing the left mouse button.

> Closing applications in the Windows 8 Start screen is different than closing applications on the desktop. Dragging an application down to the bottom of the screen closes it, while dragging an application to the left or right portion of the screen resizes the application and positions it on the side to which it was dragged.

In Brief
Start Program
1. Display Windows 8 Start screen.
2. Click desired program tile.

Shut Down Windows
1. Display Charm bar.
2. Click Settings button.
3. Click Power tile.
4. Click *Shut down*.

12 Display the Charm bar by positioning the mouse in the upper right corner of the screen and then click the Settings button on the Charm bar.

> The Settings button contains options for changing Windows 8 settings. It also contains the controls to shut down the computer.

13 Click the Power tile located toward the bottom of the Settings panel.

14 Click the *Shut down* option at the pop-up list that displays.

> The Power tile contains three options. The *Sleep* option turns off the monitor and hard drives to conserve power. The *Shut down* option turns off the computer, and the *Restart* option turns off the computer and then restarts it.

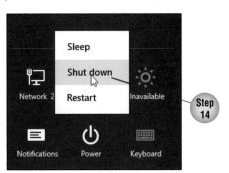

Need Help?

Check with your instructor before shutting down Windows 8. If you are working in a computer lab at your school, a shared computer lab policy may prevent you from shutting down the computer. In this case, proceed to the next activity.

In Addition

Putting the Computer to Sleep

In Windows 8, Sleep mode saves all of your work and places the computer in a low power state by turning off the monitor and hard drive. A light on the outside of the computer case blinks or turns a different color to indicate Sleep mode is active. Wake up the computer by pressing the Power button on the front of the computer case, or by moving the mouse. After you log on, the screen will display exactly as you left it when you activated Sleep mode. Sleep mode causes Windows to automatically save your work, whereas shutting down does not.

Activity 1.2

Exploring the Windows 8 Desktop

The Windows 8 desktop can be compared to the top of a desk in an office. A person places necessary tools—such as pencils, pens, paper, files, or a calculator—on his or her desktop to perform functions. Similarly, the Windows 8 desktop contains tools for operating the computer. These tools are logically grouped and placed in dialog boxes or windows that can be accessed using the icons located on the desktop. The desktop is the most common screen in Windows 8 and is the screen in which most applications and tools will open and run.

Project You decide to take some time to explore the Windows 8 desktop to familiarize yourself with this important screen of the operating system.

Tutorial 1.2
Exploring the
Windows 8 Desktop

1. If necessary, turn on the power to your computer to start Windows. At the Windows 8 Start screen, click the Desktop tile.

    When the Windows 8 Start screen is displayed, you will see a screen similar to the one in Figure 1.1 on page 2. When your Windows desktop displays, it may contain additional icons or have a different background than the desktop shown in Figure 1.2 below.

2. Move the mouse pointer to the bottom right corner of the desktop where the current day and time display at the right side of the Taskbar. After approximately one second, a pop-up box appears with the current day of the week as well as the current date.

    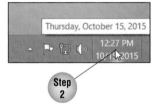

    To identify the location of the Taskbar, refer to Figure 1.2.

3. Position the mouse pointer on the Recycle Bin icon and then double-click the left mouse button.

    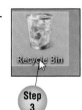

    Icons provide an easy method for opening programs or documents. Double-clicking the *Recycle Bin* icon displays the Recycle Bin window. When you open a program, a defined work area, referred to as a ***window***, appears on the screen.

FIGURE 1.2 Windows 8 Desktop

Recycle Bin icon

Position the mouse pointer here to access the Start screen.

Taskbar

4 Close the Recycle Bin window by clicking the Close button that displays in the upper right corner of the window.

In Brief
Display Windows 8 Desktop
Click Desktop tile.

5 Position the mouse pointer in the lower left corner of the screen until the Start screen thumbnail displays and then click the right mouse button.

When you right-click the Start screen thumbnail, a pop-up list displays with various options. You can use these options to access computer and operating system management features such as the Control Panel, Task Manager, and Device Manager.

6 Click the *System* option in the pop-up list to display information about your computer in a new window.

Your computer's information will appear in the System window. This information can be useful when determining if your computer is capable of running advanced software, or when you want to upgrade hardware such as RAM or a processor.

Step 6

Programs and Features
Power Options
Event Viewer
System
Device Manager
Disk Management
Computer Management
Command Prompt
Command Prompt (Admin)

Task Manager
Control Panel
File Explorer
Search
Run

Desktop

7 Close the System window by clicking the Close button that displays in the upper right corner of the window.

8 Right-click in a blank area of the desktop (not on an icon or the Taskbar).

A shortcut menu will display with various options you can use to manage files and/or change the way the desktop appears on your monitor.

9 Click the *Personalize* option at the shortcut menu.

The Personalization window contains options such as the Desktop Background, Color, Sounds, and Screen Saver, which you can customize.

10 Close the Personalization window by clicking the Close button in the upper right corner of the window.

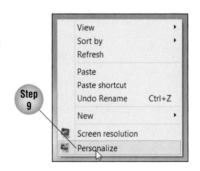

Step 9

View ▶
Sort by ▶
Refresh

Paste
Paste shortcut
Undo Rename   Ctrl+Z

New ▶

Screen resolution
Personalize

In Addition

Changing the Appearance of Windows 8

You can change the appearance of Windows 8 with options that display when you right-click a blank area of the desktop. Click the *Personalize* option at the shortcut menu if you want to change the Windows theme, desktop background, color, sounds, or screen saver. You can also change how the desktop icons and mouse pointers display. Click the *Screen resolution* option at the shortcut menu if you want to change the screen resolution, the monitor orientation, or the size of text or other items. The Screen Resolution window also contains controls for setting up multiple displays. Customizing how Windows 8 appears on your monitor by increasing the size of certain elements or changing certain colors can make Windows easier to use.

Activity 1.3

Opening and Manipulating Windows

When you open a program, a defined work area, referred to as a *window*, appears on the screen. You can move a window on the desktop and change the size of a window. The top of a window is called the Title bar and generally contains buttons at the right side for closing, minimizing, maximizing, and/or restoring the size of the window. More than one window can be open at a time, and open windows can be cascaded or stacked. When a window is moved to the left or right side of the screen, the Snap feature in Windows 8 causes it to "stick" to the edge of the screen. When the window is moved to the top of the screen, the window is automatically maximized, and when a maximized window is dragged down, the window is automatically restored down.

Project You decide to continue your exploration of the Windows 8 desktop by opening and manipulating windows.

Tutorial 1.3
Opening and Using Windows

1 At the Windows 8 desktop, double-click the Recycle Bin icon.

This opens the Recycle Bin window on the desktop. If the Recycle Bin window fills the entire desktop, click the Restore Down button, which is the second button from the right (immediately left of the Close button) in the upper right corner of the window.

Step 1

2 Move the window on the desktop. To do this, position the mouse pointer on the window's Title bar (the bar along the top of the window), hold down the left mouse button, drag the window to a different location on the desktop, and then release the mouse button.

3 Position the mouse pointer in the lower left corner of the desktop to display the Start screen thumbnail, click the right mouse button, and then click the *File Explorer* option in the pop-up list.

If the Computer window fills the entire desktop, click the Restore Down button in the upper right corner of the window. You now have two windows open on the desktop—Computer and Recycle Bin.

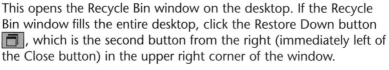
Step 3

Programs and Features
Power Options
Event Viewer
System
Device Manager
Disk Management
Computer Management
Command Prompt
Command Prompt (Admin)

Task Manager
Control Panel
File Explorer
Search
Run

Desktop

4 Make sure the Title bar of the Recycle Bin window is visible (if not, move the Computer window) and then click the Recycle Bin Title bar.

Clicking the Recycle Bin Title bar makes the Recycle Bin window active and moves it in front of the Computer window.

5 Minimize the Recycle Bin window to the Taskbar by clicking the Minimize button (located toward the right side of the Recycle Bin Title bar).

The minimized Recycle Bin window is positioned behind the File Explorer button (displays as a group of file folders) on the Taskbar. Notice the File Explorer button now appears with another button stacked behind it.

Step 5

6 Minimize the Computer window to the Taskbar (behind the File Explorer button) by clicking the Minimize button located at the right side of the Title bar.

7 Move the pointer over the File Explorer button at the left side of the Taskbar.

> The two minimized windows are stacked behind the File Explorer button. Resting the pointer on the File Explorer button causes a thumbnail preview of each window to display.

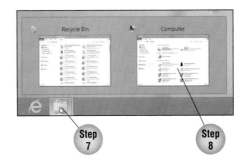

Step 7

Step 8

8 Click the thumbnail preview for the Computer window to redisplay the window on the desktop.

9 Rest the pointer over the File Explorer button on the Taskbar and then click the thumbnail preview for the Recycle Bin window.

10 Drag the Title bar for the Recycle Bin window to the top of the desktop and then release the mouse button.

> Dragging a window to the top of the desktop causes the window to automatically maximize when you release the mouse button. The Snap feature allows you to resize a window by dragging the window to the edge of a screen. You can also maximize the window by clicking the Maximize button ☐ adjacent to the Close button at the right side of the Title bar.

11 Drag the Title bar for the Recycle Bin window down from the top of the desktop to restore the window to its previous size before it was maximized.

12 Right-click a blank, unused section of the Taskbar and then click *Show windows stacked* at the shortcut menu.

> The Taskbar shortcut menu provides three options to display windows: *Cascade windows,* which places the windows in a fanned, single stack with the title bar of each open window visible; *stacked,* which places windows in a horizontal stack with a portion of each window visible; or *side by side,* which places open windows next to each other.

Toolbars	▶
Cascade windows	
Show windows stacked	
Show windows side by side	
Show the desktop	
Task Manager	
✔ Lock all taskbars	
Properties	

Step 12

13 Drag the Recycle Bin window off the right edge of the screen and then release the mouse button. When you release the mouse button, the window resizes to fill one-half the width of the screen.

14 Drag the Computer window off the left edge of the screen and then release the mouse button. When you release the mouse button, the window resizes to fill the remaining width of the screen.

15 Close each of the two windows by clicking the Close button ☒ located at the right side of the Title bar.

In Brief

Move Window
1. Position mouse pointer on window Title bar.
2. Hold down left mouse button.
3. Drag window to desired position.
4. Release mouse button.

Stack Windows
1. Right-click an unused section of Taskbar.
2. Click *Show windows stacked* at shortcut menu.

Cascade Windows
1. Right-click an unused section of Taskbar.
2. Click *Cascade windows* at shortcut menu.

In Addition

Sizing a Window

Using the mouse, you can increase or decrease the size of a window. To change the width, position the mouse pointer on the border at the right or left side of the window until the mouse turns into a left-and-right-pointing arrow. Hold down the left mouse button, drag the border to the right or left, and then release the mouse button. Complete similar steps to increase or decrease the height of the window using the top or bottom borders. To change the width and height of the window at the same time, position the mouse pointer at the left or right corner of the window until the pointer turns into a diagonally pointing, double-headed arrow and then drag in the desired direction to change the size.

Activity 1.4

Exploring the Taskbar, Charm Bar, and Dialog Box Components

The bar that displays at the bottom of the desktop is called the *Taskbar* and it is divided into three sections: the Start screen area, the task button area, and the notification area. Position the mouse in the Start screen area to display the Start screen thumbnail. Open programs display as task buttons in the task button area of the Taskbar. The notification area displays at the right side of the Taskbar and contains a clock and the program icons for programs that run in the background on your computer. You can right-click a blank, unused portion of the Taskbar to display a shortcut menu with options for customizing the Taskbar. The bar that displays at the right side of the desktop when the mouse pointer is positioned in the upper or lower right corner of the desktop is called the *Charm bar*. Click buttons in the Charm bar to access common operating system features. Some settings are changed in a window called a *dialog box*. Dialog boxes contain similar features such as tabs, text boxes, and option buttons that you can use to change settings.

Project

Worldwide Enterprises

SNAP

Tutorial 1.4
Exploring the Taskbar and the Charm Bar

As you continue exploring Windows 8, you want to learn more about the features available on the Taskbar.

1. At the Windows 8 desktop, click the current time that displays at the far right side of the Taskbar and then click the <u>Change date and time settings</u> hyperlink in the pop-up box.

   Figure 1.3 identifies the components of the Taskbar. Clicking the current time and then clicking the <u>Change date and time settings</u> hyperlink causes the Date and Time dialog box to display. Refer to Table 1.3 on the next page for information on dialog box components. Each listed component will not be present in every dialog box.

2. Check to make sure the correct date and time display in the Date and Time dialog box.

   If the date is incorrect, click the Change date and time button. At the Date and Time Settings dialog box, click the correct date in the calendar box. If necessary, use the left- or right-pointing arrows to change the calendar display to a different month. To change the time, double-click the hour, minutes, or seconds and then type the correct entry or use the up- or down-pointing arrows to adjust the time. Click OK when finished.

3. Click the Additional Clocks tab located toward the top of the Date and Time dialog box.

   At this tab, you can add the ability to show a second clock when you hover over or click the current time in the Taskbar. For example, you could show the current time for Cairo, Egypt, in addition to the current time for your time zone.

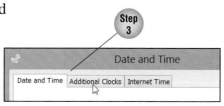

Step 3

Date and Time

Date and Time | Additional Clocks | Internet Time

FIGURE 1.3 Taskbar

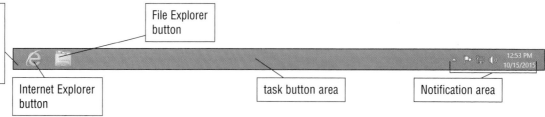

Position the mouse pointer here to access the Start screen.

File Explorer button

Internet Explorer button

task button area

Notification area

TABLE 1.3 Possible Dialog Box Components

Name	Image	Function
tabs	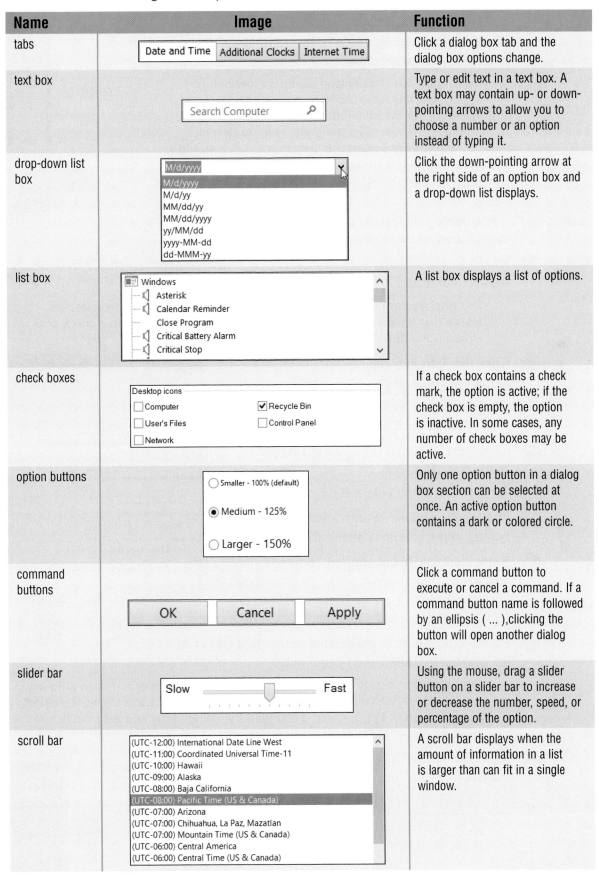	Click a dialog box tab and the dialog box options change.
text box		Type or edit text in a text box. A text box may contain up- or down-pointing arrows to allow you to choose a number or an option instead of typing it.
drop-down list box		Click the down-pointing arrow at the right side of an option box and a drop-down list displays.
list box		A list box displays a list of options.
check boxes		If a check box contains a check mark, the option is active; if the check box is empty, the option is inactive. In some cases, any number of check boxes may be active.
option buttons		Only one option button in a dialog box section can be selected at once. An active option button contains a dark or colored circle.
command buttons		Click a command button to execute or cancel a command. If a command button name is followed by an ellipsis (...),clicking the button will open another dialog box.
slider bar		Using the mouse, drag a slider button on a slider bar to increase or decrease the number, speed, or percentage of the option.
scroll bar		A scroll bar displays when the amount of information in a list is larger than can fit in a single window.

continues

4 Click the OK button to close the Date and Time dialog box.

5 Position the mouse pointer on the Speakers button 🔊 located toward the right side of the Taskbar and then click the left mouse button.

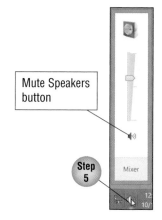

> Clicking the Speakers button causes a slider bar to display. Use this slider bar to increase or decrease the volume. Click the Mute Speakers button located at the bottom of the slider bar if you want to turn off the sound. If the Speakers button is not visible on the Taskbar, click the up-pointing arrow located near the left side of the notification area. This expands the area to show hidden icons.

Mute Speakers button

Step 5

6 After viewing the Speakers slider bar, click in a blank, unused area on the desktop to hide the slider bar.

7 Right-click in a blank, unused section of the Taskbar and then click *Properties* at the shortcut menu.

> This displays the Taskbar Properties dialog box with the Taskbar tab selected. Notice that the dialog box contains check boxes. A check mark in a check box indicates that the option is active.

8 Click the *Auto-hide the taskbar* check box to insert a check mark.

9 Click the Apply button located toward the bottom of the dialog box.

Step 8

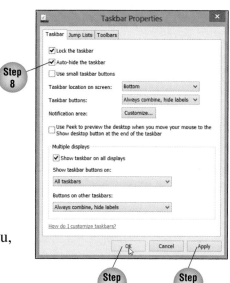

10 Click the OK button to close the Taskbar Properties dialog box.

> Notice that the Taskbar is no longer visible.

11 Display the Taskbar by moving the mouse pointer to the bottom of the desktop.

12 Right-click in a blank, unused section of the Taskbar, click *Properties* at the shortcut menu, click the *Auto-hide the taskbar* check box to remove the check mark, and then click OK.

Step 10   Step 9

13 Position the mouse pointer in the upper right corner of the desktop to display the Charm bar.

> The Charm bar displays transparently until the mouse pointer is moved onto any area of the bar, which activates the bar. When the Charm bar is active, it changes from transparent to black, and a box with the current time and date displays in the lower left corner of the screen.

14 Make the Charm bar active by moving the mouse onto the bar and then click the Search button.

> Clicking the Search button opens the Windows 8 Start screen and makes the search text box active. You can search for applications, settings, or files by clicking the desired option below the search text box.

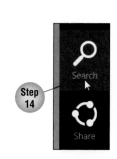

Step 14

15 Type **snipping tool** in the search text box.

> Notice that Windows 8 actively narrows the search results in the *Apps* section of the screen as you type.

Step 15

16 Press the Enter key on the keyboard.

> Pressing the Enter key opens the Snipping Tool in a new window on the desktop. If the search does not return a match for what you typed in the text box, a list of possible results will display.

17 Close the Snipping Tool window by clicking the Close button in the upper right corner of the window.

18 Make the Charm bar active and then click the Settings button.

19 At the Settings panel, click the *Change PC settings* option located at the bottom of the panel.

> When you click the *Change PC settings* option in the Settings panel, the PC settings screen displays. This screen contains a variety of options for changing the settings of your computer. These options are grouped into categories that display at the left side of the PC settings screen.

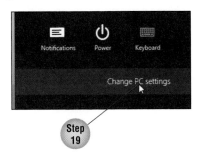

Step 19

20 Close the PC settings screen by positioning the mouse pointer at the top of the screen until it turns into a hand, holding down the left mouse button, dragging the PC settings screen to the bottom of the screen until it dims, and then releasing the left mouse button.

> In Windows 8, certain applications and tools open in the Start screen instead of in a window on the desktop. To close applications or tools that open in the Start screen, drag the top of the screen to the bottom of the screen until it becomes dim and then release the mouse button.

In Brief

Display Date and Time Dialog Box
1. Click current time at right side of Taskbar.
2. Click <u>Change date and time settings</u>.

Display Speakers Slider Bar
Click Speakers button on Taskbar.

Display Taskbar Properties Dialog Box
1. Right-click an unused section on Taskbar.
2. Click *Properties* at shortcut menu.

In Addition

Managing Devices Using the Charm Bar

The Charm bar contains the Devices button 🔲, which you can use to manage devices plugged into your computer. Click the Devices button on the Charm bar and the Devices panel displays at the right side of the screen. Devices plugged into your computer display as a list in the Devices panel.

Click a device in the Devices list to display options for a particular device. Devices that are commonly listed in the Devices panel are monitors, projectors, and other peripheral devices that may be plugged into your computer.

Activity 1.5

Getting Help in Windows; Displaying File Extensions

Windows 8 includes an on-screen reference guide, called Windows Help and Support, that provides information, explanations, and interactive help on learning Windows features. The Windows Help and Support feature contains complex files with hypertext that can be clicked to display additional information. Display the Windows Help and Support window by right-clicking a blank area of the Start screen, clicking the All apps icon and then clicking the Help and Support tile in the Windows System section. You can also press F1 at the desktop and the Windows Help and Support window will display with information on your current task. At the Windows Help and Support window, you can perform such actions as choosing a specific help topic, searching for a keyword, and displaying a list of help topics.

Project

You decide to use the Windows Help and Support feature to learn how to pin an application to the Taskbar. You also want to find out how to turn on the display of file extensions.

Worldwide Enterprises

Tutorial 1.5
Getting Help
in Windows 8

1. Display the Windows 8 Start screen, right-click a blank area of the screen, and then click the All apps icon.

2. Use the horizontal scroll bar at the bottom of the screen to display the *Windows System* section and then click the Help and Support tile.

3. At the Windows Help and Support window with the insertion point positioned in the search text box, type **taskbar** and press Enter.

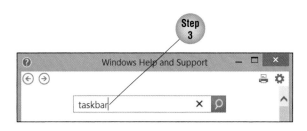

4. Click the How to use the taskbar hyperlink in the search results list.

5. Scroll down the Windows Help and Support window and then read the information under the heading *Pin an app to the taskbar*.

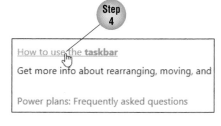

You will open and then pin the Snipping Tool application to the Taskbar in the following steps.

6. Open the Snipping Tool from the Windows 8 Start screen or by using the Charm bar to conduct a search for the Snipping Tool application.

7. Return to the Windows Help and Support window by clicking the Windows Help and Support button on the Taskbar.

8. Follow the instructions in the *Pin an app to the taskbar* section of the Windows

Help and Support window to pin the Snipping Tool to the Taskbar.

When you pin an application to the Taskbar, the button for the application will be added to and remain on the Taskbar until it is unpinned (even if you restart the computer). Pinning applications you use often to the Taskbar reduces the steps required to open them.

In Brief
Display Help and Support Window
1. Open Start screen.
2. Right-click blank area of Start screen.
3. Click All apps icon.
4. Click Help and Support tile.

9 Read information in the *Pin an app to the taskbar* section of the Windows Help and Support Window on how to remove a pinned application from the Taskbar and then unpin the Snipping Tool.

Note that unpinning the Snipping Tool application while the application is still open will unpin the button, but the button will display on the taskbar until the Snipping Tool application is closed.

10 Close the Windows Help and Support window and the Snipping Tool application by clicking the Close button located in the upper right corner of each window.

Worldwide Enterprises requires that employees work with the display of file extensions turned on. This practice helps employees identify source applications associated with files and can prevent employees from accidentally opening email attachments that contain harmful data. In the next steps, you will turn on the display of file extensions.

11 Click the File Explorer button on the Taskbar.

12 Click the View tab on the ribbon.

Windows 8 File Explorer contains a ribbon with four tabs: File, Home, Share, and View. These tabs contain options and buttons to change File Explorer settings and manage folders and files.

13 Click the *File name extensions* check box in the Show/hide group to insert a check mark. ***Note: If the check box appears with a check mark in it, then file extensions are already turned on—click the Cancel button.***

Inserting a check mark in a check box makes the option active.

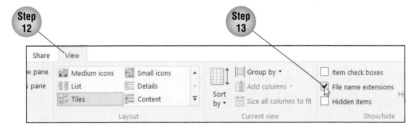

14 Close the File Explorer window by clicking the Close button located at the right side of the Title bar.

In Addition

Browsing the Windows Help and Support Window by Topic Lists

You can locate Help information by browsing the Contents list of topics instead of typing key words in the search text box. Click the Browse help button (located below the search text box) in the Windows Help and Support window. This displays the Windows Help topics list. Click the hyperlink to a topic category in the Windows Help topics list and then continue clicking hyperlinks until you find the information you need.

Features Summary

Feature	Button	Action
close window	☒	Click Close button on Title bar.
Computer window		Right-click Start screen thumbnail, click *File Explorer*.
Date and Time dialog box		Click time on Taskbar, click <u>Change date and time settings</u>.
maximize window	☐	Drag window to top of screen or click Maximize button on Title bar.
minimize window	—	Click Minimize button on Title bar.
move window on desktop		Drag window Title bar.
restore window	☐	Drag maximized window down or click Restore Down button on Title bar.
shut down computer		Click Settings button on Charm bar, click Power, click *Shut down*.
Start screen		Click Start screen area on Taskbar.
Taskbar and Start Menu Properties dialog box		Right-click unused section of Taskbar, click *Properties* at shortcut menu.
Taskbar shortcut menu		Right-click unused section of Taskbar.
Speakers slider bar	🔊	Click Speakers button on Taskbar.
Windows Help and Support window		Open Start screen, right-click blank area, click All apps icon, click *Help and Support*.

Knowledge Check (SNAP)

Completion: In the space provided at the right, indicate the correct term, command, or option.

1. This mouse term refers to tapping the left mouse button twice in quick succession. _____
2. Click this button on a window Title bar to reduce the window to a task button on the Taskbar. _____
3. Click this button on a window Title bar to expand the window so it fills the entire screen. _____
4. Click the time located at the right side of the Taskbar and then click this option to open the Date and Time dialog box. _____
5. This is the name of a bar you can display on the desktop for quick access to a variety of Windows 8 features. _____
6. Windows Help and Support is accessed from this screen. _____

Skills Review

Review 1 Opening and Manipulating Windows

1. At the Windows 8 desktop, click the File Explorer button on the Taskbar. (If the Libraries window fills the desktop, drag the window down from the top of the screen or click the Restore Down button located in the upper right corner of the window.)
2. Double-click the Recycle Bin icon on the desktop. (If the Recycle Bin window fills the desktop, drag the window down from the top of the screen or click the Restore Down button.)
3. Position the mouse pointer on the Recycle Bin Title bar, hold down the left mouse button, and then drag the Recycle Bin window so the Libraries Title bar is visible.
4. Click the Libraries Title bar to make the window active.
5. Right-click in a blank, unused section of the Taskbar and then click *Cascade windows* at the shortcut menu.
6. Click the Minimize button (located toward the right side of the Title bar) on the Libraries Title bar to reduce the window to a task button behind the File Explorer button on the Taskbar.
7. Click the Minimize button on the Recycle Bin window to reduce the window to a task button behind the File Explorer button on the Taskbar.
8. Point to the File Explorer button on the Taskbar and then click the thumbnail preview for the Recycle Bin window to restore the Recycle Bin window on the desktop.
9. Point to the File Explorer button on the Taskbar and then click the thumbnail preview for the Libraries window to restore the Libraries window on the desktop.
10. Drag the Libraries window to the top of the screen and then release the mouse button. (The window expands to fill the entire screen.)
11. Drag the Libraries window down from the top of the screen to restore the window to its previous size and then release the mouse button.
12. Drag the Libraries window off the right edge of the screen until a transparent box displays on the right half of the screen and then release the mouse button.
13. Drag the Recycle Bin window off the left edge of the screen until a transparent box displays on the left half of the screen and then release the mouse button.
14. Close the Libraries window.
15. Close the Recycle Bin window.

Review 2 Exploring the Taskbar

1. At the Windows 8 desktop, click the time that displays in the notification area at the right side of the Taskbar and then click <u>Change date and time settings</u> hyperlink in the pop-up box.
2. At the Date and Time dialog box, click the Change date and time button.
3. At the Date and Time Settings dialog box, click the right arrow in the calendar to display the next month (from the current month).
4. Click the OK button twice.
5. Click the Start screen thumbnail, right-click in a blank area of the Start screen, click the All apps icon, and then click the Notepad tile in the *Windows Accessories* section. (Notepad is a program used for creating and editing text files.)
6. Close Notepad by clicking the Close button at the right side of the Notepad Title bar.

Skills Assessment

Assessment 1 Manipulating Windows

1. Click the File Explorer button on the Taskbar and then double-click the Pictures icon. (If the Pictures window fills the entire desktop, drag the window down from the top of the screen or click the Restore Down button.)
2. Right-click the File Explorer button on the Taskbar, click *File Explorer* in the pop-up list, and then double-click the Music icon. (If the Music window fills the entire desktop, drag the window down from the top of the screen or click the Restore Down button.)
3. Stack the two windows.
4. Make the Pictures window active and then reduce it to a task button on the Taskbar.
5. Reduce the Music window to a task button on the Taskbar.
6. Restore the Pictures window.
7. Restore the Music window.
8. Arrange the two windows side-by-side on the desktop with each window filling one-half the width of the screen.
9. Close the Music window and then close the Pictures window.

Assessment 2 Customizing the Taskbar

1. At the Windows 8 desktop, display the Date and Time dialog box.
2. Change the current hour to one hour ahead and then close the dialog box.
3. Display the Speakers slider bar, drag the slider to increase the volume, and then click the desktop outside the slider to hide the slider bar.
4. Display the Taskbar Properties dialog box, use the *Taskbar location on screen* option box to change the Taskbar location on the screen to *Top*, and then close the dialog box. (Notice that the Taskbar is now positioned along the top edge of the screen.)
5. Display the Charm bar and then click the Search button.
6. At the Search panel, type **calculator** in the text box and then press Enter.
7. Close the Calculator application.

Assessment 3 Restoring the Taskbar

1. At the Windows 8 desktop, display the Date and Time dialog box and then change the date and time to today's date and the current time.
2. Display the Speakers slider bar and then drag the slider button back to the original position.
3. Display the Taskbar Properties dialog box and change the Taskbar location so that the Taskbar displays back at the bottom of the screen.

Windows SECTION 2

Maintaining Files and Customizing Windows

- Browse the contents of storage devices
- Change folder and view options
- Create a folder
- Rename a folder or file
- Select, move, copy, and paste folders or files
- Delete files/folders to and restore files/folders from the Recycle Bin
- Explore the Control Panel
- Use search tools to find applications, folders, and/or files
- Customize the desktop
- Change screen resolution

Student Resources

Before beginning the activities in Windows Section 2, copy to your storage medium the Windows folder on the Student Resources CD. This folder contains the data files you need to complete the projects in Windows Section 2.

Projects Overview

Explore options for browsing and viewing folders and files and then organize folders and files for your department at Worldwide Enterprises. This organization includes creating and renaming folders, as well as moving, copying, renaming, deleting, and restoring files. You will also search for specific files and customize your desktop to the corporate computer standard.

Organize files for Performance Threads including creating folders and copying, moving, renaming, and deleting files.

Organize files for First Choice Travel including creating folders and copying, moving, renaming, and deleting files. Assist your supervisor by searching for information on how to set up a computer for multiple users and how to work with libraries.

Activity 2.1

Browsing Storage Devices and Files in a Computer Window

Open a Computer window to view the various storage devices connected to your computer. The Content pane of the Computer window displays an icon for each hard disk drive and each removable storage medium such as a CD, DVD, or USB device. Next to each storage device icon, you can see the amount of storage space available as well as a bar with the amount of used space shaded with color. This visual cue allows you to see at a glance the proportion of space available relative to the capacity of the device. Double-click a device icon in the Content pane to show the contents stored on the device. You can display contents from another device or folder using the Navigation pane or the Computer window Address bar.

Project You decide to explore the contents of the various storage devices on the computer you are using as you become familiar with the Windows 8 environment.

Note: To complete the projects in this section, you will need to use a USB flash drive or computer hard drive rather than your SkyDrive. Before beginning the projects in this section, make sure you have copied the WindowsS2 folder from the Student Resources CD to your storage medium. If necessary, refer to the inside back cover of this textbook for instructions on how to copy a folder from the Student Resources CD to your storage medium.

Tutorial 2.1
Browsing Devices and Files

1. If necessary, insert into an empty USB port the storage medium that you are using for the files in this course.

FIGURE 2.1 Computer Window

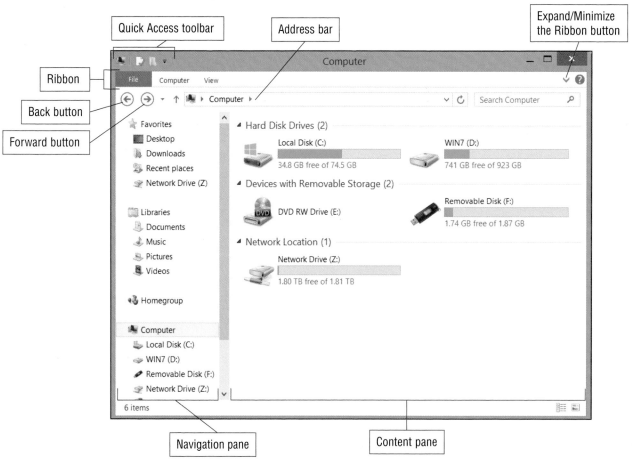

2 At the Windows desktop, position the mouse in the lower left corner of the screen to display the Start screen thumbnail, right-click the thumbnail to display a pop-up list, and then click *File Explorer*.

> The Computer window displays. It should appear similar to the one shown in Figure 2.1.

3 Double-click the icon for the hard disk drive named *Local Disk (C:)*.

> The Computer window changes so that the Content pane displays the files and folders that are stored on the local hard disk drive assigned drive letter C:. Notice also that the Address bar in the Computer window updates to show the location where you are viewing *Local Disk (C:)* within *Computer* (your drive name may vary). You can navigate back using either the Back button or by clicking *Computer* in the Address bar.

4 Click the Back button to return to the Computer window.

5 Double-click the icon for the storage medium onto which you copied the WindowsS2 folder. *Note: The screens shown in this section show* **Removable Disk (F:)** *as the storage medium in the Computer window. Your icon label and drive letter may vary.*

> USB flash drives are shown in the section of the Content pane labeled *Devices with Removable Storage*. Each device is assigned a drive letter by Windows, usually starting at E or F and continuing through the alphabet depending on the number of removable devices that are currently in use. The label that displays next to the drive letter depends on the manufacturer of the USB flash drive. If no manufacturer label is present, Windows displays *Removable Disk*.

6 Double-click the *WindowsS2* folder to view the contents of the folder in the Content pane.

7 Look at the Address bar and notice how it displays the path to the current content list: Computer ▶ Removable Disk (F:) ▶ WindowsS2.

> You can use the Address bar to navigate to any other device or folder by clicking a drive or folder name or by clicking the right-pointing black arrow to view a drop-down list of folders or other devices.

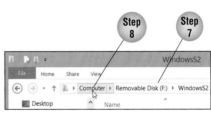

8 Click *Computer* in the Address bar.

9 Click the right-pointing arrow ▶ next to *Computer* in the Address bar (the arrow becomes a down-pointing arrow when clicked) and then click the drive letter representing the removable storage device that contains the WindowsS2 folder.

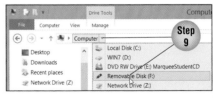

10 Click *Desktop* in the *Favorites* section of the Navigation pane.

> You can also change what displays in the Content pane by clicking the device or folder name in the Navigation pane. Click the white right-pointing arrow next to a device or folder name in the Navigation pane to expand the list and view what is stored within the item.

11 Close the Computer window.

In Brief
Display Computer Window
1. Right-click Start screen thumbnail.
2. Click *File Explorer* at pop-up list.

Programs and Features
Power Options
Event Viewer
System
Device Manager
Disk Management
Computer Management
Command Prompt
Command Prompt (Admin)
Task Manager
Control Panel
File Explorer
Search
Run
Desktop

Activity 2.2

Changing Folder and View Options

You can change the view of the File Explorer window to show the contents of your current location (drive or folder) in various formats, including icons, tiles, or a list, among others. With the Content pane in Details view, you can click the column headings to change how the contents are sorted and whether they are sorted in ascending or descending order. You can customize a window's environment by using buttons and options on the File Explorer View tab. You can change how panes are displayed, how content is arranged in the Content pane, how content is sorted, and which features are hidden.

Project You decide to experiment with various folder and view options as you continue to become acquainted with the Windows 8 environment.

Tutorial 2.2
Changing Folder and View Options

1. Click the File Explorer button [icon] on the Taskbar.

   A Libraries window opens. For a description of libraries, refer to the In Addition section at the end of this activity.

2. Click the drive letter representing your storage medium in the *Computer* section in the Navigation pane.

3. Double-click the *WindowsS2* folder in the Content pane.

4. Click the View tab located below the WindowsS2 Title bar.

5. Click the *Large icons* option in the Layout group.

   After you click an option on the View tab, the View tab collapses to provide more space in the File Explorer window.

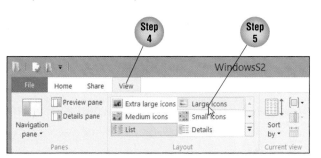

Step 4   Step 5

6. Click the View tab.

7. Click the *Details* option in the Layout group.

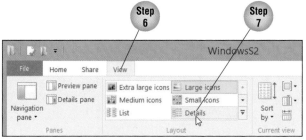

Step 6   Step 7

8. With folders now displayed in Details view, click the *Name* column heading to sort the list in descending order by name.

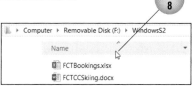

Step 8

9 Click the *Name* column heading again to restore the list to ascending order by name.

10 Click the View tab and then click the Options button [icon] to open the Folder Options dialog box.

11 Click the *Open each folder in its own window* option in the *Browse folders* section on the General tab and then click OK.

12 Close the WindowsS2 window.

13 Click the File Explorer button on the Taskbar and then click the drive representing your storage medium in the *Computer* section in the Navigation pane.

14 Double-click the *WindowsS2* folder.

> Notice that this time a new window opens with the WindowsS2 content list layered on top of the original window.

15 Close the WindowsS2 folder window.

16 Click the View tab, click the Options button, click the Restore Defaults button located near the bottom of the General tab, and then click OK.

17 Close the Removable Disk (F:) window.

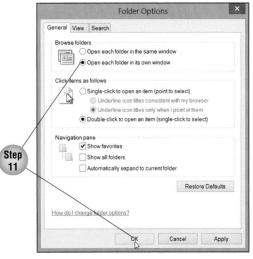

Step 10

Step 11

In Brief

Change Current View
Click desired view in Layout group on View tab.

Change Folder and View Options
1. Click View tab.
2. Click Options button.
3. Click desired option(s).
4. Click OK.

Step 16

In Addition

Windows Libraries

While browsing the Computer window you may have noticed a section in the Navigation pane with the title *Libraries*. Libraries are tools you can use to keep track of and/or organize files that have something in common, regardless of where they are stored. A library does not store the actual files but instead keeps track of locations where the source files are stored. When you click the library name in the Navigation pane, the library displays all of the files in the locations that it is keeping track of associated with that library. For example, in the Pictures library, you could have Windows show you the contents of a Pictures folder on the local disk, from another folder on an external hard disk, and from a folder on a networked computer. Four default libraries are created when Windows 8 is installed: Documents, Music, Pictures, and Videos. You can create your own library and customize the locations associated with the default libraries. You will explore Libraries further in an assessment at the end of this section.

Changing the Default View for All Folders

You can set a view to display by default for all folders of a similar type (such as all disk drive folders or all documents folders). To do this, change the current view to the desired view for the type of folder that you want to set, such as a disk drive folder or a documents folder. Next, click the Options button on the View tab and then click the View tab at the Folder Options dialog box. Click the Apply to Folders button in the *Folder views* section and then click OK. Click Yes at the Folder Views message asking if you want all folders of this type to match this folder's view settings.

Activity 2.3

Creating a Folder;
Renaming a Folder or File

As you begin working with programs, you will create files in which data (information) is saved. A file might be a Word document, an Excel workbook, or a PowerPoint presentation. Files can also be pictures or videos that you transfer from your digital camera to your computer. As you begin creating files, developing a system by which to organize those files becomes important so that you can easily retrieve a document or photograph when you need it. The first step in organizing your files is to create folders. Creating a folder is like creating a separate container in which you can place similar types of files. File management tasks such as creating a folder, renaming a folder or file, and copying and moving files and folders can be completed at a variety of locations, including the Computer and Documents windows.

Project You need to organize files for your department at Worldwide Enterprises, so you decide to start by creating a folder.

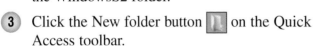

(1) At the Windows desktop, position the mouse in the lower left corner of the screen to display the Start screen thumbnail, right-click the thumbnail, and then click *File Explorer* in the pop-up list.

(2) Double-click the icon representing the storage medium onto which you copied the WindowsS2 folder.

(3) Click the New folder button [image] on the Quick Access toolbar.

> A new folder icon is added to the Content pane with the text *New folder* already selected.

Step 3

(4) With the text *New folder* selected next to the folder icon, type **Revenue** and then press Enter. (As soon as you type the *R* in *Revenue*, the existing text *New folder* is immediately deleted.)

> This changes the folder name from *New folder* to *Revenue*.

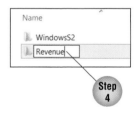

Step 4

(5) You can also create a new folder using a shortcut menu. To begin, right-click in a blank, unused area of the Content pane, point to *New*, and then click *Folder*.

(6) With the text *New folder* already selected next to the folder icon, type **Contracts** and then press Enter.

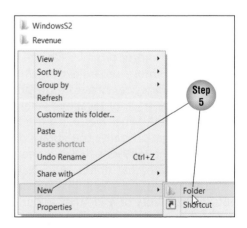

Step 5

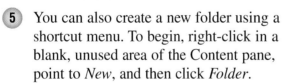

Step 6

(7) Click once on the *Revenue* folder to select the folder.

(8) Click the Home tab and then click the Rename button in the Organize group.

Step 8

Tutorial 2.3
Creating a Folder and Renaming a Folder or File

9 With the text *Revenue* selected, type **Income** and then press Enter.

You can also use the shortcut menu to rename a file or folder.

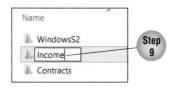
Step 9

10 Right-click the *Contracts* folder and then click *Rename* at the shortcut menu.

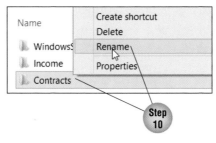
Step 10

11 With the text *Contracts* selected, type **Administration** and then press Enter.

12 Double-click the *WindowsS2* folder.

13 Right-click the file ***FCTExcelSalesCom.xlsx*** and then click *Rename* at the shortcut menu.

14 Type **FCTSalesCommissions** and then press Enter.

Step 11

Notice when you rename a file that Windows does not select the file extension. Programs such as Microsoft Word and Microsoft Excel automatically assign a file extension to each file (in this case, Word documents or Excel workbooks). These file extensions should remain intact. If you rename or remove a file extension by accident, Windows prompts you with a message that the file may no longer be usable and asks you if you are sure.

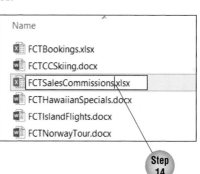
Step 14

15 Close the Computer window.

In Brief

Create New Folder
1. Display Computer window.
2. Double-click device in which to create folder.
3. Click New folder button on Quick Access toolbar.
4. Type folder name and press Enter.

Rename Folder or File
1. Display Computer window.
2. Navigate to desired drive and/or folder.
3. Right-click file to be renamed.
4. At shortcut menu, click *Rename*.
5. Type new file name and press Enter.

In Addition

More about Organizing Files into Folders

Think of a *folder* on the computer the same way you think of a file folder in which you would store paper documents in your filing cabinet. Generally, you put similar types of documents into the same folder. For example, all of your rent receipts might be placed inside a file folder on which you have written the label *Rent* on the folder tab. Similarly, on the computer, you could create a folder named *Rent* and store all of the electronic copies of all of your rental documents within that folder. On the computer, a folder can have another folder stored inside it. The folder within the folder is referred to as a *subfolder*. For example, you may have thousands of pictures stored on your computer. Saving all of the pictures in one folder named *Pictures* would be too cumbersome when the content list contains thousands of images. You would be scrolling a long time to locate a particular picture. Instead, consider creating subfolders in the Pictures folder so that related pictures are grouped together in one place.

Activity 2.4

Selecting and Copying Folders and Files

In addition to creating and renaming files and folders, file management activities include selecting, moving, copying, and deleting files or folders. Open a Computer or Documents window to perform file management tasks. Use options on the Home tab or at a shortcut menu. More than one file or folder can be moved, copied, or deleted at one time. Select adjacent files and folders using the Shift key, and select nonadjacent files and folders using the Ctrl key. When selecting multiple files or folders, you may want to change the view to *List* in the Computer window.

Project As you continue to organize files for your department, you will copy files to the Income folder you created in Activity 2.3.

Worldwide Enterprises

SNAP

Tutorial 2.4
Selecting, Copying, and Moving Folders and Files

1. At the Windows desktop, open a Computer window.

   You can open a Computer window by either right-clicking the Start screen thumbnail and then clicking *File Explorer* or by clicking the File Explorer button on the Taskbar and then clicking *Computer* in the Navigation pane.

2. Double-click the icon representing the storage medium onto which you copied the WindowsS2 folder.

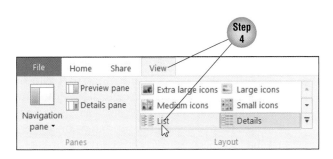

3. Double-click the *WindowsS2* folder in the Content pane.

4. Click the View tab and then click the *List* option in the Layout group.

5. Click the file named **WEExcelRevenues.xlsx** in the Content pane.

   Click once to select a file. Windows displays file properties for the selected file in the bottom left corner of the WindowsS2 window.

6. Hold down the Shift key, click the file named **WETable02.docx**, and then release the Shift key.

   Clicking **WETable02.docx** while holding down the Shift key causes all files from **WEExcelRevenues.xlsx** through **WETable02.docx** to be selected.

7. Position the mouse pointer within the selected group of files, right-click, and then click *Copy* at the shortcut menu.

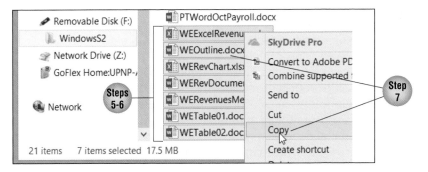

8 Click the Back button located left of the Address bar.

9 Double-click the *Income* folder.

10 Right-click in the Content pane and then click *Paste* at the shortcut menu.

When a large file or large group of files is copied, Windows displays a message box with a progress bar to indicate the approximate time required to copy the files, as shown in Figure 2.2. The message box closes when the copying process is complete.

In Brief

Copy Adjacent Files to New Folder
1. Display Computer window.
2. Navigate to desired drive and/or folder.
3. If necessary, change current view to *List*.
4. Click first file name.
5. Hold down Shift key and then click last file name.
6. Right-click in selected group of files and click *Copy*.
7. Navigate to desired destination drive and/or folder.
8. Right-click in blank area of Content pane and click *Paste*.

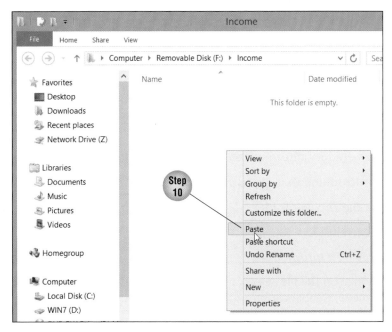

11 Click in a blank area of the Content pane to deselect the file names.

12 Close the Computer window.

FIGURE 2.2 Time to Complete Message Box

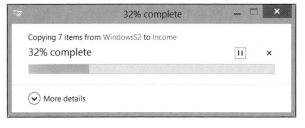

In Addition

Copying by Dragging

You can also copy a file or folder to another location using a drag-and-drop technique. To do this, open a Computer or Documents window and display the desired file or folder in the Content pane. Position the mouse pointer on the file or folder to be copied, hold down the left mouse button, drag to the destination drive or folder name in the *Favorites, Libraries,* or *Computer* list in the Navigation pane, and then release the mouse button. By default, if you drag a file from one disk drive to another, Windows copies the file. However, to copy a file from one folder to another on the same disk drive, you must hold down the Ctrl key as you drag. To make dragging and dropping easier, you can open two windows and arrange them side-by-side on the desktop. In one window, display the files you want to copy. In the other window, display the destination folder. Select the files to be copied and then hold down the Ctrl key while dragging them to the destination window.

Drag and drop to copy a file.

Activity 2.5

Moving Folders and Files

Move files in a Computer or Documents window in a manner similar to copying files. Select the file(s) or folder(s) you want to move, position the mouse pointer over the selected file(s) or folder(s), right-click, and then click *Cut* at the shortcut menu. Navigate to the desired destination location, right-click a blank area in the Content pane, and then click *Paste* at the shortcut menu. You can also use the Copy, Cut, and Paste buttons in the Clipboard group on the Home tab.

Project

After further review of the files you copied into the Income folder, you decide to create another folder and move some of the files from the Income folder into the new folder.

Review Tutorial 2.4
Selecting, Copying, and Moving Folder and Files

1. At the Windows desktop, display a Computer window.

2. Double-click the icon representing the storage medium onto which you copied the WindowsS2 folder.

3. Click the New folder button on the Quick Access toolbar.

4. Type **Distribution** and then press Enter.

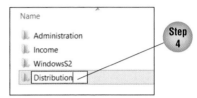

5. Double-click the *Income* folder.

6. Change the current view to *List*.

7. Click once on *WEOutline.docx*.

   Clicking once on the file selects the file name, thereby identifying the item you want to move; double-clicking the file would instruct Windows to open Word and then open the document.

8. Hold down the Ctrl key, click once on *WETable01.docx*, click once on *WETable02.docx*, and then release the Ctrl key.

   Using the Ctrl key, you can select nonadjacent files.

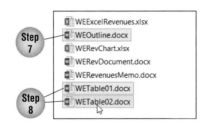

9. Click the Home tab and then click the Cut button in the Clipboard group.

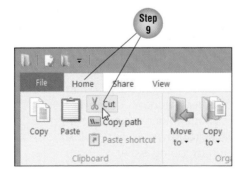

10 Click the Back button at the left of the Address bar.

11 Double-click the *Distribution* folder.

12 Click the Home tab and then click the Paste button in the Clipboard group.

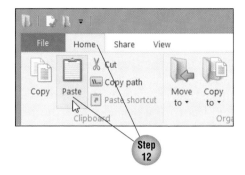

Step 12

In Brief

Move Nonadjacent Files to New Folder
1. Display Computer window.
2. Navigate to desired drive and/or folder.
3. If necessary, change current view to *List*.
4. Click first file name.
5. Hold down Ctrl key, click each additional file name, and then release Ctrl key.
6. Click Cut button in Clipboard group on Home tab.
7. Navigate to desired destination drive and/or folder.
8. Click Paste button in Clipboard group on Home tab.

13 Click in a blank area of the Content pane to deselect the file names.

14 Click the Back button at the left of the Address bar.

15 Double-click the *Income* folder.

16 Notice the three files ***WEOutline.docx***, ***WETable01.docx***, and ***WETable02.docx*** no longer reside in the Income folder.

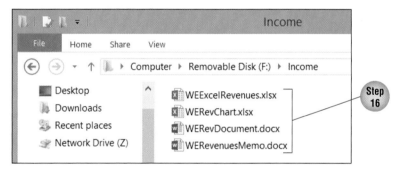

Step 16

17 Close the Computer window.

In Addition

Displaying Disk or Drive Properties

Information such as the amount of used space and free space on a disk or drive and the disk or drive hardware is available at the Properties dialog box. To display the Local Disk (C:) Properties dialog box, similar to the one shown at the right, open a Computer window. At the Computer window, right-click *Local Disk (C:)* and then click *Properties* at the shortcut menu. With the General tab selected, information displays about used and free space on the drive. Click the Tools tab to display error-checking, backup, and defragmentation options. The Hardware tab displays the name and type of all disk drives as well as the device properties. The Sharing tab displays options for sharing folders, and change user permissions at the Security tab. To enable quota management wherein you can assign space limits for each user, click the Quota tab.

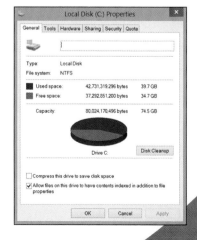

Activity 2.6

Deleting Folders and Files to the Recycle Bin

Deleting the wrong file can be a disaster, but Windows helps protect your work with the Recycle Bin. The Recycle Bin acts just like an office wastepaper basket: you can "throw away" (delete) unwanted files, but you also can "reach in" to the Recycle Bin and take out (restore) a file if you threw it away by accident. Files or folders deleted from a hard disk drive are automatically sent to the Recycle Bin. However, files or folders deleted from a removable disk such as your USB flash drive are deleted permanently.

To delete a file or folder, display a Computer or Documents window and then display in the Content pane the file(s) or folder(s) you want to delete. Select the file(s) or folder(s) and then press the Delete key on the keyboard or right-click the selected files or folders and click *Delete* at the shortcut menu. At the message asking you to confirm the deletion, click the Yes button.

Project

As you continue to organize your files, you will copy a file and a folder from your storage medium to the My Documents folder on the hard drive and then delete a file and folder, moving them to the Recycle Bin.

Tutorial 2.6
Using the Recycle Bin

1 At the Windows desktop, display a Computer window.

2 Double-click the icon representing the storage medium onto which you copied the WindowsS2 folder.

3 Click once to select the *Distribution* folder.

4 Position the mouse pointer over the selected folder name, hold down the left mouse button, drag to *Documents* in the *Libraries* section of the Navigation pane, and then release the mouse button.

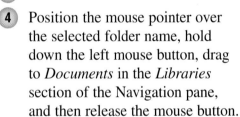

As you point to the Documents library in the Navigation pane, Windows displays the ScreenTip *Copy to My Documents*. If you drag a file or folder from a removable storage device to a location on the computer's hard drive, the file or folder is copied. However, if you drag a file or folder from a location on the hard drive to another location on the hard drive, the file or folder is moved rather than copied.

5 Double-click the *Income* folder.

6 Click once to select **WERevDocument.docx**.

7 Position the mouse pointer over the selected file name, hold down the left mouse button, drag to *Documents* in the *Libraries* section of the Navigation pane, and then release the mouse button.

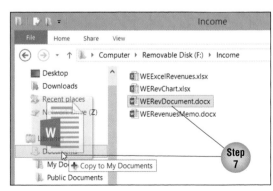

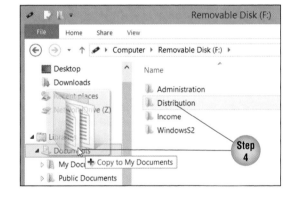

8 Click *Documents* in the *Libraries* section of the Navigation pane to display the files and folders associated with the Documents library in the Content pane.

> The Documents library displays the contents of two folders by default: *My Documents* and *Public Documents*. My Documents is the default folder in which files and folders associated with the Documents library are stored. You can add and remove folders associated with a library. You will learn more about libraries in an assessment at the end of this section.

9 Click once to select the *Distribution* folder.

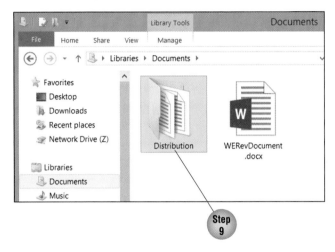

10 Press the Delete key on the keyboard.

11 Right-click ***WERevDocument.docx*** in the Content pane and then click *Delete* at the shortcut menu.

12 Close the Documents library window.

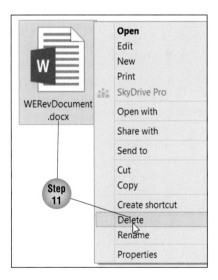

In Brief

Delete File/Folder
1. Display Computer window and navigate to desired drive and/or folder.
2. Click file/folder to select it.
3. Press Delete key.
4. At confirmation message, click Yes.

In Addition

Dragging and Dropping Files and Folders

Another method for deleting a file or folder is to drag the file or folder to the Recycle Bin icon on the desktop. This moves the file into the Recycle Bin. You can also select multiple files or folders and then drag and drop the selected items into the Recycle Bin.

Activity 2.7

Restoring Folders and Files; Emptying Files from the Recycle Bin

A file or folder deleted to the Recycle Bin can be restored. Restore a file or folder with options at the Recycle Bin window. Display this window by double-clicking the Recycle Bin icon on the Windows desktop. Once you restore a file or folder, it is removed from the Recycle Bin and returned to its original location. Just like a wastepaper basket can overflow, the Recycle Bin can contain too many files and folders. Emptying the Recycle Bin permanently deletes all files and folders. You can also delete a single file or folder from the Recycle Bin (rather than all files and folders).

Project You decide to experiment with the Recycle Bin by learning how to restore a file and how to empty the Recycle Bin.

1. At the Windows desktop, display the contents of the Recycle Bin by double-clicking the Recycle Bin icon.

   The Recycle Bin window displays, similar to the one shown in Figure 2.3.

2. At the Recycle Bin window, change the current view to *List*.

3. Click once to select **WERevDocument.docx**.

Review Tutorial 2.4
Selecting, Copying, and Moving Folders and Files

   Depending on the contents of the Recycle Bin, you may need to scroll down the list to display this document.

FIGURE 2.3 Recycle Bin Window

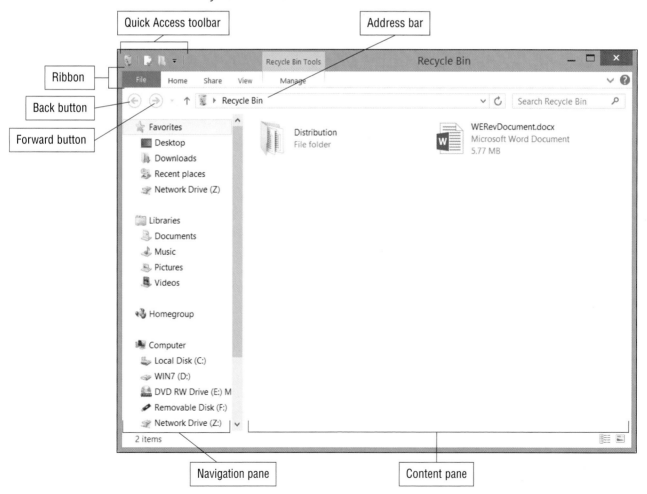

④ Click the Recycle Bin Tools Manage tab and then click the Restore the selected items button in the Restore group.

> The file is removed from the Recycle Bin and returned to the location from which it was deleted. Once a file or folder is moved into the Recycle Bin, you are limited to the following options: Restore, Cut, or Delete.

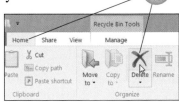

⑤ Click once to select the *Distribution* folder.

⑥ Click the Restore the selected items button in the Restore group.

⑦ Close the Recycle Bin window.

⑧ At the Windows desktop, open a Computer window.

⑨ Click *Documents* in the *Libraries* section of the Navigation pane.

> Notice that the file and folder have been restored from the Recycle Bin.

⑩ Delete the file and folder you restored. To do this, click once on the *Distribution* folder, hold down the Ctrl key, click once on the ***WERevDocument.docx*** file name, and then release the Ctrl key.

⑪ Press the Delete key.

⑫ Close the Documents window.

⑬ At the Windows desktop, double-click the Recycle Bin icon.

⑭ Click once on the *Distribution* folder, hold down the Ctrl key, click once on the ***WERevDocument.docx*** file name, and then release the Ctrl key.

⑮ Click the Home tab and then click the Delete button in the Organize group.

⑯ At the Delete Multiple Items message box asking if you are sure you want to permanently delete the two items, click Yes.

> To empty the entire contents of the Recycle Bin, click the Empty Recycle Bin button in the Manage group on the Recycle Bin Tools Manage tab.

⑰ Close the Recycle Bin window.

In Brief
Restore File/Folder from Recycle Bin
1. At Windows desktop, double-click Recycle Bin icon.
2. At Recycle Bin window, click file/folder to select it (or select multiple files/folders).
3. Click Restore the selected items button on Recycle Bin Tools Manage tab.

Delete File/Folder from Recycle Bin
1. At Windows desktop, double-click Recycle Bin icon.
2. At Recycle Bin window, click file/folder to select it (or select multiple files/folders).
3. Press Delete key.
4. At confirmation message, click Yes.

In Addition

Showing or Hiding the Recycle Bin on the Desktop

The Recycle Bin icon is displayed on the desktop by default. To remove it, right-click a blank area of the desktop and then click *Personalize* at the shortcut menu. At the Personalization window, click <u>Change desktop icons</u> in the left pane. At the Desktop Icon Settings dialog box, shown at the right, click the *Recycle Bin* check box to remove the check mark and then click OK. Note the other desktop icons you can choose to show or hide at this dialog box.

Activity 2.8

Exploring the Control Panel

The Control Panel offers a variety of categories, each containing icons you can use to customize the functionality of your computer. Display the Control Panel window by right-clicking the Start screen thumbnail and then clicking *Control Panel* at the pop-up list. At the Control Panel window, available categories display in the Content pane. (By default, the Control Panel window opens in Category view. If your window opens in Large icons view or Small icons view, click the down-pointing arrow next to *View by*, located near the top right of the Control Panel window, and then click *Category* at the drop-down list.) Click a category or hyperlinked option below a category and a list of tasks, a list of icons, or a separate window displays.

Project

You want to know how to customize your computer, so you decide to explore the Control Panel window.

① At the Windows desktop, right-click the Start screen thumbnail and then click *Control Panel* at the pop-up list.

The Control Panel window displays, similar to the one shown in Figure 2.4.

② At the Control Panel window, click the Appearance and Personalization hyperlink.

Tutorial 2.8
Exploring the
Control Panel

③ After viewing the tasks and icons available in the Appearance and Personalization category, click the Back button.

④ Click the Hardware and Sound hyperlink.

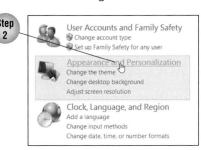

FIGURE 2.4 Control Panel Window

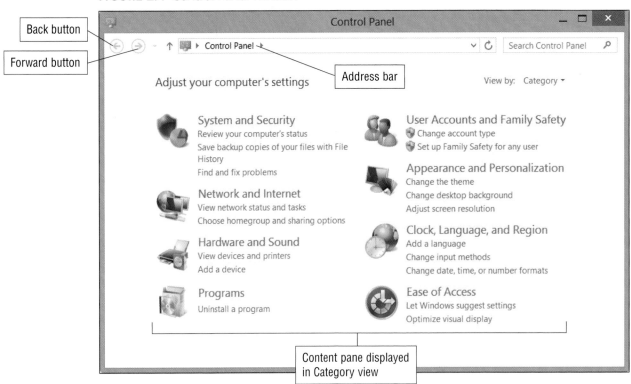

5 Click the <u>Mouse</u> hyperlink in the Devices and Printers category.

> This displays the Mouse Properties dialog box.

In Brief

Display Control Panel Window
1. Right-click Start screen thumbnail.
2. Click *Control Panel*.

6 At the Mouse Properties dialog box, click each tab and review the available options.

7 Click the Cancel button to close the Mouse Properties dialog box.

8 Click the Back button.

9 Click the <u>Programs</u> hyperlink in the Content pane.

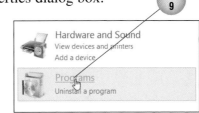

10 At the Programs window, click the <u>Programs and Features</u> hyperlink.

> This is where you would uninstall a program on your computer.

11 Click the Back button twice.

12 Click the <u>System and Security</u> hyperlink.

13 Click the <u>System</u> hyperlink.

14 Maximize the window.

15 Close the System window.

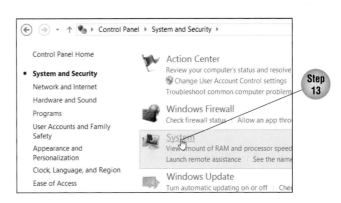

In Addition

Changing the Control Panel View

By default, the Control Panel window displays categories of tasks in what is called Category view. This view can be changed to *Large icons* or *Small icons*. In the Large icons view, shown at the right, options in the Control Panel window are shown alphabetically by icon name. To change from Category view to Large icons or Small icons, click the down-pointing arrow next to *View by* located near the top right of the Control Panel window and then click the desired option at the drop-down list.

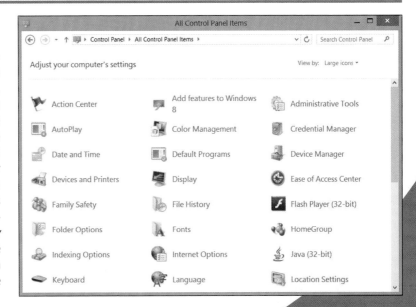

Activity 2.9

Using Windows Search Tools

Windows includes a Search feature you can access through the Charm bar. You can quickly find an application, setting, or file by typing the first few letters of the application, setting, or file name. You can choose whether to search for an application, setting or file by selecting one of the three tiles located below the search text box—Apps, Settings, or Files. If your computer has many applications and files stored on the hard disk, using the search tool allows you to locate what you need in a few seconds and with minimal mouse clicks. At the right of the Address bar in a Computer or Documents window is a search text box. Type in this text box the first few letters of a file you need to locate. The Content pane is filtered instantly to display items that match your criterion.

Windows performs fast searching because the operating system maintains an index in the background in which all of the key words associated with the applications, settings, and files on your computer are referenced. This index is constantly updated as you work. When you type an entry in a search text box, Windows consults the index rather than conducting a search of the entire hard drive.

Project

You want to experiment with the search capabilities of Windows to see how you can quickly locate applications and files.

Worldwide Enterprises

SNAP

Tutorial 2.9
Using Windows Search Tools

(1) At the Windows desktop, display the Charm bar and then click the Search button.

(2) With the insertion point positioned in the search text box located at the top of the Search panel, make sure the Apps tile is selected below the search text box, and then type **calc** in the search text box.

As soon as you begin typing an entry in the search text box, Windows begins to display relevant results. Notice that the Calculator program is shown below the heading *Apps* at the top of the list. Depending on the contents stored in the computer you are using, additional items may be displayed below *Calculator*.

Step 2

(3) Click the Calculator tile in the *Apps* list at the upper left side of the Start screen.

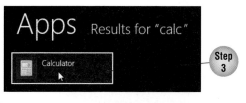

Step 3

(4) Close the Calculator window.

(5) Display the Charm bar and then click the Search button.

(6) Make sure the Apps tile is selected below the search text box and then type **note** in the search text box.

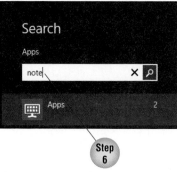

Windows lists all app elements stored on the computer you are using that are associated with the text *note*, including the Notepad application, which you can use to create, edit, and save simple, text-based documents.

Step 6

(7) Press the Esc key.

Pressing the Esc key clears the search results list and the search text box.

(8) Display the desktop and then open a Computer window.

(9) Double-click the icon representing the storage medium onto which you copied the WindowsS2 folder.

10 Double-click the *WindowsS2* folder and then change the view to Large Icons.

11 Click in the Search WindowsS2 text box located at the right of the Address bar.

12 Type **werev**.

> As soon as you begin typing in the search WindowsS2 text box, Windows filters the list of files in the Content pane to those that begin with the letters you type. Notice that the Address bar displays *Search Results in WindowsS2* to indicate that the files displayed that match your criteria were limited to the current folder. If you want to search other locations or by other file properties, click one of the option buttons located on the Search Tools Search tab.

In Brief

Search for Applications or Documents from Charm bar
1. Click Search button on Charm bar.
2. Click Apps, Settings, or Files tile.
3. Type search criteria in search text box.

Search for Document
1. Open Computer or Documents library window.
2. Type search criteria in search text box.

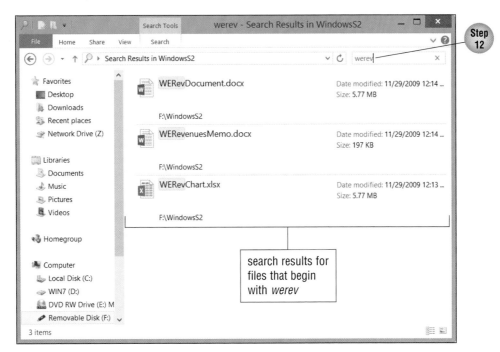

search results for files that begin with *werev*

13 With the insertion point still positioned in the search text box, press the Backspace key to remove *werev* and then type **pte**.

> The list of files in the Content pane is updated to display those files that begin with *pte*.

14 Double-click the file named ***PTExcelOctPayroll.xlsx***.

> The file opens in Microsoft Excel.

15 Close Microsoft Excel by clicking the Close button at the right side of the Title bar.

16 Close the Computer window.

In Addition

Using a Wildcard Character in a Search

When conducting a search, you can type an asterisk (*) in place of any number of letters, numbers, or symbols within a file name to find files based on a pattern of characters. For example, typing ***hours*** would locate the files listed at the right in your WindowsS2 folder. Notice the pattern is that all files have *hours* in the middle of the file name but any number of other characters before and after *hours*.

PTWordHours.docx
PTExcelHours.xlsx
PTCostumeHours.xlsx

Activity 2.10

Customizing the Desktop

The Windows operating environment is customizable. You can change background patterns and colors; specify a screen saver that will display when the screen sits idle for a specific period of time; change the scheme for windows, title bars, and system fonts; and change screen resolution and text size. Make these types of changes at the Control Panel Personalization window. Many companies adopt a corporate standard for display properties on their computers.

Project

You decide to look at the customization options available for the desktop and set the screen resolution to the corporate standard for computers at Worldwide Enterprises.

Note: Before completing this activity, check with your instructor to determine if you can customize the desktop. If necessary, practice these steps on your home computer.

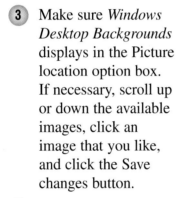

Tutorial 2.10
Customizing the Desktop

① At the Windows desktop, position the arrow pointer in a blank area of the desktop, right-click the mouse, and then click *Personalize* at the shortcut menu.

② At the Personalization window, click the <u>Desktop Background</u> hyperlink located along the bottom of the window.

Make a note of the current background.

③ Make sure *Windows Desktop Backgrounds* displays in the Picture location option box. If necessary, scroll up or down the available images, click an image that you like, and click the Save changes button.

④ Click the <u>Screen Saver</u> hyperlink.

Make a note of the current screen saver name.

⑤ At the Screen Saver Settings dialog box, click the option box arrow below *Screen saver* and then click *Ribbons* at the drop-down list.

A preview of the screen saver displays in the screen located toward the top of the dialog box.

⑥ Click the up- or down-pointing arrow next to the *Wait* measurement box until *1* displays.

⑦ Click the OK button.

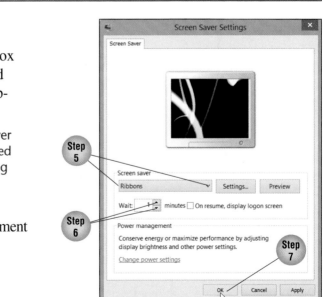

8 Click the Color hyperlink.

Make a note of the color box that is currently selected.

9 Click the *Color 9* color box (second column in the bottom row) and then click the Save changes button. *Note: Skip this step if your window does not display as shown below.*

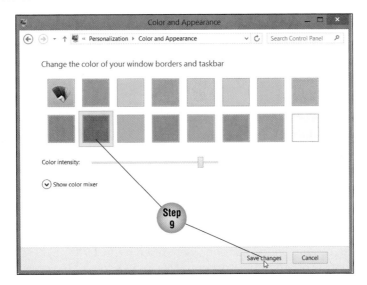

10 Close the Personalization window. Let the screen remain idle for one minute so that the screen saver displays.

11 Move the mouse to deactivate the screen saver and then double-click the Recycle Bin icon.

Notice the Color 9 color scheme applied to the Taskbar and the window borders.

12 Close the Recycle Bin window.

13 Reinstate the original desktop settings by right-clicking a blank area of the desktop, clicking *Personalize* at the shortcut menu, and then returning the desktop background, screen saver, and window color to the original settings.

In the next steps, you will set the screen resolution to *1600 × 900 pixels,* which is the corporate standard for all desktop computers at Worldwide Enterprises. Standardizing display properties is considered a best practice in large companies that support many computer users.

14 Right-click a blank area of the desktop and then click *Screen resolution* at the shortcut menu.

15 At the Screen Resolution window, look at the current setting displayed in the *Resolution* option box. For example, your screen may be currently set at *1920 × 1080*. If your screen is already set to *1600 × 900*, click OK to close the window and complete this activity.

Screen resolution is set in pixels. *Pixel* is the abbreviation of *picture element* and refers to a single dot or point on the display monitor. Changing the screen resolution to a higher number of pixels means that more information can be seen on the screen as items are scaled to a smaller size.

continues

16 Click the *Resolution* option box and then drag the slider bar up or down as necessary until the screen resolution is set to *1600 × 900*. If necessary, check with your instructor for alternate instructions.

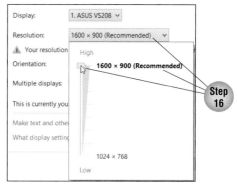

Step 16

17 Click in the window outside the slider box, click OK, and then click the Keep changes button at the Display Settings message box asking if you want to keep the display settings.

18 At the Screen resolution window, click the Make text and other items larger or smaller hyperlink located toward the lower left corner of the window.

19 At the display window, click the Medium – 125% option.

20 Click the Apply button.

21 At the message indicating that you must sign out of your computer, click the Sign out now button.

22 Log back into your account.

> The screen captures in this textbook were taken using 1600 × 900 screen resolution and the display of text and items set to Medium - 125%. If the computer you are using has a different screen resolution, what you will see on your screen may not match the textbook illustrations. For additional information, refer to the In Addition section below.

In Addition

Windows Screen Resolution and the Microsoft Office Ribbon

Before you begin learning the applications in the Microsoft Office 2013 suite, take a moment to check the display settings on the computer you are using. The ribbon in the Microsoft Office suite adjusts to the screen resolution setting of your computer monitor. A computer monitor set at a high resolution will have the ability to show more buttons in the ribbon than will a monitor set to a low resolution. The screen captures in this textbook were taken at a resolution of 1600 x 900 pixels. Below, the Word ribbon is shown three ways: at a lower screen resolution (1366 x 768 pixels), at the screen resolution featured throughout this textbook, and at a higher screen resolution (1920 x 1080 pixels). Note the variances in the ribbon in all three examples. If possible, set your display to 1600 x 900 pixels to match the illustrations you will see in this textbook.

Appearance of Microsoft Word ribbon with computer monitor set at:

1366 x 768 screen resolution

1600 x 900 screen resolution (featured in this textbook)

1920 x 1080 screen resolution

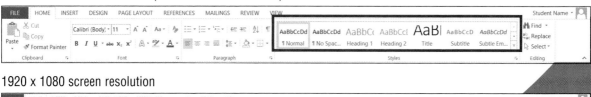

Features Summary

Feature	Button/Icon	Action
Computer window		Right-click Start screen thumbnail, click *File Explorer*.
Control Panel window		Right-click Start screen thumbnail, click *Control Panel*.
copy selected files/folders		At Computer or Documents library window, select files/folders to be copied, right-click in selected group, click *Copy*, navigate to destination folder, right-click in Content pane, click *Paste*.
create new folder		At Computer or Documents library window, click New Folder button on Quick Access toolbar.
delete selected files/folders		At Computer or Documents library window, select files to be deleted, press Delete key, click Yes.
folder options		Click View tab, click Options button.
move selected files/folders		At Computer or Documents library window, select files/folders to be moved, right-click in selected group, click *Cut*, navigate to destination folder, right-click in Content pane, click *Paste*.
Recycle Bin		Double-click *Recycle Bin* icon.
rename file/folder		At Computer or Documents library window, right-click file or folder, click *Rename,* type new name, press Enter.
restore files/folders from Recycle Bin		At Recycle Bin, select desired files/folders, click Recycle Bin Tools Manage tab, click Restore the selected items button on tab.
search for programs or documents		Display Charm bar, click Search button, type search criterion in search text box; or open Computer or Documents library window, type search criterion in search text box.
select adjacent files/folders		Click first file/folder, hold down Shift key, click last file/folder.
select nonadjacent files/folders		Click first file/folder, hold down Ctrl key, click any other files/folders.

Knowledge Check (SNAP)

Completion: In the space provided at the right, indicate the correct term, command, or option.

1. Navigate to any other device or folder from the current device and folder using the Navigation pane or this bar in the Computer window. _____

2. Specify the option to open each folder in its own window at this dialog box. _____

3. Click this button on the Quick Access toolbar to create a new folder in the Computer window. _____

4. Change the display of files and folders in the Computer window to *List* or *Details* using this group on the View tab. _____

5. To select adjacent files, click the first file, hold down this key, and then click the last file. _____

6. To select nonadjacent files, click the first file, hold down this key, and then click any other desired files. _____

7. Click this button to display in the Content pane the files in the previous folder viewed. _____

8. Click this button in the Clipboard group on the Home tab to move selected files. _____

9. Files deleted from the hard drive are sent here. _____

10. Open this window to display a list of categories or icons in which you can customize the appearance and functionality of your computer. _____

11. Access search tools using this bar at the desktop. _____

12. Customize the desktop by changing the background, screen saver, and/or color option at this window. _____

Skills Review

Review 1 Browsing Devices and Changing the View

1. Open the Computer window.
2. Change to Large Icons view.
3. Change the folder option to open each folder in its own window.
4. Display the contents of your storage medium.
5. Display the contents of the WindowsS2 folder.
6. Change to Details view.
7. Close the WindowsS2 window.
8. Close the window for your storage medium.
9. Change the folder option to open each folder in the same window.
10. Change to Tiles view and then close the Computer window.

Review 2 Creating a Folder

1. Open the Computer window.
2. Display the contents of your storage medium.
3. Right-click a blank area in the Content pane, point to *New*, and then click *Folder*.
4. Type **Worksheets** and then press Enter.
5. Close the window.

Review 3 Selecting, Copying, Moving, and Deleting Files

1. Open the Computer window.
2. Display the contents of your storage medium.
3. Display the contents of the WindowsS2 folder.
4. Change the current view to List if the display is not already set to List.
5. Click once on *FCTBookings.xlsx* to select it, hold down the Shift key, and then click *FCTPackages.docx*.
6. Right-click within the selected group of files and then click *Copy* at the shortcut menu.
7. Click the Back button.
8. Double-click the *Worksheets* folder.
9. Right-click in the Content pane, click *Paste*, and then click in a blank area to deselect the files.
10. Click the Back button and then double-click *WindowsS2*.
11. Click *WEExcelRevenues.xlsx* in the Content pane, hold down the Ctrl key, and then click *WERevChart.xlsx*.
12. Click the Cut button in the Clipboard group on the Home tab.
13. Click the Back button and then double-click *Worksheets*.
14. Click the Paste button in the Clipboard group on the Home tab.
15. Click the right-pointing arrow next to your storage medium in the Address bar and then click *WindowsS2* at the drop-down list.
16. Click *FCTCCSkiing.docx* in the Content pane, hold down the Ctrl key, and then click *FCTNorwayTour.docx*.
17. Press the Delete key and then click Yes at the Delete Multiple Items confirmation message.
18. Close the Computer window.

Review 4 Renaming a File

1. Open the Computer window.
2. Display the contents of your storage medium.
3. Display the contents of the WindowsS2 folder.
4. Right-click *WETable01.docx* and then click *Rename*.
5. Type **WEPreviewDistribution** and then press Enter.
6. Right-click *WETable02.docx* and then click *Rename*.
7. Type **WEGeneralDistribution** and then press Enter.
8. Close the Computer window.

Review 5 Searching for Files

1. Open the Computer window.
2. Display the contents of the WindowsS2 folder on your storage medium.
3. Type ***rev*** in the search WindowsS2 text box.
4. Press the Esc key until the filter is cleared and all files are redisplayed.
5. Type ***excel*** in the search WindowsS2 text box.
6. Close the Computer window.
7. Click the Search button on the Charm bar.
8. Type ***word*** in the search text box. Notice the applications displayed in the Start screen.
9. Press the Esc key and then click in the Start screen area outside the Search panel to close the Search panel.

Skills Assessment

Assessment 1 Managing Folders and Files

1. Create a new folder on your storage medium named PerformanceThreads.
2. Display the contents of the WindowsS2 folder.
3. If necessary, change to List view.
4. Copy all files beginning with *PT* to the PerformanceThreads folder.
5. If necessary, display the contents of the PerformanceThreads folder and change to List view.
6. Create a new folder within PerformanceThreads named Payroll. (A folder created within a folder is referred to as a subfolder.)
7. Move **PTExcelOctPayroll.xlsx** and **PTWordOctPayroll.docx** from the PerformanceThreads folder into the Payroll subfolder.
8. Delete **PTMarqueeLetter.docx** from the PerformanceThreads folder.
9. Rename the file named **PTAgreement.docx** located in the PerformanceThreads folder to **CostumeAgreement.docx**.

Assessment 2 Managing Folders and Files

1. Display the contents of your storage medium.
2. Create a new folder named FirstChoiceTravel.
3. Display the contents of the WindowsS2 folder.
4. Copy all files beginning with *FCT* to the FirstChoiceTravel folder.
5. If necessary, display the contents of the FirstChoiceTravel folder and change to List view.
6. Create a new folder within FirstChoiceTravel and name it *Accounting*.
7. Create a new folder within the Accounting folder and name it *Commissions*.
8. Move **FCTBookings.xlsx** from the FirstChoiceTravel folder into the Accounting subfolder.
9. Move **FCTSalesCommissions.xlsx** from the FirstChoiceTravel folder into the Commissions subfolder.
10. Delete **FCTIslandFlights.docx** from the FirstChoiceTravel folder.
11. Rename the file named **FCTPackages.docx** located in the FirstChoiceTravel folder to **FCTOregonNevadaPkgs.docx**.

Assessment 3 Managing Folders and Files

1. Display the contents of your storage medium.
2. Create a new folder named WorldwideEnt.
3. Display the contents of the WindowsS2 folder.
4. Copy all files beginning with *WE* to the WorldwideEnt folder.
5. If necessary, display the contents of the WorldwideEnt folder and change to List view.
6. Delete **WEOutline.docx** from the WorldwideEnt folder.
7. Change the name of the WorldwideEnt folder to *WorldwideEnterprises*.

Assessment 4 Deleting Folders and Files

Note: Check with your Instructor before completing this assessment in case you need to show him or her that you completed the activities within this section before deleting the folders.

1. Display the contents of your storage medium.
2. Delete the folder named Administration.
3. Delete the folder named Distribution.
4. Delete the folder named Income.

Assessment 5 Copying Folders from the Student CD to Storage Medium

1. Display the contents of the Marquee student CD that accompanies this textbook in the Computer window.
2. Display the contents of the Word folder in the Content pane.
3. Select all of the subfolders in the Word folder and then copy them to your storage medium.
4. Display the contents of the Excel folder in the Content pane and then copy all of the subfolders in the Excel folder to your storage medium.
5. Display the contents of the Access folder in the Content pane and then copy all of the subfolders in the Access folder to your storage medium.
6. Display the contents of the PowerPoint folder in the Content pane and then copy all of the subfolders in the PowerPoint folder to your storage medium.
7. Copy the AudioandVideo folder to your storage medium.
8. Display the contents of the Integrating folder and then copy all of the subfolders to your storage medium.

Assessment 6 Searching for Information on User Accounts

1. You have been asked by your supervisor at First Choice Travel to learn about sharing your computer with other users. Your supervisor is considering adding an evening shift and wants to find out how existing computer equipment can be set up for other users. Using the Windows Help and Support feature, search for information on user accounts. ***Hint: Type user accounts in the search text box and press Enter. Consider reading the topic*** **Which user account is right for me** *as your first step*.
2. Locate topics with information about the three types of user accounts: *Standard*, *Administrator*, and *Guest*. Specifically, your supervisor is interested in which type of account would be best suited for day-to-day work and why this type of account is your recommendation.
3. Create a new folder on your storage medium named WindowsEOS.
4. Using WordPad or Word, compose a memo to your instructor that describes the differences among the three types of user accounts and then provide your recommendation for which type of account should be used for individuals on each shift.
5. Save the memo in the WindowsEOS folder and name it **WS2-UserAccounts**.
6. Print the memo and then close the application you used to compose the memo.

Assessment 7 Searching for Information on Windows Libraries

HELP

1. You have been asked by your supervisor at First Choice Travel to learn about a feature in Windows 8 called Libraries. Your supervisor is not sure about the difference between a library and a normal folder for managing folders and files. She wants you to find out how a library can be useful to her and how to create her own library and add folders to it. She also wonders if the default libraries Windows created can have other folders added to them. Using the Windows Help and Support feature, search for information on libraries. ***Hint: Type*** *libraries* ***in the search text box and then press Enter. Consider reading the topic*** **Library basics** *as your first step*.
2. Locate topics with information about libraries.
3. Using WordPad or Word, compose a memo to your instructor that provides her or him with answers to the following questions:
   a. What is the difference between a library and a folder?
   b. How can I create my own library?
   c. How can I add or remove folders in a library?
   d. What is the limit on the number of folders that can be added to a library?
4. Save the memo and name it **WS2-Libraries** in the WindowsEOS folder.
5. Print the memo and then close the application you used to compose the memo.

Marquee Series

MICROSOFT®

INTERNET EXPLORER 10

Nita Rutkosky
Pierce College at Puyallup,
Puyallup, Washington

Denise Seguin
Fanshawe College,
London, Ontario

Audrey Roggenkamp
Pierce College at Puyallup,
Puyallup, Washington

Ian Rutkosky
Pierce College at Puyallup,
Puyallup, Washington

Paradigm
PUBLISHING

St. Paul

Contents

Managing Editor	Christine Hurney
Director of Production	Timothy W. Larson
Production Editor	Sarah Kearin
Cover and Text Designer	Leslie Anderson
Copy Editor	Sid Korpi, Proof Positive Editing
Design and Production Specialists	Jack Ross and Sara Schmidt Boldon
Testers	Desiree Carvel; Ann E. Mills, Ivy Tech Community College of Indiana, Indianapolis, IN; Brienna McWade
Indexer	Terry Casey
VP & Director of Digital Projects	Chuck Bratton
Digital Project Manager	Tom Modl

Internet Explorer

Browsing the Internet Using Internet Explorer 10

Skills

- Visit sites by typing a web address
- Use hyperlinks to navigate to web pages
- Search for information using search tools
- Narrow a search using advanced search options
- Download content from a web page
- Evaluate content found on a web page

Projects Overview

Visit websites for two national parks. Search for websites pertaining to historical costume design. Use advanced search options to locate information on skydiving companies in the state of Oregon. Locate and save images of Banff National Park. Find information on Apollo lunar missions and evaluate the source and date of publication of the information.

Visit the home pages for the *New York Times* and *USA Today* and read a current article.

Search for and locate the web page for the Theatre Department at York University and the web page for the Department of Drama at New York University.

Locate a website for a snow skiing resort in Utah and then download an image from the web page.

Navigating the Internet Using Web Addresses

In today's world, the Internet is used for a variety of tasks, including locating information about any topic one can imagine, communicating with others through email or social networking sites, and buying and selling goods and services. In this section, you will use Microsoft's Internet Explorer web browser to locate information on the Internet. A *web browser* is software that allows you to view the text, images, and other content that has been stored on a web page on the Internet. *Uniform Resource Locators*, referred to as URLs, identify web servers that have content on the Internet. A URL is often referred to as a *web address*. Just as you need a specific mailing address to identify your location to the post office, a web server needs a unique web address to identify its location to the Internet.

Project

Tutorial 1.1
Navigating the
Internet Using
Web Addresses

Dennis Chun, the location director for Marquee Productions, is gathering information for a new movie project. He has asked you to browse the websites for Yosemite National Park and Glacier National Park.

Note: Printing instructions are not included in the project steps in this section. Check with your instructor to find out if you need to print the web pages you visit.

1. Make sure you are connected to the Internet and that the Windows desktop displays.

   Check with your instructor to determine if you need to complete steps to access the Internet.

2. Open Microsoft Internet Explorer by clicking the Internet Explorer icon ⓔ on the Windows Taskbar.

   Figure 1.1 identifies the elements of the Internet Explorer window. The web page that displays in your Internet Explorer window may vary from what you see in Figure 1.1. Refer to Figure 1.2 on the next page for descriptions of the tools available in Internet Explorer.

3. At the Internet Explorer window, click in the Address bar (refer to Figure 1.1), type **www.nps.gov/yose**, and then press Enter.

Step 3

FIGURE 1.1 Internet Explorer Window

navigation buttons

Address bar

browser controls

tab

④ Scroll down the home page for Yosemite National Park by pressing the Down Arrow key on the keyboard, or by clicking the down-pointing arrow on the vertical scroll bar located at the right side of the Internet Explorer window.

The first web page that appears for a website is called the site's *home page*.

⑤ Display the home page for Glacier National Park by clicking in the Address bar, typing **www.nps.gov/glac**, and then pressing Enter.

As you begin to type the first few characters in the Address bar, a drop-down list appears with the names of websites you have already visited that are spelled the same. Matched characters are displayed in blue for quick reference. If the web address you want displays in the drop-down list, you do not need to type the entire address—simply click the desired web address in the drop-down list.

Step 5

⑥ Click the <u>History & Culture</u> hyperlink in the navigation area at the left side of the page.

Most web pages contain hyperlinks that you click to connect to another page within the website or to another site on the Internet. Hyperlinks display in a web page in a variety of ways such as underlined text, text in a navigation bar, buttons, images, or icons. To use a hyperlink, position the mouse pointer on the hyperlink until the mouse pointer turns into a hand and then click the left mouse button.

⑦ Scroll down and view the content on the History & Culture web page.

⑧ Click the Back button located in the upper left corner of the screen (see Figure 1.2) to return to the Glacier National Park home page.

⑨ Click the Forward button located to the right of the Back button to return to the History & Culture page.

Step 8

Step 9

In Brief
Display Specific Website
1. At Windows desktop, click *Internet Explorer* icon on Taskbar.
2. Click in Address bar, type web address, and then press Enter.

FIGURE 1.2 Browsing, Navigating, and Other Internet Explorer Tools

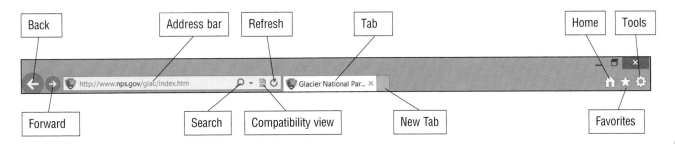

In Addition

Using Internet Explorer in the Modern UI

Windows 8 contains a new user interface, which has been optimized for touch devices. If you access Internet Explorer through the Windows 8 start screen, the Modern UI version of Internet Explorer displays. This version displays differently than the desktop version of Internet Explorer and is designed for use on touch devices. To open the Modern UI version of Internet Explorer, display the Windows 8 start screen and then click the Internet Explorer tile. The address bar and buttons appear at the bottom of the screen and are increased in size. All of the activities in this section use the desktop version of Internet Explorer. If the Internet Explorer button does not appear on the Taskbar, ask your instructor for help on how to access the desktop version of Internet Explorer.

Activity 1.2

Finding Information Using Search Tools

If you do not know the web address for a specific site or you want to find information on the Internet but do not know what site to visit, you can search the Internet using a search engine. A variety of search engines are available, and each offers the opportunity to search for specific information. One method for searching for information is to click in the Address bar, type a keyword or phrase related to your search, and then press Enter. Another method for completing a search is to go to the home page for a search engine and use options at the search engine's site.

Project

Allan Herron, research coordinator for Marquee Productions, has asked you to locate sites with historical costumes for a new movie project. Specifically, she has asked you to locate information on Elizabethan and Renaissance costumes.

1. With the Internet Explorer window active, click in the Address bar.

2. Type **Renaissance costumes** and then press Enter.

   When you press the Enter key, a Bing page with the search results displays. Bing is Microsoft's online search portal and is the default search engine used by Internet Explorer. Bing organizes search results by topic category and provides related search suggestions.

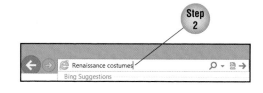

3. Scroll down the search results list and click a hyperlink that interests you by positioning the mouse pointer on the hyperlink text until the pointer turns into a hand and then clicking the left mouse button.

4. Browse the content at the page you selected.

5. Use the Yahoo! search engine to find sites on Renaissance costumes by clicking in the Address bar, typing **www.yahoo.com**, and then pressing Enter.

6. At the Yahoo! website, type **Renaissance costumes** in the search text box and then press Enter.

   As you begin to type, the Yahoo! search assist feature displays search suggestions in a list below the search text box. You can click a suggested phrase in the list instead of completing your typing. Characters in each suggested search phrase that match your typing are displayed in another font style for quick reference. Notice that Bing and Yahoo!'s suggested search phrases are different. Each search engine has its own way of cataloging and indexing search terms.

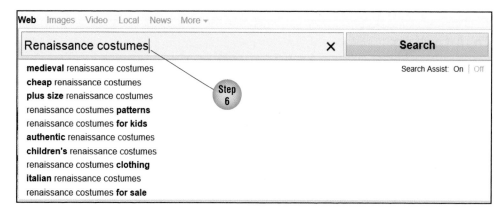

7 Click a hyperlink to a site that interests you.

8 Use the Google search engine to find sites on Elizabethan costumes by clicking in the Address bar, typing **www.google.com**, and then pressing Enter.

9 At the Google website, type **Elizabethan costumes** in the search text box and then press Enter.

In Brief

Search for Website
At Internet Explorer window, type search terms text in the Address bar and then press Enter.

Notice that Google also provides a drop-down list of suggested search phrases based on the characters you type.

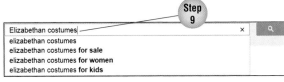

Step 9

10 Click a hyperlink to a site that interests you.

11 Use the Dogpile search engine to find sites on Elizabethan costumes by clicking in the Address bar, typing **www.dogpile.com**, and then pressing Enter.

Dogpile is a metasearch search engine. A *metasearch search engine* sends your search phrase to other search engines and then compiles the results into one list, allowing you to type the search phrase once and access results from a variety of search engines that index web pages. Dogpile provides search results from Google, Yahoo!, and Yandex.

12 At the Dogpile website, type **Elizabethan costumes** in the search text box and then press Enter.

Step 12

13 Click a hyperlink to a site that interests you.

In Addition

Customizing Internet Explorer

Internet Explorer 10 has been streamlined to provide users with more browsing space and reduced clutter. By default, Microsoft has turned off many features in Internet Explorer 10 such as the Menu bar, Command bar, and Status bar. You can turn these features on by right-clicking the empty space above the Address bar (see Figure 1.1 on page 2) and then clicking the desired option at the drop-down list that displays. For example, if you want to turn on the Menu bar (the bar that contains File, Edit, and so on), right-click the empty space above the Address bar and then click *Menu bar* at the drop-down list. (This inserts a check mark next to *Menu bar*.)

Adding Frequently Used Web Pages to Favorites

If you visit a web page on a regular basis, add the page to the Favorites Center or add a button to the web page on the Favorites bar. To display the Favorites bar, right-click the empty space above the Address bar and then click *Favorites bar* at the drop-down list. To add the web page to the Favorites bar, display the web page and then click the Favorites button (which displays as a white star located in the upper right corner of the window). When the Favorites Center displays, click the down-pointing arrow on the Add to favorites button and then click *Add to Favorites bar* at the drop-down list. If you prefer, you can add the website to the Favorites Center list. To do this, click the Favorites button and then click the Add to favorites button at the Favorites Center. At the Add a Favorite dialog box that displays, make sure the information in the *Name* text box is the title by which you want to refer to the website (if not, type your own title for the page) and then click the Add button. The new website is added to the Favorites Center drop-down list. Jump quickly to the site by clicking the Favorites button and then clicking the site name at the drop-down list.

Activity 1.3

Refining Your Search Using Advanced Search Tools

The Internet contains an extraordinary amount of information. Depending on what you are searching for on the Internet and the search engine you use, some searches can result in several thousand "hits" (sites). Wading through a large number of sites can be very time-consuming. You can achieve a more targeted search results list if you hone your search technique using the advanced search options offered by a search engine. Look for an advanced search options link at your favorite search engine site the next time you need to locate information, and experiment with various methods to limit the search results. Effective searching is a skill you obtain through practice.

Project

James Vecchio, stunt coordinator at Marquee Productions, has asked you to locate information on skydiving companies in the state of Oregon.

Tutorial 1.3
Researching Information Using Advanced Search Tools

1. With the Internet Explorer window active, click in the Address bar, type **www.yahoo.com**, and then press Enter.

2. At the Yahoo! home page, click the Search button [Search] next to the search text box.

3. Click the *More* option located above the Search text box and then click *Advanced Search* at the drop-down list.

4. At the Advanced Web Search page, click in the *the exact phrase* text box and then type **skydiving in Oregon**.

   This limits the search to websites with the exact phrase "skydiving in Oregon."

5. Click the *Only .com domains* option.

   Clicking this option tells Yahoo! to only display websites with a *.com* extension and to ignore any other extension.

6. Click the Yahoo! Search button.

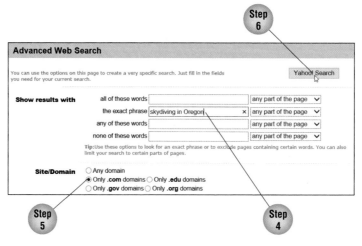

7 When the list of websites displays, click a hyperlink that interests you.

8 Click the Back button until the Yahoo! Advanced Web Search page displays.

9 Select and then delete the text *skydiving in Oregon* located in the *the exact phrase* text box.

10 Click in the *all of these words* text box and then type **skydiving Oregon tandem static line**.

> You want to focus on websites that offer tandem and static line skydiving in Oregon. Enter specific text in the *all of these words* text box to limit the search only to those websites containing all of the words.

11 Click the *Any domain* option.

12 Click the Yahoo! Search button.

In Brief

Complete Advanced Search Using Yahoo!
1. At Internet Explorer window, click in Address bar, type *www.yahoo.com*, then press Enter.
2. Click Search button, click *More* option, click *Advanced Search*.
3. Click in desired search text box, type search criteria text.
4. Select search method and search options.
5. Click Yahoo! Search button.

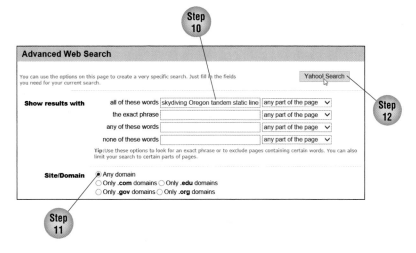

13 When the list of websites displays, click a hyperlink that interests you.

In Addition

Displaying a List of Sites Visited

As you view various web pages, Internet Explorer keeps track of the websites you visit. Display the History pane by clicking the Favorites button and then clicking the History tab in the Favorites Center. Click a timeframe to expand the list and display the sites visited during that period. For example, click *Last Week* to expand the list and view the pages you visited within the past week. Click a hyperlink to revisit the page. At the top of the History pane, click the View option box (currently displays *View By Date*) to change the order in which the history list is displayed. You can display websites in the History pane to *View By Date*, *View By Site*, *View By Most Visited*, or *View By Order Visited Today*. Click *Search History* at the View button drop-down list to search the websites in the History pane by keyword or phrase.

Activity 1.4

Downloading Content from a Web Page

Downloading content from a web page can involve saving to your hard disk or other storage medium images, text, video, audio, or an entire web page. Copyright laws protect much of the information on the Internet. Before using information or media files you have downloaded from the Internet, check the source site for restrictions. When in doubt, contact the website administrator or another contact person identified on the site and request permission to use the content. Finally, make sure to credit the source of any content you use that was obtained from a web page. Generally, you can use content from a website that is considered public domain, such as a government website, without obtaining permission.

Project

Tutorial 1.4
Downloading Content from a Web Page

Chris Greenbaum, the production manager of the new movie project at Marquee Productions, has asked you to locate on the Internet a picture of Banff National Park and an image that shows a map of the park. She wants you to save the images as separate files she can insert into her presentation for the next production meeting.

1 With the Internet Explorer window active, click in the Address bar, type **www.google.com**, and then press Enter.

2 At the Google home page, click the Images hyperlink at the top left of the home page.

Step 2

3 At the Google images page, type **Banff National Park** in the search text box and then press Enter or click the Search button.

4 Browse the images that display in the search results.

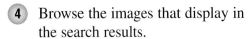

Your image may vary.

5 Position the mouse pointer over an image you want to download, right-click the mouse, and then click *Save picture as* at the shortcut menu.

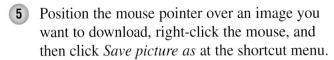

Step 5

The image you choose may vary from the one shown here.

6 At the Save Picture dialog box, click *Desktop* in the *Favorites* section of the Navigation pane, select the current text in the *File name* text box, type **BanffPicture1**, and then click Save or press Enter.

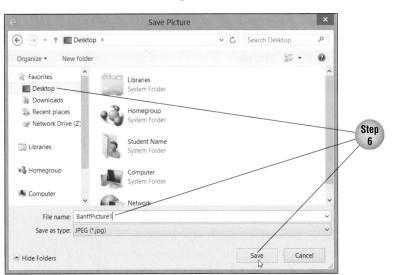

Step 6

7 Click in the Address bar, type **www.dogpile.com**, and then press Enter.

8 Click the Images tab at the Dogpile home page.

9 Click in the search text box, type **Banff National Park map**, and then press Enter or click the Go Fetch! button.

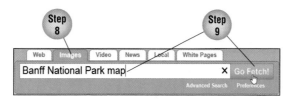

In Brief
Downloading Images from Web Page
1. Display desired web page in Internet Explorer window.
2. Right-click desired image.
3. Click *Save picture as*.
4. Navigate to desired drive and/or folder.
5. Type file name in *File name* text box.
6. Click Save.

10 Browse the map images that display in the search results, right-click the mouse over one of the maps you want to download, and then click *Save picture as* at the shortcut menu.

11 At the Save Picture dialog box, with *Desktop* already selected in the Address bar and with the current file name already selected in the *File name* text box, type **BanffMap1** and then click Save or press Enter.

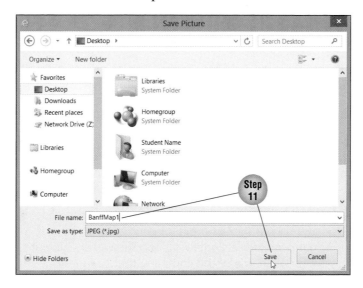

In Addition

Downloading an Application

Using Internet Explorer, you can download applications and programs to install onto your computer. When an application is downloaded, Internet Explorer displays the download bar toward the bottom of the screen (as shown below) asking if you want to run or save the application. If you want to install the application, click the Run button. Click the Save button if you want Internet Explorer to save the application in a temporary folder. If you want to save the application in a spe-cific location on your computer, click the down-pointing arrow on the Save button and then click *Save As* at the drop-down list that displays. This displays the Save As dialog box where you can specify the drive or file in which you want to save the file. Applications downloaded from the Internet can potentially contain viruses, so make sure the website and file are from a trusted source.

Activity 1.5

Evaluating Content on the Web

The Web is a vast repository of information that is easily accessible and constantly changing. Although a wealth of accurate and timely information is available at your fingertips, some information on the Internet may be outdated, inaccurate, or of poor quality, and therefore should not be relied upon. Since anyone with an Internet connection and the right software can publish information on the Web, knowing the clues to recognizing accurate and current content is a worthwhile skill. The following are some tips to help you develop this skill.

First, look for an author, publisher, or website owner name and consider if the source is credible. For example, is the author associated with a recognizable company, government, or news organization? Second, look for the date the information was published. Is the content outdated? If yes, consider the impact that more current information might have on the information you are evaluating. Third, look for indications that a bias may exist in the content. For example, is there a sponsor on the site that might indicate the information is one-sided? Can the information be validated by another source?

Project

Allan Herron, research coordinator at Marquee Productions, is working on research for a new documentary about the Apollo space missions. She has asked you to locate information on the Web that she can add to her research. You want to be careful that the information you provide for the project is credible.

1. With the Internet Explorer window active, click in the Address bar, type **www.google.com**, and then press Enter.

2. At the Google home page, type **Apollo lunar missions** in the search text box and then click the Search button or press Enter.

3. Click a hyperlink to a page that interests you.

4. At the web page, try to locate the author or publisher name, the date the article was published, and/or the date the page was last updated. If the web page contains any ads or sponsors, consider if this advertising has an impact on the content you are reading.

   > Some pages put this information at the bottom of the page, while other pages place the author and date at the beginning of the article. If you cannot find an author or date, look for a Contact link on the website you are viewing to see if you can determine the name of the company that has published the information. Also, look over the web address to see if the address provides a clue to the authorship. For example, a web address with a *.edu* domain indicates the source is from a page connected with an educational institution.

5. Click the New Tab tab to open a new browsing window.

   Your tab name may vary.

   Step 5

   Apollo Missions to t... ✕

6. Click in the Address bar, type **www.nasa.gov/ mission_pages/apollo**, and then press Enter.

7. Scroll to the bottom of the page and read the information in the banner next to the NASA logo that provides information about the date the page was last updated, the page editor, and the NASA official.

Step 7

8 Click the tab for the first web page you visited about Apollo lunar missions and click the Back button to return to the search results list.

9 Click another link that interests you and try to locate information about the date, author, and publisher similar to that which you viewed at NASA's website.

10 Compare the two pages shown side by side in Figure 1.3 below. Note that one page provides details about dates and authors while the other page does not have the same references.

> The page without the references may not necessarily have inaccurate data or be an otherwise poor-quality source of information about the Apollo missions; however, the absence of an author or date of revision means that you would have difficulty citing this source for a research paper or other academic assignment.

11 Close Internet Explorer. Click the Close all tabs button at the Internet Explorer dialog box.

FIGURE 1.3 Step 10

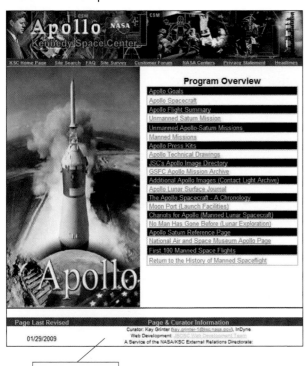

This page has source and date references.

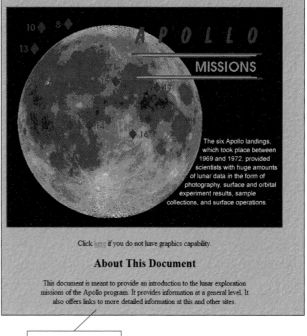

This page has no author, publisher, or date reference.

Features Summary

Feature	Button	Keyboard Shortcut
go back to previous web page	←	Alt + Left Arrow OR Backspace
go forward to next web page	→	Alt + Right Arrow
go to home page	🏠	Alt + Home
display Favorites Center	★	Alt + C
display Tools drop-down list	⚙	Alt + X

Knowledge Check

Completion: In the space provided at the right, indicate the correct term, command, or option.

1. The letters *URL* stand for this.
2. Type a URL in this bar at the Internet Explorer window.
3. Click this button on the Internet Explorer toolbar to display the previous web page.
4. Bing is the default search engine in Internet Explorer. List two other search engines.
5. Reduce the number of search results by looking for these options at the search engine's website.
6. Download an image from a website to a file on your computer by right-clicking the image and then selecting this option at the shortcut menu.

Skills Review

Note: Check with your instructor before completing the Skills Review activities to find out if you have to print the pages you visit.

Review 1 Browsing the Internet and Navigating with Hyperlinks

1. Open Internet Explorer.
2. Click in the Address bar, type **www.si.edu**, and then press Enter. (This is the home page for the Smithsonian Institution.)
3. Click a hyperlink to a topic that interests you and then read the page.
4. Click another hyperlink and then read the page.
5. Click the Back button until the Smithsonian Institution home page displays.

Review 2 Searching for Specific Sites

1. At the Internet Explorer window, search for websites on mountain climbing.
2. In the search results, click a hyperlink to a site that interests you.
3. Display the Yahoo! website and then use advanced options to search for websites with the *.com* domain on mountain climbing in British Columbia, Canada.
4. Visit at least two sites in the search results that interest you.

Review 3 Downloading Content from a Web Page

1. Using your favorite search engine, search for websites on parasailing in Hawaii. Find a site that contains a parasailing image that you like.
2. Download the parasailing image to the desktop, saving it as **ParasailImage1**.
3. Search for maps of Hawaii.
4. Browse the map images and then select one to download to the desktop, saving it as **HawaiiMap1**.
5. Close Internet Explorer.

Skills Assessment

Note: Check with your instructor before completing the Skills Assessment activities to find out if you have to print the pages you visit.

Assessment 1 Visiting Web Pages for Current News Articles

1. Sam Vestering, a manager at Worldwide Enterprises, likes to keep up to date with current events by reading the daily headlines for various newspapers. He has asked you to scan the home pages for two online newspapers—the *New York Times* and *USA Today*—for articles of interest. To begin, open Internet Explorer.
2. Go to the website of the *New York Times* at www.nytimes.com. Scan the headlines for today's publication, click the hyperlink to an article that interests you, and then read the article.
3. Visit the website of *USA Today* at www.usatoday.com, click the hyperlink to an article that interests you, and then read the article.

Assessment 2 Navigating Websites for Theatre Programs

1. Cal Rubine, the chair of the Theatre Arts Division at Niagara Peninsula College, has asked you to visit the web pages for the theatre and/or drama departments at two universities to compare programs. Visit the home page for York University, Toronto, Canada, at www.yorku.ca.
2. Locate the web page for the Theatre Department and then read about the program.
3. Visit the home page for New York University at www.nyu.edu.
4. Using NYU's home-page search feature, locate the web page for the Department of Drama (undergraduate) and then read about the program. If necessary, click hyperlinks to more pages to find program details.

Assessment 3 Downloading Content on Ski Resorts

1. You work for First Choice Travel and are preparing a brochure on snow skiing vacations. You need some information and images for the brochure. Search for information on snow-skiing resorts in Utah.
2. Visit a website that interests you and that contains an image of a resort or mountains.
3. Download an image from the web page to the desktop, saving it as **UtahResortImage1**.
4. Close Internet Explorer.

Assessment 4 Deleting Downloaded Content on the Desktop

1. At the Windows 8 desktop, right-click the ***UtahResortImage1*** file and then click *Delete* at the shortcut menu. Click *Yes* at the Delete File dialog box to move the file to the Recycle Bin.
2. Delete all of the other downloaded files you saved to the desktop during this section.

Marquee Series

MICROSOFT®

PowerPoint® 2013

Nita Rutkosky
Pierce College at Puyallup,
Puyallup, Washington

Denise Seguin
Fanshawe College,
London, Ontario

Audrey Roggenkamp
Pierce College at Puyallup,
Puyallup, Washington

Ian Rutkosky
Pierce College at Puyallup,
Puyallup, Washington

Paradigm
PUBLISHING

St. Paul

Managing Editor	Christine Hurney
Director of Production	Timothy W. Larson
Production Editor	Sarah Kearin
Cover and Text Designer	Leslie Anderson
Copy Editor	Sid Korpi, Proof Positive Editing
Design and Production Specialists	Jack Ross and Sara Schmidt Boldon
Testers	Desiree Carvel; Ann E. Mills, Ivy Tech Community College of Indiana, Indianapolis, IN; Brienna McWade
Indexer	Terry Casey
VP & Director of Digital Projects	Chuck Bratton
Digital Projects Manager	Tom Modl

The authors, editors, and publisher thank the following instructors for their helpful suggestions during the planning and development of the Marquee Office 2013 series: Olugbemiga Adekunle, Blue Ridge Community College, Harrisonburg, VA; Letty Barnes, Lake WA Institute of Technology, Kirkland, WA; Erika Nadas, Wilbur Wright College, Chicago, IL; Carolyn Walker, Greenville Technical College, Greenville, SC; Carla Anderson, National College, Lynchburg, VA; Judy A. McLaney, Lurleen B. Wallace Community College, Opp, AL; Sue Canter, Guilford Technical Community College, Jamestown, NC; Reuel Sample, National College, Knoxville, TN; Regina Young, Wiregrass Georgia Technical College, Valdosta, GA; William Roxbury, National College, Stow, OH; Charles Adams, II, Danville Community College, Danville, VA; Karen Spray, Northeast Community College, Norfolk, NE; Deborah Miller, Augusta Technical College, Augusta, GA; Wanda Stuparits, Lanier Technical College, Cumming, GA; Gale Wilson, Brookhaven College, Farmers Branch, TX; Jocelyn S. Pinkard, Arlington Career Institute, Grand Prairie, TX; Ann Blackman, Parkland College, Champaign, IL; Fathia Williams, Fletcher Technical Community College, Houma, LA; Leslie Martin, Gaston College, Dallas, NC; Tom Rose, Kellogg Community College, Battle Creek, MI; Casey Thompson, Wiregrass Georgia Technical College, Douglas, GA; Larry Bush, University of Cincinnati, Clermont College, Amelia, OH; Tim Ellis, Schoolcraft College, Liconia, MI; Miles Cannon, Lanier Technical College, Oakwood, GA; Irvin LaFleur, Lanier Technical College, Cumming, GA; Patricia Partyka, Schoolcraft College, Prudenville, MI.

Text: ISBN 978-0-76385-249-8
Text & CD: ISBN 978-0-76385-270-2

© 2014 by Paradigm Publishing, Inc.
875 Montreal Way
St. Paul, MN 55102
Email: educate@emcp.com
Website: www.emcp.com

Printed in the United States of America

22 21 20 19 18 17 16 15 14 13   1 2 3 4 5 6 7 8 9 10

Contents

PowerPoint® 2013

Create colorful and powerful presentations using PowerPoint, Microsoft's presentation program that is included in the Office 2013 suite. Use PowerPoint to organize and present information and create visual aids for a presentation. PowerPoint is a full-featured presentation program that provides a wide variety of editing and formatting features as well as sophisticated visual elements such as clip art, pictures, SmartArt, WordArt, and drawn objects. While working in PowerPoint, you will produce presentations for the following six companies.

 First Choice Travel is a travel center offering a full range of traveling services from booking flights, hotel reservations, and rental cars to offering travel seminars.

 The Waterfront Bistro offers fine dining for lunch and dinner and also offers banquet facilities, a wine cellar, and catering services.

 Worldwide Enterprises is a national and international distributor of products for a variety of companies and is the exclusive movie distribution agent for Marquee Productions.

 Marquee Productions is involved in all aspects of creating movies from script writing and development to filming. The company produces documentaries, biographies, as well as historical and action movies.

 Performance Threads maintains an inventory of rental costumes and also researches, designs, and sews special-order and custom-made costumes.

 The mission of the Niagara Peninsula College Theatre Arts Division is to offer a curriculum designed to provide students with a thorough exposure to all aspects of the theater arts.

In Section 1 you will learn how to
Prepare a Presentation

Prepare a presentation using a template provided by PowerPoint or create your own presentation and apply formatting with a design theme. Preparing a presentation consists of general steps such as creating and editing slides; adding enhancements to slides; and saving, running, previewing, printing, and closing a presentation. When running a presentation, the way in which one slide is removed from the screen and the next slide is displayed is referred to as a *transition*. You can add interesting transitions to slides as well as sound to a presentation.

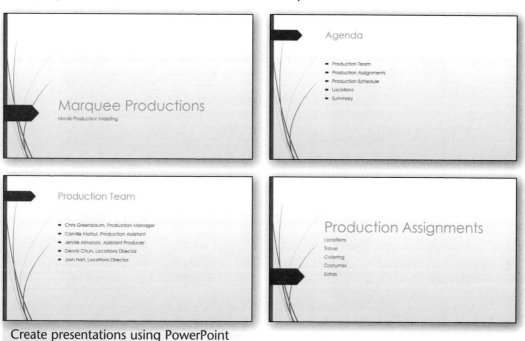

Create presentations using PowerPoint design themes and apply various slide layouts to change the appearance of slides.

In Section 2 you will learn how to
Edit and Enhance Slides

Edit slides and slide elements in a presentation to customize and personalize the presentation. Editing can include such functions as rearranging and deleting slides; cutting, copying, and pasting text; changing the font, paragraph alignment, and paragraph spacing; and changing the design theme, theme color, and theme font. Add visual appeal to a presentation by inserting clip art images, pictures, and SmartArt organizational charts and graphics.

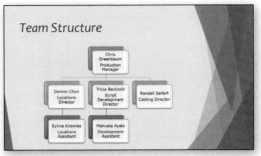

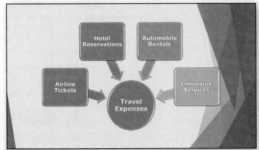

Edit slides by performing such actions as rearranging and deleting slides and changing slide size. Perform editing tasks on text in slides such as changing the font, paragraph alignment, and spacing. Enhance the visual appeal of a presentation by inserting such elements as a company logo, clip art, an organizational chart, and a graphic.

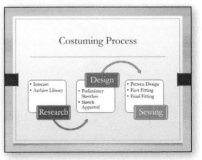

In Section 3 you will learn how to
Customize Presentations

Customize a presentation with the WordArt feature and by drawing and formatting objects and text boxes. Additional features for customizing a presentation include using the Clipboard; inserting and formatting a table; inserting actions buttons, hyperlinks, and headers and footers; and inserting audio and video files.

Further customize presentations with features such as headers and footers, audio and video files, WordArt, shapes, text boxes, and tables.

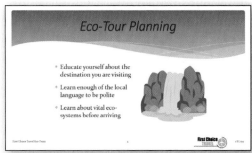

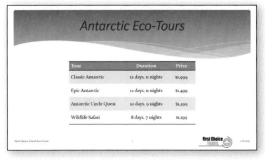

PowerPoint® SECTION 1
Preparing a Presentation

Skills

- Complete the presentation cycle
- Choose a design theme
- Add a new slide to a presentation
- Navigate in a presentation
- Insert a slide in a presentation
- Change the slide layout
- Change the presentation view
- Rearrange, delete, and hide slides
- Use the Help feature
- Check spelling in a presentation
- Use Thesaurus to display synonyms for words
- Run a presentation and use the pen during a presentation
- Add transitions and sound to a presentation
- Print and preview a presentation

Student Resources

Before beginning the activities in PowerPoint, copy to your storage medium the PowerPoint folder on the Student CD. This folder contains the data files you will need to complete the projects in each PowerPoint section.

Projects Overview

Use an installed template to prepare a presentation about the new features in PowerPoint 2013; prepare a movie production meeting presentation and a location team meeting presentation.

Prepare an executive meeting presentation for Worldwide Enterprises.

Prepare a presentation containing information on the accommodations and services offered by The Waterfront Bistro.

Prepare a presentation on Toronto, Ontario, Canada.

Prepare a presentation for a costume meeting.

Model Answers for Projects

These model answers for the projects you complete in Section 1 provide a preview of the finished projects before you begin working and also allow you to compare your own results with these models to ensure you have created the materials accurately.

PS1-MPProdMtg.pptx (a two-page document) is the project in Activities 1.2 to 1.10.

POWERPOINT SECTION 1
Project Model Answers

Activity 1.1

Completing the Presentation Cycle

PowerPoint is a presentation graphics program you can use to organize and present information. With PowerPoint, you can create visual aids for a presentation and then print copies of the aids as well as run the presentation. Preparing a presentation in

PowerPoint generally follows a presentation cycle. The steps in the cycle vary but generally include opening PowerPoint; creating and editing slides; saving, printing, running, and closing the presentation; and then closing PowerPoint.

Project You are an employee of Marquee Productions and Office 2013 has just been installed on your computer. You need to prepare a presentation in the near future so you decide to open a PowerPoint file and experiment with running the presentation.

SNAP

Tutorial 1.1
Opening, Running, and Closing a Presentation

1 Open PowerPoint by clicking the PowerPoint 2013 tile at the Windows 8 Start screen.

> This step may vary. Check with your instructor for specific instructions.

2 At the PowerPoint 2013 opening screen, click the *Welcome to PowerPoint* template.

> If this template is not visible, you will need to search for it. To do this, click in the search text box, type **Welcome to PowerPoint**, and then press the Enter key.

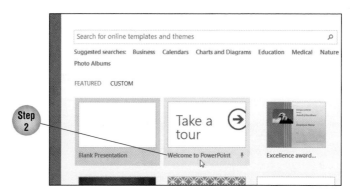

3 Click the Create button.

> The Welcome to PowerPoint template opens in the PowerPoint window. What displays in the PowerPoint window will vary depending on what type of presentation you are creating. However, the PowerPoint window contains some consistent elements, as identified in Figure 1.1. Refer to Table 1.1 for a description of the window elements.

4 Run the presentation by clicking the Start From Beginning button on the Quick Access toolbar.

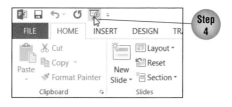

(5) When the first slide fills the screen, read the information and then click the left mouse button. Continue reading the information in each slide and clicking the left mouse button to advance to the next slide. When a black screen displays, click the left mouse button to end the slide show.

FIGURE 1.1 PowerPoint Window

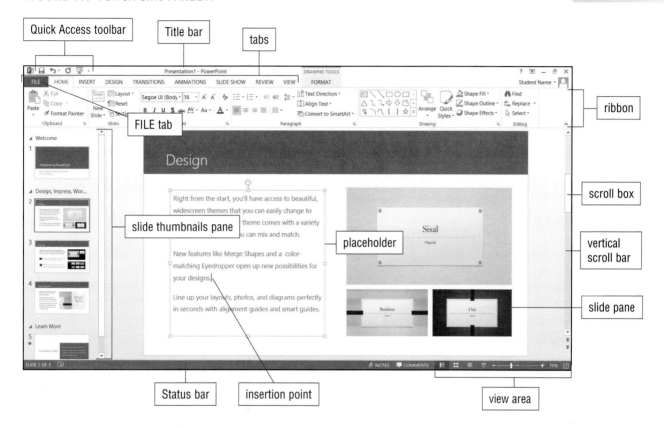

TABLE 1.1 PowerPoint Window Elements

Feature.	Description
FILE tab	when clicked, displays backstage area with options for working with and managing files
I-beam pointer	used to move the insertion point or to select text
insertion point	indicates location of next character entered at the keyboard
placeholder	location on a slide with a dotted border that holds text or objects
Quick Access toolbar	contains buttons for commonly used commands
ribbon	area containing the tabs with commands and buttons divided into groups
slide pane	displays the slide and slide contents
slide thumbnails pane	left side of the screen that displays slide thumbnails
Status bar	displays slide number, design theme, view buttons, and Zoom slider bar
tabs	contain commands and features organized into groups
Title bar	displays file name followed by program name
vertical scroll bar	display specific slides using this scroll bar
view area	located toward right side of Status bar; contains buttons for changing the presentation view

continues

6 Save the presentation by clicking the Save button 🔲 on the Quick Access toolbar.

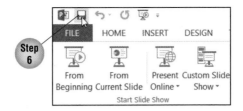

7 At the Save As backstage area, click the *SkyDrive* option preceded by your name if you are saving to your SkyDrive or click the *Computer* option if you are saving to a USB flash drive.

8 Click the Browse button.

9 At the Save As dialog box, navigate to your PowerPointS1 folder (if necessary), type **PS1-MPPowerPoint2013** in the *File name* text box, and then press Enter.

> The Address bar at the Save As dialog box displays the active folder and the folder path.

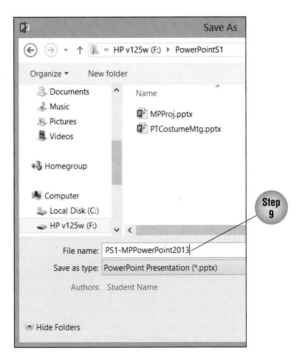

10 At the PowerPoint window, print the presentation information in outline view by clicking the FILE tab and then clicking the *Print* option.

> The FILE tab is located in the upper left corner of the screen at the left side of the HOME tab. When you click the FILE tab, the backstage area displays with options for working with and managing files.

11 At the Print backstage area, click the second gallery in the *Settings* category (the gallery containing the text *Full Page Slides*) and then click *Outline* in the *Print Layout* section of the drop-down list.

12 Click the Print button. ***Note: Always check with your instructor before printing.***

13 Close the presentation by clicking the FILE tab and then clicking the *Close* option.

If a message displays asking if you want to save the presentation, click Yes.

14 Close PowerPoint by clicking the Close button that displays in the upper right corner of the screen.

In Addition

Using Tabs

The ribbon area displays below the Quick Access toolbar. The buttons and options in the ribbon area vary depending on the tab selected and the width of the window displayed on the screen. PowerPoint commands and features are organized into tabs that display in the ribbon area. Commands and features are organized into groups within a tab. For example, the HOME tab, which is the default tab, contains the Clipboard, Slides, Font, Paragraph, Drawing, and Editing groups. When you hover the mouse over a button, a ScreenTip displays with the name of the button, a keyboard shortcut (if any), and a description of the purpose of the button.

Activity 1.2

Choosing a Design Theme; Creating Slides; Closing a Presentation

Create a PowerPoint presentation using an installed template as you did in the previous activity or begin with a blank presentation and apply your own formatting or a slide design theme. To display a blank PowerPoint presentation, use the keyboard shortcut Ctrl + N, or click the FILE tab, click the *New* option, and then click the *Blank Presentation* template in the New backstage area. A PowerPoint presentation screen displays in Normal view with the slide pane in the center and the slide thumbnails pane located at the left side of the screen.

Project Chris Greenbaum, production manager for Marquee Productions, has asked you to prepare slides for a movie production meeting. You decide to prepare the presentation using a design template offered by PowerPoint.

Tutorial 1.2
Creating and Saving
a Presentation

1. Open PowerPoint.

2. At the PowerPoint 2013 opening screen, click the *Blank Presentation* template.

3. At the PowerPoint window, click the DESIGN tab.

4. Click the More button located at the right side of the theme thumbnails in the Themes group.

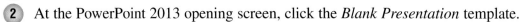

5. Click the *Wisp* thumbnail in the *Office* section of the drop-down gallery. (Design thumbnails display in alphabetic order at the drop-down gallery.)

When you click the More button, a drop-down gallery displays. This gallery is an example of the **live preview** feature. When you hover your mouse pointer over one of the design themes, the slide in the slide pane displays with the design theme formatting applied. With the live preview feature, you can view a design theme before actually applying it to the presentation.

6. Click the third thumbnail from the left in the Variants group (the light blue option).

This changes the slide background to a light blue color.

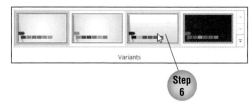

7 Click anywhere in the *Click to add title* placeholder that displays in the slide in the slide pane and then type **Marquee Productions**.

> A *placeholder* is a location on a slide that is marked with a border and holds text or an object.

8 Click anywhere in the *Click to add subtitle* placeholder that displays in the slide and then type **Movie Production Meeting**.

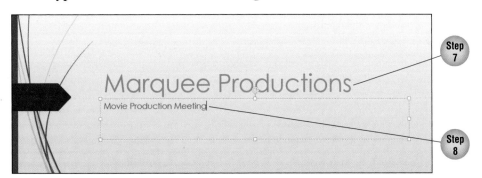

9 Click the HOME tab and then click the New Slide button in the Slides group.

> When you click this button, a new slide displays in the slide pane with the Title and Content layout. You will learn more about slide layouts in Activity 1.3.

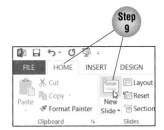

10 Click anywhere in the *Click to add title* placeholder that displays in the slide and then type **Agenda**.

11 Click anywhere in the *Click to add text* placeholder that displays in the slide and then type **Production Team**.

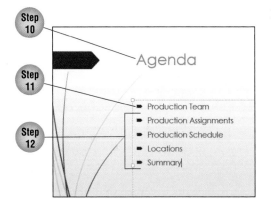

12 Press the Enter key and then type the following agenda items, pressing the Enter key after each item except the last item: **Production Assignments, Production Schedule, Locations,** and **Summary**.

> You can use keys on the keyboard to move the insertion point to various locations within a placeholder in a slide. Refer to Table 1.2 on the next page for a list of insertion point movement commands.

13 Click the New Slide button in the Slides group on the HOME tab.

continues

Activity 1.2 9

TABLE 1.2 Insertion Point Movement Commands

To move insertion point	Press
One character left	Left Arrow
One character right	Right Arrow
One line up	Up Arrow
One line down	Down Arrow
One word to the left	Ctrl + Left Arrow
One word to the right	Ctrl + Right Arrow
To end of a line of text	End
To beginning of a line of text	Home
To beginning of current paragraph in placeholder	Ctrl + Up Arrow
To beginning of previous paragraph in placeholder	Ctrl + Up Arrow twice
To beginning of next paragraph in placeholder	Ctrl + Down Arrow
To beginning of text in placeholder	Ctrl + Home
To end of text in placeholder	Ctrl + End

14 Click anywhere in the *Click to add title* placeholder that displays in the slide and then type **Department Reports**.

15 Click anywhere in the *Click to add text* placeholder that displays in the slide and then type the bulleted text as shown in the slide below. Press the Enter key after each item except the last item.

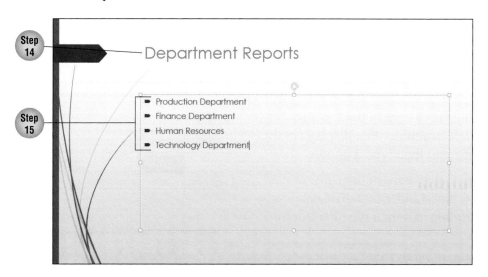

16 Click the New Slide button in the Slides group on the HOME tab.

17 Click anywhere in the *Click to add title* placeholder that displays in the slide and then type **Locations**.

18 Click anywhere in the *Click to add text* placeholder that displays in the slide, type **Studio Shoots**, and then press the Enter key.

19 Press the Tab key, type **Vancouver Studio**, and then press Enter.

   Pressing the Tab key demotes the insertion point to a second-level bullet, while pressing Shift + Tab promotes the insertion point back to the first level.

20 Type **Los Angeles Studio** and then press Enter.

21 Press Shift + Tab, type **Location Shoots**, and then press Enter.

22 Press the Tab key, type **Stanley Park**, and then press Enter.

23 Type **Downtown Streets**.

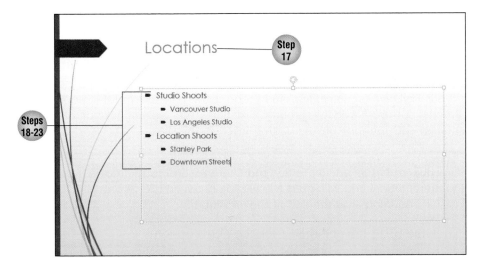

In Brief

Choose Slide Design
1. Click DESIGN tab.
2. Click More button at right side of theme thumbnails.
3. Click desired theme at drop-down gallery.

Add Slide
1. Click HOME tab.
2. Click New Slide button.

Save Presentation
1. Click Save button on Quick Access toolbar.
2. Click desired location.
3. Click Browse button.
4. At Save As dialog box, type presentation file name.
5. Press Enter.

Close PowerPoint
1. Click FILE tab.
2. Click *Close* option.

24 Click the Save button on the Quick Access toolbar.

25 At the Save As backstage area, click the desired location such as your SkyDrive or the *Computer* option and then click the Browse button.

26 At the Save As dialog box, make sure the PowerPointS1 folder is active, type **PS1-MPProdMtg** in the *File name* text box, and then press Enter.

27 Close the presentation by clicking the FILE tab and then clicking the *Close* option.

In Addition

Planning a Presentation

Consider the following basic guidelines when preparing the content for a presentation:

- **Determine the main purpose of the presentation.** Do not try to cover too many topics. Identifying the main point of the presentation will help you stay focused and convey a clear message to the audience.
- **Determine the output.** To help decide the type of output needed, consider the availability of equipment, the size of the room where you will make the presentation, and the number of people who will be attending the presentation.
- **Show one idea per slide.** Each slide in a presentation should convey only one main idea. Too many ideas on a slide may confuse the audience and cause you to stray from the purpose of the slide.

- **Maintain a consistent design.** A consistent design and color scheme for slides in a presentation will create continuity and cohesiveness. Do not use too much color or too many pictures or other graphic elements.
- **Keep slides easy to read and uncluttered.** Keep slides simple and easy for the audience to read. Keep words and other items, such as bullets, to a minimum.
- **Determine printing needs.** Will you be providing audience members with handouts? If so, will these handouts consist of a printing of each slide? an outline of the presentation? a printing of each slide with space for taking notes?

Activity 1.3

Opening, Navigating, and Inserting Slides in a Presentation; Choosing a Slide Layout

Open a saved presentation by displaying the Open dialog box and then double-clicking the desired presentation. Display the Open dialog box by clicking the FILE tab and then clicking the *Open* option. At the Open backstage area, click the desired location (your SkyDrive or *Computer*), and then click the Browse button. Navigate through slides in a presentation with buttons on the vertical scroll bar, by clicking desired slide thumbnails in Normal view, or using keys on the keyboard. Insert a new slide with a specific layout by clicking the New Slide button arrow located in the Slides group on the HOME tab and then clicking the desired layout at the drop-down list. Choose the layout that matches the type of text or object you want to insert in the slide.

Project

Tutorial 1.3
Navigating and Inserting Slides in a Presentation

Chris Greenbaum has asked you to add more information to the movie production meeting presentation. You will insert a new slide between the second and third slides in the presentation and another at the end of the presentation.

1 Click the FILE tab and then click the *Open* option.

> You can also open a presentation by inserting an Open button on the Quick Access toolbar and then clicking the button. To insert the button, click the Customize Quick Access Toolbar button that displays at the right side of the toolbar and then click *Open* at the drop-down list.

2 At the Open backstage area, click the desired location such as your SkyDrive or the *Computer* option, and then click the Browse button.

3 At the Open dialog box, make sure the PowerPointS1 folder on your storage medium is active and then double-click *PS1-MPProdMtg.pptx* in the Content pane.

4 With **PS1-MPProdMtg.pptx** open, click the Next Slide button 🔽 located at the bottom of the vertical scroll bar.

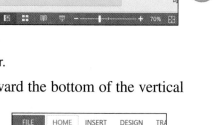
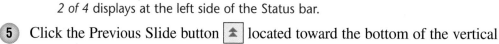

Step 4

> Clicking this button displays the next slide, Slide 2, in the presentation. Notice that *SLIDE 2 of 4* displays at the left side of the Status bar.

5 Click the Previous Slide button 🔼 located toward the bottom of the vertical scroll bar to display Slide 1.

> When you click the Previous Slide button, *SLIDE 1 of 4* displays at the left side of the Status bar.

6 Display Slide 2 in the slide pane by clicking the second slide in the slide thumbnails pane (the slide titled *Agenda*).

7 Insert a new slide between Slides 2 and 3 by clicking the New Slide button in the Slides group on the HOME tab.

> When you select a slide in the slide thumbnails pane and then click the New Slide button, the new slide is inserted after the selected slide.

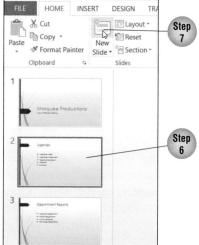

Step 7

Step 6

8 Click anywhere in the *Click to add title* placeholder in the slide in the slide pane and then type **Production Schedule**.

9 Click anywhere in the *Click to add text* placeholder located in the slide and then type the bulleted text as shown in the slide at the right. Press the Enter key after typing each item except the last item.

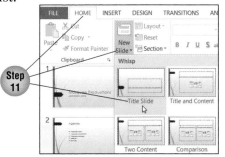

In Brief

Open Presentation
1. Click FILE tab.
2. Click *Open* option.
3. Click the desired location.
4. Click the Browse button.
5. At Open dialog box, double-click desired presentation.

10 Click below the last thumbnail in the slide thumbnails pane. (You may need to scroll down the slide thumbnails pane to display the last slide.)

> When you click below the slide thumbnail, an orange horizontal line displays below Slide 5.

11 Click the HOME tab, click the New Slide button arrow, and then click the *Title Slide* layout that displays in the drop-down list.

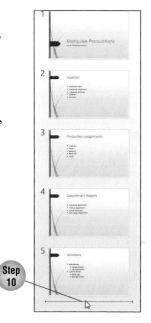

12 Click the *Click to add title* placeholder and then type **Production Leader**.

13 Click the *Click to add subtitle* placeholder and then type **Chris Greenbaum**.

14 Click the Save button on the Quick Access toolbar to save **PS1-MPProdMtg.pptx**.

In Addition

Correcting Errors in PowerPoint

PowerPoint's AutoCorrect feature automatically corrects certain words as you type them. For example, type *teh* and press the spacebar, and AutoCorrect changes it to *the*. PowerPoint also contains a spelling feature that inserts a wavy red line below words that are not contained in the Spelling dictionary or not corrected by AutoCorrect. If the word containing a red wavy line is correct, you can leave it as written since the red wavy line does not print. If the word is incorrect, edit it.

Activity 1.4

Changing Views

PowerPoint provides different viewing options for a presentation. Change the presentation view with buttons in the Presentation Views group on the VIEW tab or with buttons in the view area on the Status bar. The Normal view is the default view, and you can change the view to Outline view, Slide Sorter view, Notes Page view, or Reading view. Choose the view based on the type of activity you are performing in the presentation. Another method for entering text in a slide is in Outline view. When Outline view is active, the slide thumbnails pane changes to an outline pane for entering text. Insert speaker's notes into a presentation using the notes pane, which can be displayed by clicking the NOTES button on the Status bar.

Project

After reviewing the movie production presentation, Chris Greenbaum has asked you to add a new slide and edit an existing slide.

Tutorial 1.4
Changing Views and Slide Layout

1 With **PS1-MPProdMtg.pptx** open, click the VIEW tab and then click the Outline View button in the Presentation Views group.

2 Click immediately right of the text *Music* in the third slide located toward the middle of the outline pane, press the Enter key, and then press Shift + Tab.

> This moves the insertion point back a level and inserts the number *4* followed by a slide icon.

3 Type **Production Assignments**, press the Enter key, and then press the Tab key. Type the remaining text for Slide 4 as shown at the right. Do not press the Enter key after typing *Extras*.

> When you are finished typing the text, the presentation will contain seven slides.

4 Click immediately right of the text *Location Shoots* in the third slide.

5 Press the Enter key and then type **Editing**.

> This inserts *Editing* between *Location Shoots* and *Dubbing*.

6 Make Slide 6 the active slide in the slide pane, click anywhere in the text *Click to add notes* in the notes pane, and then type **Camille Matsui will report on the park location.**

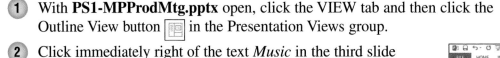

Step 1

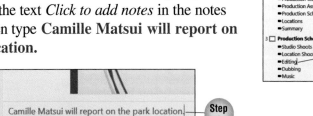

Step 3

Step 5

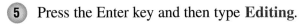

Camille Matsui will report on the park location.

Step 6

7 Display the slides in Notes Page view by clicking the Notes Page button in the Presentation Views group.

> In Notes Page view, an individual slide displays on a page with any added notes displayed below the slide. Notice that the note you created about Camille Matsui displays below the slide in the page.

8 Click the Previous Slide button on the vertical scroll bar until Slide 1 displays.

9 Increase the zoom by clicking the Zoom button 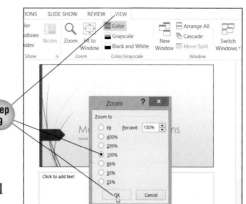 in the Zoom group on the VIEW tab, clicking *100%* at the Zoom dialog box, and then clicking OK.

In Brief

Display in Normal View
1. Click VIEW tab.
2. Click Normal button.
OR
Click Normal button in view area on Status bar.

Display in Outline View
1. Click VIEW tab.
2. Click Outline View button.

Display in Slide Sorter View
1. Click VIEW tab.
2. Click Slide Sorter button.
OR
Click Slide Sorter button in view area on Status bar.

Display in Notes Page View
1. Click VIEW tab.
2. Click Notes Page button.

10 You can also change the zoom using the Zoom slider bar. Change the zoom by positioning the mouse pointer on the Zoom slider bar button located at the right side of the Status bar. Hold down the left mouse button, drag to the right until the zoom percentage at the right side of the Zoom slider bar displays as approximately *138%*, and then release the mouse button.

11 Click the Zoom Out button 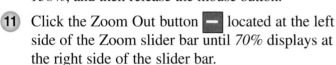 located at the left side of the Zoom slider bar until *70%* displays at the right side of the slider bar.

> Click the Zoom Out button to decrease the zoom display and click the Zoom In button to increase the display.

12 View all slides in the presentation in slide thumbnails by clicking the Slide Sorter button 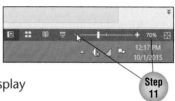 in the view area on the Status bar.

13 View the presentation in Reading view by clicking the Reading View button in the Presentation Views group.

> Use Reading view to show the presentation to someone viewing the presentation on his or her own computer. You can also use Reading view to view a presentation in a window with controls that make the presentation easy to view. In Reading view, navigation buttons display in the lower right corner of the screen immediately left of the view area on the Status bar.

14 View the slides in the presentation in Reading view by clicking the left mouse button on the slides until a black screen displays. At the black screen, click the mouse button again.

> This returns the presentation to the previous view—in this case, Slide Sorter view.

15 Return the presentation to the Normal view by clicking the Normal button in the Presentation Views group.

16 Close the Notes pane by clicking the NOTES button on the Status bar.

17 Save **PS1-MPProdMtg.pptx**.

In Addition

Navigating in a Presentation Using the Keyboard

You can also use the keyboard to display slides in a presentation. In Normal view, press the Down Arrow or Page Down key to display the next slide or press the Up Arrow or Page Up key to display the previous slide in the presentation. Press the Home key to display the first slide in the presentation and press the End key to display the last slide in the presentation. Navigate in Outline view and Slide Sorter view by using the arrow keys on the keyboard. Navigate in Reading view by using the Right Arrow key to move to the next slide or the Left Arrow key to move to the previous slide.

Activity 1.5

Changing the Slide Layout; Selecting and Moving a Placeholder

So far, you have created slides based on a default slide layout. Change the slide layout by clicking the Layout button in the Slides group on the HOME tab and then clicking the desired layout at the drop-down list. Objects in a slide, such as text, charts, tables, and other graphic elements, are generally positioned in placeholders. Click the text or object to select the placeholder and a dashed border will surround the placeholder. You can move, size, and/or delete a selected placeholder.

Project

You have decided to make a few changes to the layout of slides in the movie production presentation.

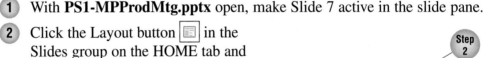

Tutorial 1.5
Modifying Placeholders

1. With **PS1-MPProdMtg.pptx** open, make Slide 7 active in the slide pane.

2. Click the Layout button 📧 in the Slides group on the HOME tab and then click the *Title and Content* layout at the drop-down list.

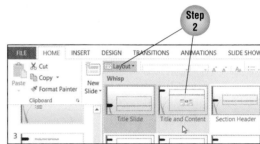

Position the mouse pointer on a slide layout and the name of the layout displays in a box.

3. Click immediately right of the *r* in *Leader* (this selects the placeholder), press the Backspace key until *Leader* is deleted, and then type **Team**.

   Sizing handles display around the selected placeholder. Use these sizing handles to increase and/or decrease the size of the placeholder.

4. Click immediately right of the *m* in *Greenbaum*.

5. Type a comma (,), press the spacebar, and then type **Production Manager**.

6. Press the Enter key and then type the remaining names and titles shown in the slide at the right. (Do not press the Enter key after typing *Josh Hart, Locations Director*.)

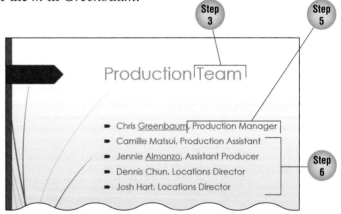

7. Click the Previous Slide button on the vertical scroll bar until Slide 4 displays.

8. Change the slide layout by clicking the Layout button in the Slides group and then clicking the *Title Slide* layout at the drop-down list.

9. Click anywhere in the title *Production Assignments*.

   This selects the placeholder.

10. Decrease the size of the placeholder by positioning the mouse pointer on the middle sizing handle that displays at the top of the placeholder until the pointer turns into a up-and-down-pointing arrow. Hold down the left mouse button, drag down to the approximate location shown on the next page, and then release the mouse button.

11 Move the title placeholder so it positions the title as shown in Figure 1.2 below. To do this, position the mouse pointer on the placeholder border until the mouse pointer displays with a four-headed arrow

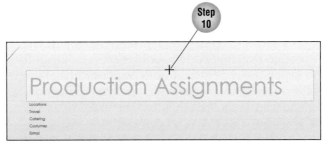

Step 10

attached, hold down the left mouse button, drag to the approximate location shown in the figure, and then release the mouse button.

12 Increase the size of the subtitle placeholder (and the size of the text). Begin by clicking on any character in the text *Locations*.

> This selects the placeholder containing the text.

13 Position the mouse pointer on the middle sizing handle that displays at the top of the placeholder until the pointer turns into an up-and-down-pointing arrow. Hold down the left mouse button, drag up approximately one inch, and then release the mouse button.

> Increasing the size of the placeholder automatically increased the size of the text in the placeholder. This is because, by default, PowerPoint automatically sizes the contents to fit the placeholder. Read the In Addition at the bottom of this page for information on the AutoFit Options button.

14 Move the content placeholder so it positions the text as shown in Figure 1.2. To do this, position the mouse pointer on the placeholder border until the mouse pointer displays with a four-headed arrow attached, hold down the left mouse button, drag to the approximate location shown in the figure, and then release the mouse button.

15 Click outside the placeholder to deselect it.

> If you are not satisfied with the changes you make to a placeholder, click the Reset button in the Slides group on the HOME tab. This resets the position, size, and formatting to the default settings.

16 Save **PS1-MPProdMtg.pptx**.

FIGURE 1.2 Slide 4

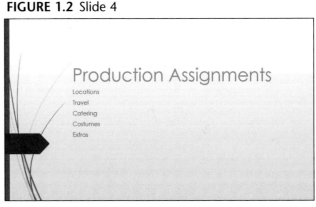

In Brief

Change Slide Layout
1. Make desired slide active.
2. Click HOME tab.
3. Click Layout button.
4. Click desired layout at drop-down list.

Move Placeholder
1. Click inside placeholder.
2. Drag with mouse to desired position.

Size Placeholder
1. Click inside placeholder.
2. Drag sizing handles to increase/decrease size.

In Addition

Using the AutoFit Options Button

If you decrease the size of a placeholder so the existing text does not fit within it, PowerPoint will automatically decrease the size of the text so it fits in the placeholder. If you click on any character in the text that has been decreased in size, an AutoFit Options button displays at the left side of the placeholder. Click the AutoFit Options button and a list of choices displays for positioning objects in the placeholder, as shown at the right. The *AutoFit Text to Placeholder* option is selected by default and tells PowerPoint to fit text within the boundaries of the placeholder. Click the middle choice, *Stop* *Fitting Text to This Placeholder*, and PowerPoint will not automatically fit the text or object within the placeholder. Choose the last option, *Control AutoCorrect Options*, to display the AutoCorrect dialog box with the AutoFormat As You Type tab selected. Additional options may display depending upon the placeholder and the type of data it contains.

Activity 1.6

Rearranging, Deleting, and Hiding Slides

As you edit a presentation, you may need to rearrange, delete, or hide specific slides. PowerPoint provides various views for creating and managing a presentation. Manage slides in the slide thumbnails pane or in Slide Sorter view. Switch to Slide Sorter view by clicking the Slide Sorter button in the view area on the Status bar or by clicking the VIEW tab and then clicking the Slide Sorter button in the Presentation Views group.

Project

Chris Greenbaum has asked you to make some changes to the presentation, including rearranging the slides, deleting a slide, and hiding a slide.

Tutorial 1.6
Rearranging, Deleting, and Hiding Slides

1. With **PS1-MPProdMtg.pptx** open, right-click Slide 5 in the slide thumbnails pane and then click *Delete Slide* at the shortcut menu.

    You can also delete a selected slide by pressing the Delete key on the keyboard.

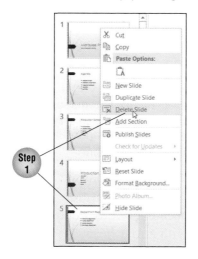

2. Click the Slide Sorter button in the view area on the Status bar.

3. Click Slide 6 to make it active.

    A selected slide displays with an orange border.

4. Position the mouse pointer on Slide 6, hold down the left mouse button, drag the slide (the arrow pointer will display with a square attached) to the left of Slide 3, and then release the mouse button.

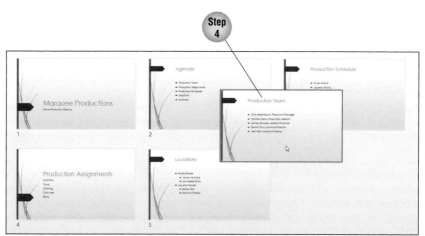

5 Click the Normal button located in the view area on the Status bar.

6 Position the mouse pointer on the Slide 5 thumbnail in the slide thumbnails pane, hold down the left mouse button, drag up until the slide displays immediately below the Slide 3 thumbnail, and then release the mouse button.

7 With the Slide 4 thumbnail selected in the slide thumbnails pane (thumbnail displays with an orange border), hide the slide by clicking the SLIDE SHOW tab and then clicking the Hide Slide button 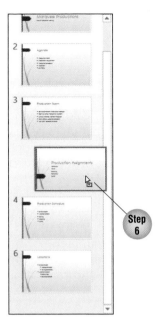 in the Set Up group.

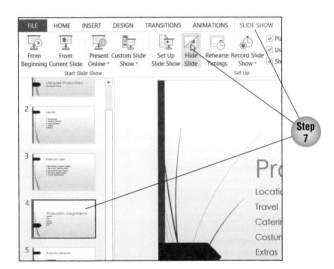

When a slide is hidden, the slide thumbnail displays dimmed and the slide number displays with a diagonal line across the number.

8 Run the presentation by clicking the From Beginning button 🖵 in the Start Slide Show group. Click the left mouse button to advance each slide until a black screen displays. At the black screen, click the left mouse button again.

9 After running the presentation, you decide to redisplay the hidden slide. To do this, make sure the Slide 4 thumbnail is selected in the slide thumbnails pane and then click the Hide Slide button in the Set Up group.

10 Save **PS1-MPProdMtg.pptx**.

In Addition

Copying Slides within a Presentation

Copying a slide within a presentation is similar to moving a slide. To copy a slide, position the arrow pointer on the desired slide and hold down the Ctrl key and the left mouse button. Drag to the location where you want the slide copied, release the left mouse button, and then release the Ctrl key. When you drag with the mouse, the mouse pointer displays with a square and a plus symbol attached.

Activity 1.7

Using Help; Checking Spelling; Using Thesaurus

Use the PowerPoint Help feature to display information about PowerPoint. To use the Help feature, click the Microsoft PowerPoint Help button (a circle with a question mark inside) located toward the upper right corner of the screen. At the PowerPoint Help window that displays, type the topic on which you want information and then press Enter or click the Search online help button. A list of topics related to the search text displays in the results window. Click the desired topic and information displays in the PowerPoint Help window. Use PowerPoint's spelling checker to find and correct misspelled words and find duplicated words (such as *and and*). The spelling checker compares words in your slide with words in its dictionary. If a match is found, the word is passed over. If no match is found, the spelling checker stops, selects the word, and offers replacements. Use Thesaurus to find synonyms, antonyms, and related words for a particular word. To use Thesaurus, click the word for which you want to display synonyms and antonyms, click the REVIEW tab, and then click the Thesaurus button in the Proofing group. This displays the Thesaurus task pane with information about the word in which the insertion point is positioned.

Project

Tutorial 1.7A
Using Help in PowerPoint

Tutorial 1.7B
Using the Spelling and Thesaurus Features

You have decided to create a new slide in the movie production presentation. Because several changes have been made to the presentation, you know that checking the spelling of all the slide text is important, but you are not sure how to do it. You will use the Help feature to learn how to complete a spelling check and then use Thesaurus to replace a couple of words with synonyms.

1. With **PS1-MPProdMtg.pptx** open, position the mouse pointer on the scroll box located on the vertical scroll bar at the right side of the screen. Hold down the left mouse button, drag the scroll box to the bottom of the scroll bar, and then release the mouse button.

   This displays Slide 6 in the slide pane. As you drag the scroll box on the vertical scroll bar, a box displays indicating the slide number and slide title (if the slide contains a title).

2. Click the HOME tab and then click the New Slide button in the Slides group.

   This inserts a new slide at the end of the presentation.

3. Click the *Click to add title* placeholder and then type **Summary**.

4. Click the *Click to add text* placeholder and then type the text shown in the slide below.

   Type the words exactly as shown. You will check the spelling in a later step.

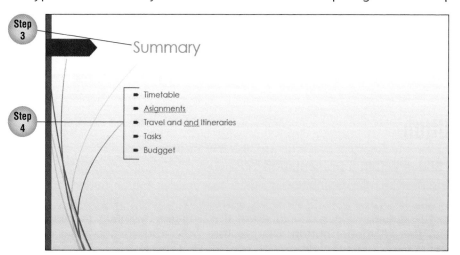

5 Learn how to complete a spelling check by clicking the Microsoft PowerPoint Help button ? located toward the upper right corner of the screen.

6 At the PowerPoint Help window, type **check spelling** in the search text box and then press Enter.

7 Click a hyperlink in the PowerPoint Help window that will display information on checking spelling.

8 Read the information that displays about checking spelling and then click the Close button ☒ located in the upper right corner of the PowerPoint Help window.

9 Complete a spelling check by moving the insertion point to the beginning of *Timetable*, clicking the REVIEW tab, and then clicking the Spelling button in the Proofing group.

10 When the spelling checker selects *Asignments* in Slide 7 and displays *Assignments* in the list box in the Spelling task pane, click the Change button.

Refer to Table 1.3 for a description of the Spelling task pane options.

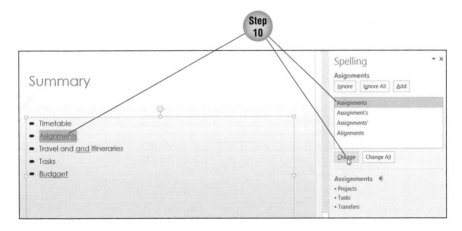

TABLE 1.3 Spelling Task Pane Options

Button	Function
Ignore	skips that occurrence of the word and leaves currently selected text as written
Ignore All	skips that occurrence of the word and all other occurrences of the word in the presentation
Delete	deletes the currently selected word(s)
Change	replaces selected word in sentence with selected word in the suggestions list box
Change All	replaces selected word with selected word in suggestions list box and all other occurrences of the word in the presentation
Add	adds selected word to the main spelling check dictionary

continues

11 When the spelling checker selects the second *and* in the slide, click the Delete button.

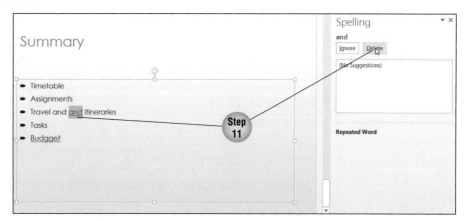

12 When the spelling checker selects *Budgget* in Slide 7 and displays *Budget* in the list box in the Spelling task pane, click the Change button.

13 When the spelling checker selects *Greenbaum* in Slide 3, click the Ignore button.

Greenbaum is a proper name and is spelled correctly. Clicking the Ignore button tells the spelling checker to leave the name as spelled.

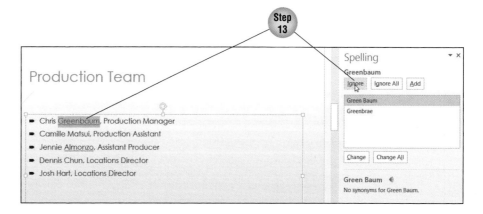

14 When the spelling checker selects *Almonzo* in Slide 3, click the Ignore button.

15 At the message telling you that the spelling check is complete, click OK.

16 Display Slide 7 in the slide pane and then click the word *Timetable*.

17 Look up synonyms for *Timetable* by clicking the Thesaurus button in the Proofing group.

This displays the Thesaurus task pane containing lists of synonyms for *Timetable*. Depending on the word you are looking up, the words in the Thesaurus task pane list box may display followed by *(n.)* for *noun*, *(adj.)* for *adjective*, or *(adv.)* for *adverb*. Antonyms may display in the list of related synonyms, usually toward the end and followed by *(Antonym)*.

18 Position the mouse pointer on the word *Schedule* in the Thesaurus task pane, click the down-pointing arrow at the right of the word, and then click *Insert* at the drop-down list.

> This replaces *Timetable* with *Schedule*.

19 Close the Thesaurus task pane by clicking the Close button located in the upper right corner of the task pane.

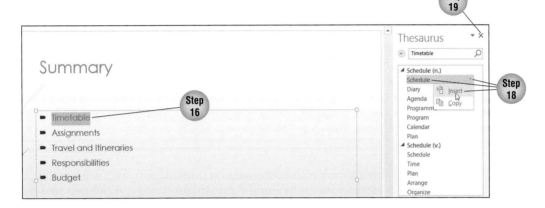

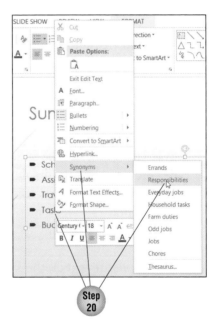

20 Right-click in the word *Tasks*, point to *Synonyms*, and then click *Responsibilities*.

> The shortcut menu offers another method for displaying synonyms for words.

21 Save **PS1-MPProdMtg.pptx**.

In Brief

Use Help
1. Click Microsoft PowerPoint Help button.
2. Click in search box.
3. Type text for desired information.
4. Press Enter.

Complete Spelling Check
1. Click REVIEW tab.
2. Click Spelling button.
3. Change or ignore highlighted words.
4. When spelling check is completed, click OK.

Use Thesaurus
1. Click desired word.
2. Click REVIEW tab.
3. Click Thesaurus button.
4. Position mouse pointer on desired replacement word in Thesaurus task pane, click down-pointing arrow at right of word, and then click *Insert*.

In Addition

Changing Spelling Options

Control spelling options at the PowerPoint Options dialog box with the *Proofing* option selected. Display this dialog box by clicking the FILE tab and then clicking *Options*. At the PowerPoint Options dialog box, click *Proofing* at the left side of the dialog box. With options in the dialog box, you can tell the spelling checker to ignore certain types of text, create custom dictionaries, and hide spelling errors in the presentation.

Editing While Checking Spelling

When spell checking a presentation, you can temporarily leave the Spelling task pane by clicking in the slide. To resume the spelling check, click the Resume button in the Spelling task pane.

Activity 1.8

Running a Presentation; Using the Pen During a Presentation

You can run a presentation in PowerPoint manually, advance the slides automatically, or set up a slide show to run continuously for demonstration purposes. In addition to the Start From Beginning button on the Quick Access toolbar, you can run a slide show with the From Beginning button on the SLIDE SHOW tab or the Slide Show button on the Status bar. You can also run the presentation beginning with the currently active slide by clicking the From Current Slide button in the Start Slide Show group or clicking the Slide Show button in the view area. Use the mouse or keyboard to advance through the slides. You can also use buttons on the Slide Show toolbar that displays when you move the mouse pointer while running a presentation. Use the pen to emphasize major points or draw the attention of the audience to specific items in a slide during a presentation. To use the pen on a slide, run the presentation, and when the desired slide displays, move the mouse to display the Slide Show toolbar. Click the Pen button on the toolbar and then click *Pen*. Use the mouse to draw in the slide to underline, circle, or otherwise emphasize specific text. Options at the Pen button drop-down list also include a laser pointer and a highlighter.

Project You are now ready to run the movie production meeting presentation. You will use the mouse to perform various actions while running the presentation and use the pen to emphasize points in slides.

① With **PS1-MPProdMtg.pptx** open, click the SLIDE SHOW tab and then click the From Beginning button in the Start Slide Show group.

Clicking this button begins the presentation, and Slide 1 fills the entire screen.

Tutorial 1.8
Running a
Presentation

② After viewing Slide 1, click the left mouse button to advance to the next slide.

③ At Slide 2, move the mouse pointer until the Slide Show toolbar displays dimmed in the lower left corner of the slide and then click the Previous button (displays with a left arrow) on the toolbar to display the previous slide (Slide 1).

With buttons on the Slide Show toolbar, you can display the next slide, the previous slide, or a specific slide; use the pen, laser pointer, and highlighter to emphasize text on the slide; display slide thumbnails; and zoom in on elements of a slide. You can also display the Slide Show Help dialog box, shown in Figure 1.3, which describes all the navigation options available while running a presentation. Display this dialog box by clicking the More slide show options button on the Slide Show toolbar and then clicking *Help*.

FIGURE 1.3 Slide Show Help Dialog Box

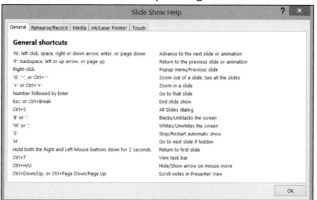

4 Click the Next button (displays with a right arrow) on the Slide Show toolbar to display the next slide (Slide 2).

5 Display the previous slide (Slide 1) by clicking the right mouse button anywhere on the slide and then clicking *Previous* at the shortcut menu.

> Clicking the right mouse button causes a shortcut menu to display with a variety of options including options to display the previous or next slide.

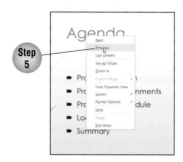

6 Display Slide 5 by pressing the number 5 key and then pressing Enter.

> Move to any slide in a presentation by typing the slide number and then pressing Enter.

7 Change to a black screen by pressing the letter B key.

> When you press the letter B key, the slide is removed from the screen and the screen displays black. This might be useful in a situation where you want to discuss something with your audience unrelated to the slide.

8 Return to Slide 5 by pressing the letter B key.

> Pressing the letter B key switches between the slide and a black screen. Press the letter W key if you want to switch between the slide and a white screen.

9 Zoom in on the bulleted items in Slide 5 by clicking the Zoom button (displays as a magnifying glass) on the Slide Show toolbar, hovering the magnification area over the bulleted items, and then clicking the left mouse button.

10 Press the Esc key to display Slide 5 without magnification.

11 Display thumbnails of all the slides in the presentation while viewing the slide show by clicking the See all slides button on the Slide Show toolbar.

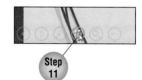

12 Click the Slide 3 thumbnail on the screen.

> This displays Slide 3 in the slide show.

13 Click the left mouse button to display Slide 4. Continue clicking the left mouse button until a black screen displays. At the black screen, click the left mouse button again.

> This returns the presentation to the Normal view.

14 Make Slide 1 active.

15 Display Slide 2 by clicking the Next Slide button located at the bottom of the vertical scroll bar.

16 Click the From Current Slide button 🖳 in the Start Slide Show group on the SLIDE SHOW tab.

> Clicking this button begins the presentation with the active slide.

continues

17. Run the presentation by clicking the left mouse button at each slide until Slide 5 is active (contains the title *Production Schedule*).

18. Move the mouse to display the Slide Show toolbar, click the Pen button, and then click *Laser Pointer*.

   This turns the mouse pointer into a red, hollow, glowing circle.

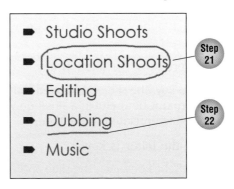

19. Practice moving the laser pointer around the screen.

20. Click the Pen button on the Slide Show toolbar and then click *Pen*.

   This turns the mouse pointer into a small circle.

21. Using the mouse, draw a circle around the text *Location Shoots*.

22. Using the mouse, draw a line below *Dubbing*.

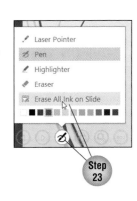

23. Erase the pen markings by clicking the Pen button on the Slide Show toolbar and then clicking *Erase All Ink on Slide*.

24. Change the color of the ink by clicking the Pen button and then clicking *Blue* in the color palette (third option from the right).

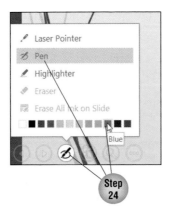

25. Draw a blue line below the word *Music*.

26. Return the mouse pointer back to an arrow by pressing the Esc key.

27 Click the left mouse button to advance to Slide 6.

28 Click the Pen button and then click *Highlighter*.

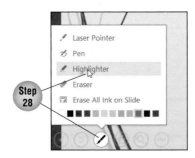

29 Using the mouse, drag through the words *Studio Shoots*.

30 Using the mouse, drag through the words *Location Shoots*.

31 Return the mouse pointer back to an arrow by pressing the Esc key.

32 Press the Esc key on the keyboard to end the presentation without viewing the remaining slides. At the message asking if you want to keep your ink annotations, click the Discard button.

In Brief

Run Presentation
Click Start From
Beginning button on
Quick Access toolbar.
OR
1. Click SLIDE SHOW
   tab.
2. Click From Beginning
   button or From
   Current Slide button.
OR
Click Slide Show
button in view area on
Status bar.

**Use Pen When
Running Presentation**
1. Run presentation.
2. At desired slide,
   move mouse.
3. Click Pen button on
   Slide Show toolbar.
4. Click *Pen* option.
5. Draw in slide with
   pen.

In Addition

Hiding/Displaying the Mouse Pointer

When running a presentation, the mouse pointer is set, by default, to be hidden after three seconds of inactivity. The mouse pointer will appear again when you move the mouse. Change this default setting by clicking the More slide show options button on the Slide Show toolbar, clicking *Arrow Options*, and then clicking *Visible* if you want the mouse pointer always visible or *Hidden* if you do not want the mouse to display at all as you run the presentation. The *Automatic* option is the default setting.

View a Presentation in Presenter View

If you are running a presentation using two monitors, you can display the presentation in Presenter view on one monitor. Use this view to control the slide show. For example, in Presenter view you can see your speaker notes, you have all the Slide Show toolbar options available, and you can advance slides and set slide timings. Press Alt + F5 to display the presentation in Presenter view.

Activity 1.9

Adding Transitions and Sound

You can apply a variety of transitions and sounds to a presentation. A transition is how one slide is removed from the screen during a presentation and the next slide is displayed. Interesting transitions such as fades, dissolves, push, cover, wipes, stripes, and bar can add interest to your presentation. You can also insert sounds that you want to play at specific points during a presentation. Add transitions and sounds with options on the TRANSITIONS tab.

Project

You have decided to enhance the movie production meeting presentation by adding transitions and sound to the slides.

Tutorial 1.9
Adding Transition Effects and Sound

1. With **PS1-MPProdMtg.pptx** open, click the TRANSITIONS tab.

2. Click the More button located at the right side of the transition thumbnails that display in the Transition to This Slide group.

3. At the drop-down gallery, click the *Ripple* option in the *Exciting* section.

   A *gallery* contains the live preview feature that shows the transition in the slide in the slide pane as you hover the mouse over each transition option.

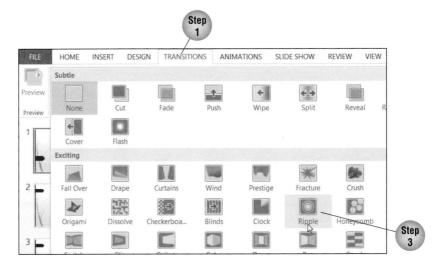

4. Click the Effect Options button in the Transition to This Slide group and then click *From Top-Left* at the drop-down list.

   The effect options change depending on the transition selected.

5. Click the down-pointing arrow at the right side of the Sound button in the Timing group.

6. At the drop-down gallery that displays, click the *Breeze* option.

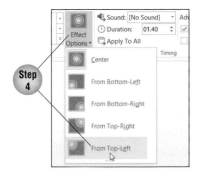

7 Apply three seconds to each slide transition by clicking in the *Duration* measurement box, typing **3**, and then pressing Enter.

8 Click the Apply To All button ⬚ in the Timing group.

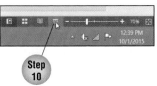
Step 7

Step 8

> Notice that play animations star icons display below the slide numbers in the slide thumbnails pane.

9 Click the Slide 1 thumbnail in the slide thumbnails pane.

10 Run the presentation by clicking the Slide Show button 🖵 in the view area on the Status bar.

Step 10

11 Click the left mouse button to advance each slide.

12 At the black screen that displays after the last slide, click the left mouse button again to return the presentation to the Normal view.

13 Click the More button located at the right side of the transition thumbnails that display in the Transition to This Slide group.

14 Click the *Curtains* option in the *Exciting* section of the drop-down gallery.

15 Click the down-pointing arrow at the right side of the Sound button and then click *Whoosh* at the drop-down gallery.

Step 14

16 Click the down-pointing arrow at the right of the *Duration* measurement box until *02.50* displays.

17 Click the Apply To All button in the Timing group.

18 With Slide 1 active, run the presentation.

19 Save **PS1-MPProdMtg.pptx**.

In Brief

Add Transition to All Slides in Presentation
1. Click TRANSITIONS tab.
2. Click More button at right side of transition thumbnails.
3. Click desired transition at drop-down gallery.
4. Click Apply To All button.

Add Transition Sound to All Slides in Presentation
1. Click TRANSITIONS tab.
2. Click Sound button arrow.
3. Click desired option at drop-down gallery.
4. Click Apply To All button.

In Addition

Running a Slide Show Automatically

Slides in a slide show can be advanced automatically after a specific number of seconds by inserting a check mark in the *After* check box in the Timing group and removing the check mark from the *On Mouse Click* check box. Change the time in the *After* measurement box by clicking the up- or down-pointing arrow at the right side of the measurement box or by selecting any number in the measurement box and then typing the desired time. If you want the transition time to affect all slides in the presentation, click the Apply To All button. In Slide Sorter view, the transition time displays below each affected slide. Click the Slide Show button to run the presentation. The first slide displays for the specified amount of time and then the next slide automatically displays.

Activity 1.10

Previewing and Printing a Presentation

You can print each slide on a separate piece of paper; print each slide at the top of the page, leaving the bottom of the page for notes; print up to nine slides or a specific number of slides on a single piece of paper; or print the slide titles and topics in outline form. Before printing a presentation, consider previewing it. Choose print options and display a preview of the presentation in the Print backstage area. Display this view by clicking the FILE tab and then clicking the *Print* option. Click the Back button or press the Esc key to exit the backstage area without clicking an option.

Project

Staff members need the movie production meeting slides printed as handouts and as an outline. You will preview and print the presentation in various formats.

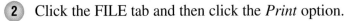
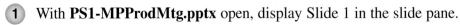

Tutorial 1.10
Previewing Slides
and Printing a
Presentation

1. With **PS1-MPProdMtg.pptx** open, display Slide 1 in the slide pane.

2. Click the FILE tab and then click the *Print* option.

   Slide 1 of your presentation displays at the right side of the screen as it will when printed. Use the Next Page button (right-pointing arrow) located below and to the left of the slide to view the next slide in the presentation, click the Previous Page button (left-pointing arrow) to display the previous slide in the presentation, use the Zoom slider bar to increase or decrease the size of the slide, and click the Zoom to Page button to fit the slide in the viewing area in the Print backstage area. The left side of the Print backstage area displays three categories—*Print*, *Printer*, and *Settings*. Galleries display below each category name. For example, the *Printer* category has one gallery that displays the name of the currently selected printer. The *Settings* category has a number of galleries that describe how the slides will print.

3. Click the Next Page button located below and to the left of the preview slide to display the next slide in the presentation.

   This displays Slide 2 in the backstage preview area.

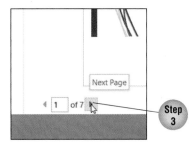

4. Click twice on the Zoom In button that displays at the right side of the Zoom slider bar.

   Click the Zoom In button to increase the size of the slide or click the Zoom Out button (displays with a minus symbol) to decrease the size of the slide.

5. Click the Zoom to Page button located at the right side of the Zoom slider bar.

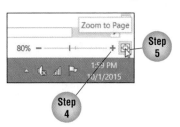

6 You decide to print the slides on two pages and you want to preview how the slides will display on the pages. To do this, click the second gallery in the *Settings* category (contains the text *Full Page Slides*) and then click *4 Slides Horizontal* in the *Handouts* section.

> Notice how four slides display on the preview page.

Step 6

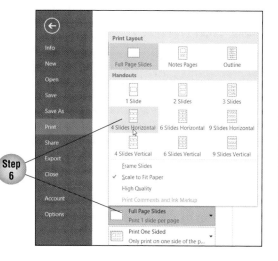

In Brief

Print Presentation
1. Click FILE tab.
2. Click *Print* option.
3. At Print backstage area, specify how you want presentation printed.
4. Click Print button.

Preview Presentation
1. Click FILE tab.
2. Click *Print* option.
3. View preview in right panel of Print backstage area.

7 Click the Print button in the *Print* category.

8 You want to print all slide text on one page to use as a reference during your presentation. To do this, click the FILE tab and then click the *Print* option.

9 At the Print backstage area, click the second gallery in the *Settings* category (contains the text *4 Slides Horizontal*) and then click *Outline* in the *Print Layout* section.

10 Click the Print button in the *Print* category.

> With the *Outline* option selected, the presentation prints on one page with slide numbers, slide icons, and slide text in outline form.

11 You want to print only Slide 6. To do this, click the FILE tab and then click the *Print* option.

12 At the Print backstage area, click the second gallery in the *Settings* category (contains the text *Outline*) and then click *Full Page Slides* in the *Print Layout* section.

13 Click in the *Slides* text box located below the first gallery in the *Settings* category, type **6**, and then click the Print button.

14 Save **PS1-MPProdMtg.pptx**.

15 Close the presentation by clicking the FILE tab and then clicking the *Close* option.

Step 13

Step 12

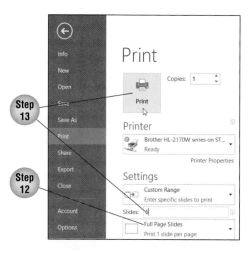

In Addition

Using Options at the Slide Size Dialog Box

You can change orientation with options at the Slide Size dialog box, shown at the right. Display this dialog box by clicking the DESIGN tab, clicking the Slide Size button in the Customize group, and then clicking *Customize Slide Size* at the drop-down list. With options at this dialog box you can specify how you want slides sized; page width and height; orientation for slides; and orientation for notes, handouts, and outlines.

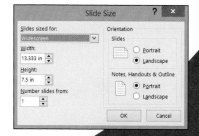

Features Summary

Feature	Ribbon Tab, Group	Button	FILE Tab Option	Keyboard Shortcut
apply transitions and sound to all slides	TRANSITIONS, Timing			
close a presentation			*Close*	Ctrl + F4
close PowerPoint		✕		
Help		?		F1
layout	HOME, Slides			
new slide	HOME, Slides			Ctrl + M
Normal view	VIEW, Presentation Views			
Notes Page view	VIEW, Presentation Views			
open blank presentation				Ctrl + N
Open backstage area			*Open*	Ctrl + O
Outline view	VIEW, Presentation Views			
Print backstage area			*Print*	Ctrl + P
run presentation from current slide	SLIDE SHOW, Start Slide Show			Shift + F5
run presentation from Slide 1	SLIDE SHOW, Start Slide Show			F5
save			*Save*	Ctrl + S
Save As backstage area			*Save As*	F12
Slide Sorter view	VIEW, Presentation Views			
spelling checker	REVIEW, Proofing	ABC		F7
themes	DESIGN, Themes			
Thesaurus	REVIEW, Proofing			Shift + F7
transitions	TRANSITIONS, Transition to This Slide			
transition sound	TRANSITIONS, Timing			
transition duration	TRANSITIONS, Timing			
Zoom dialog box	VIEW, Zoom			

Knowledge Check SNAP

Completion: In the space provided at the right, indicate the correct term, command, or option.

1. After selecting a template at the Open backstage area, click this button to begin working in the presentation. _____

2. To run a presentation beginning with Slide 1, click this button on the Quick Access toolbar. _____

3. The Normal view contains the slide thumbnails pane and this pane. _____

4. The New Slide button is located on this tab. _____

5. The Zoom slider bar is located at the right side of this bar. _____

6. Click the Microsoft PowerPoint Help button and this displays. _____

7. Use this feature to find synonyms, antonyms, and related words for a particular word. _____

8. The Spelling button is located in the Proofing group on this tab. _____

9. Move the mouse while running a presentation and this toolbar displays. _____

10. Press this key on the keyboard to change to a black screen while running a presentation. _____

11. Press this key on the keyboard to end a presentation. _____

12. Add transitions and sound to a presentation with options on this tab. _____

13. Specify the length of a transition using the *Duration* measurement box located in this group on the TRANSITIONS tab. _____

14. You can print up to this number of slides on a single piece of paper. _____

Skills Review

Review 1 Creating a Presentation for Marquee Productions

1. Create a new folder on your storage medium and name it **PowerPointEOS**.
2. With a blank presentation open in PowerPoint, click the DESIGN tab and then click the *Facet* thumbnail in the Themes group (third option from the left).
3. Type the title and subtitle for Slide 1 as shown in Figure 1.4.
4. Click the HOME tab and then click the New Slide button in the Slides group.
5. Type the text shown for Slide 2 in Figure 1.4.
6. Continue creating the slides for the presentation as shown in Figure 1.4.
7. Insert a new Slide 3 between the current Slides 2 and 3 with the text shown in Figure 1.5.
8. Display Slide 2 in the slide pane and then change the slide layout to *Title Slide*.
9. Click in the text *Current Status* to select the placeholder and then move the placeholder up approximately one inch.
10. Click in the text *Overview of Project* to select the placeholder and then move the placeholder up approximately one-half inch.
11. Change to Slide Sorter view and then move Slide 3 (*Resources*) immediately after Slide 1 (*Marquee Productions*).
12. Change to the Normal view, click the TRANSITIONS tab, click the More button located at the right side of the transition thumbnails in the Transition to This Slide group, and then click the *Orbit* option in the *Dynamic Content* section.
13. Click the down-pointing arrow at the right of the Sound button and then click *Drum Roll* at the drop-down gallery.
14. Click the down-pointing arrow at the right side of the *Duration* measurement box until *00.75* displays in the text box.
15. Apply the transition, sound, and duration to all slides in the presentation.
16. Save the presentation in the PowerPointEOS folder and name it **PS1-R-MPTeamMtg**.
17. Run the presentation beginning with Slide 1.
18. View the presentation as an outline in the Print backstage area.
19. Print the presentation with all five slides positioned horizontally on the page.
20. Save and then close **PS1-R-MPTeamMtg.pptx**.

FIGURE 1.4 Review 1

Slide 1	Title	Marquee Productions
	Subtitle	Location Team Meeting
Slide 2	Title	Current Status
	Bullets	• Overview of project
		• Tasks on schedule
		• Tasks behind schedule
Slide 3	Title	Filming Sites
	Bullets	• Gardiner Expressway
		• Kings Mill Park
		• Island Airport
		• Royal Ontario Museum
		• Black Creek Pioneer Village
		• Additional sites
Slide 4	Title	Key Issues
	Bullets	• Equipment rental
		• Budget overruns
		• Transportation concerns
		• Location agreements

FIGURE 1.5 Review 1

Slide 3	Title	Resources
	Bullets	• Location contacts
		• Movie extras
		• Catering company
		• Lodging
		• Transportation rentals

Skills Assessment

Assessment 1 Preparing a Presentation for Worldwide Enterprises

1. Prepare a presentation for Worldwide Enterprises with the information shown in Figure 1.6 below. (You determine the design template.)
2. Add a transition, sound, and transition duration time of your choosing to all slides in the presentation.
3. Run the presentation.
4. Print the presentation with all five slides positioned horizontally on one page.
5. Save the presentation in the PowerPointEOS folder and name it **PS1-A1-WEExecMtg**.
6. Close **PS1-A1-WEExecMtg.pptx**.

FIGURE 1.6 Assessment 1

Slide 1	Title	Worldwide Enterprises
	Subtitle	Executive Meeting
Slide 2	Title	Accounting Policies
	Bullets	• Cash equivalents
		• Short-term investments
		• Inventory valuation
		• Property and equipment
		• Foreign currency translation
Slide 3	Title	Financial Instruments
	Bullets	• Investments
		• Derivative instruments
		• Credit risks
		• Fair value of instruments
Slide 4	Title	Inventories
	Bullets	• Products
		• Raw material
		• Equipment
		• Buildings
Slide 5	Title	Employee Plans
	Bullets	• Stock options
		• Bonus plan
		• Savings and retirement plan
		• Defined benefits plan
		• Foreign subsidiaries

Assessment 2 Preparing a Presentation for The Waterfront Bistro

1. Prepare a presentation for The Waterfront Bistro with the information shown in Figure 1.7 below. (You determine the design template.)
2. Add a transition, sound, and transition duration time of your choosing to all slides in the presentation.
3. Run the presentation.
4. Print the presentation with all five slides positioned horizontally on one page.
5. Save the presentation in the PowerPointEOS folder and name it **PS1-A2-WBServices**.
6. Close **PS1-A2-WBServices.pptx**.

FIGURE 1.7 Assessment 2

Slide 1	Title	The Waterfront Bistro
	Subtitle	3104 Rivermist Drive
		Buffalo, NY 14280
		(716) 555-3166
Slide 2	Title	Accommodations
	Bullets	• Dining area
		• Salon
		• Two banquet rooms
		• Wine cellar
Slide 3	Title	Menus
	Bullets	• Lunch
		• Dinner
		• Wines
		• Desserts
Slide 4	Title	Catering Services
	Bullets	• Lunch
		– Continental
		– Deli
		– Hot
		• Dinner
		– Vegetarian
		– Meat
		– Seafood
Slide 5	Title	Resource
	Subtitle	Dana Hirsch, Manager

Assessment 3 Finding Information on Setting Slide Show Timings

HELP

1. Open **MPProj.pptx** and then use the Help feature to learn how to save a presentation with Save As.
2. Save the presentation with Save As in the PowerPointEOS folder and name it **PS1-A3-MPProj**.
3. Use the Help feature or experiment with the options in the TRANSITIONS tab and learn how to set slide show timings manually.
4. Set up the presentation so that, when running the slide show, each slide advances automatically after three seconds.
5. Run the presentation.
6. Save and then close **PS1-A3-MPProj.pptx**.

Assessment 4 Individual Challenge
Preparing a Presentation on Cancun, Mexico

1. You are interested in planning a vacation to Cancun, Mexico. Connect to the Internet and search for information on Cancun. (One possible site for information is www.cancun.com.) Locate information on lodging (hotels), restaurants, activities, and transportation.
2. Using PowerPoint, create a presentation about Cancun that contains the following:
   - Title slide containing the title *Vacationing in Cancun*, and your name as the subtitle
   - Slide containing the names of at least three major airlines that travel to Cancun
   - Slide containing the names of at least four hotels or resorts in Cancun
   - Slide containing the names of at least four restaurants in Cancun
   - Slide containing at least four activities in Cancun
3. Run the presentation.
4. Print all of the slides on one page.
5. Save the presentation in the PowerPointEOS folder and name it **PS1-A4-IC-Cancun**.
6. Close **PS1-A4-IC-Cancun.pptx**.

Marquee Challenge

Challenge 1 Preparing a Presentation on Toronto, Ontario, Canada

1. Create the presentation shown in Figure 1.8 on the next page. Apply the appropriate design theme and slide layouts, and size and move placeholders so your slides display as shown in the figure. (You will need to increase the size of the subtitle placeholder in Slide 6.)
2. Apply a transition, sound, and transition duration time of your choosing to each slide in the presentation.
3. Save the completed presentation in the PowerPointEOS folder and name it **PS1-C1-FCTToronto**.
4. Print the presentation as a handout with all six slides on the same page.
5. Close the presentation.

Challenge 2 Preparing a Presentation for Performance Threads

1. Open **PTCostumeMtg.pptx** and then save the presentation in the PowerPointEOS folder and name it **PS1-C2-PTCostumeMtg**.
2. Apply the Organic design theme, add and rearrange slides, change slide layouts, and move a placeholder so the presentation displays as shown in Figure 1.9 on page 41. (Read the slides in Figure 1.9 from left to right.)
3. Apply a transition, sound, and transition duration time of your choosing to each slide in the presentation.
4. Save and then print the presentation as a handout with all six slides on the same page.
5. Close the presentation.

FIGURE 1.8 Challenge 1

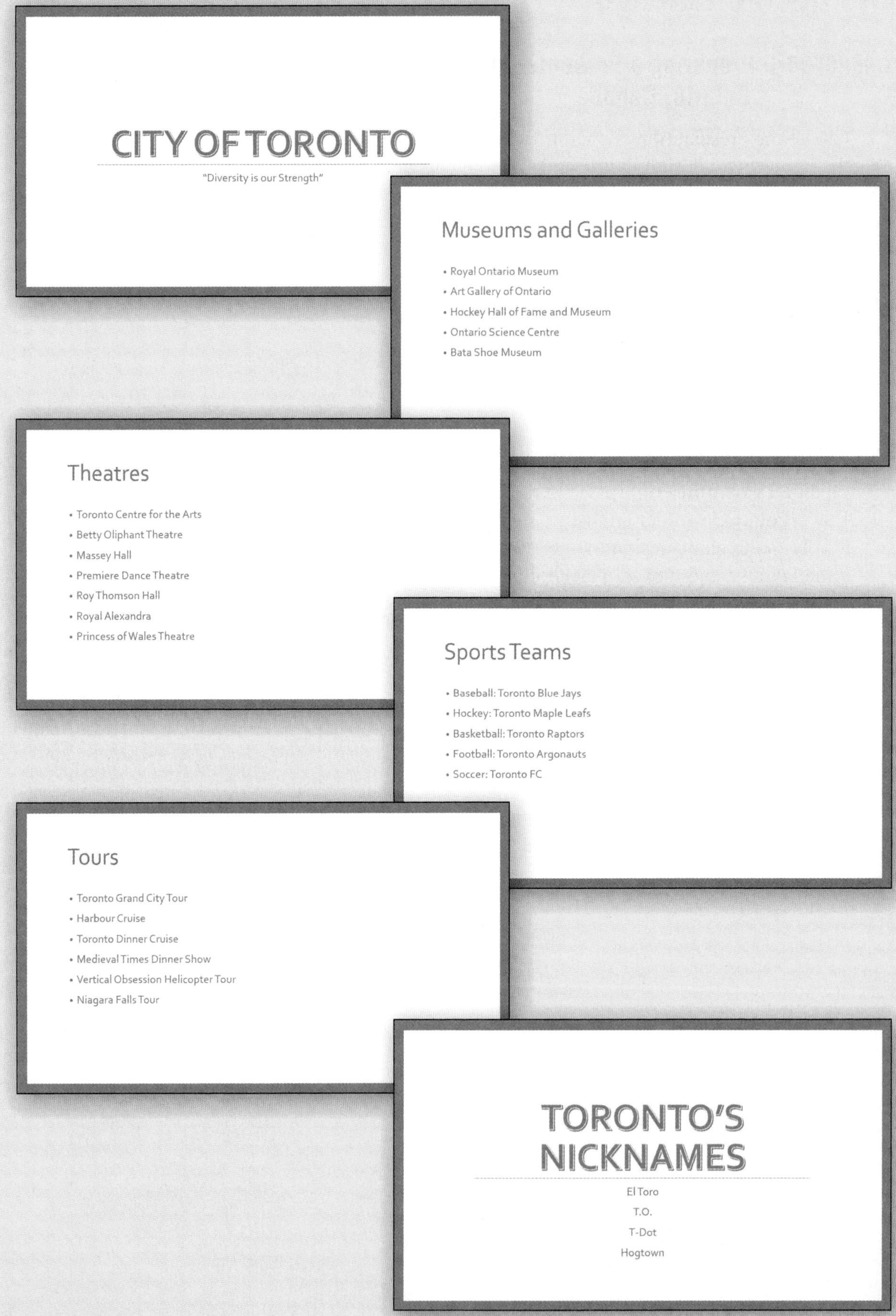

CITY OF TORONTO

"Diversity is our Strength"

Museums and Galleries

- Royal Ontario Museum
- Art Gallery of Ontario
- Hockey Hall of Fame and Museum
- Ontario Science Centre
- Bata Shoe Museum

Theatres

- Toronto Centre for the Arts
- Betty Oliphant Theatre
- Massey Hall
- Premiere Dance Theatre
- Roy Thomson Hall
- Royal Alexandra
- Princess of Wales Theatre

Sports Teams

- Baseball: Toronto Blue Jays
- Hockey: Toronto Maple Leafs
- Basketball: Toronto Raptors
- Football: Toronto Argonauts
- Soccer: Toronto FC

Tours

- Toronto Grand City Tour
- Harbour Cruise
- Toronto Dinner Cruise
- Medieval Times Dinner Show
- Vertical Obsession Helicopter Tour
- Niagara Falls Tour

TORONTO'S NICKNAMES

El Toro

T.O.

T-Dot

Hogtown

FIGURE 1.9 Challenge 2

Performance Threads

Costuming Meeting

Sewing Projects

- Costumes for current production at Lafferty Performing Arts Theatre
- Research for Pantages Art Group
- Medieval and Regency period costumes for Marquee Productions

Medieval Costume: Women

Cotton dress with gathered neckline; wide, extended sleeves; full skirt with over-bodice laces; and decorative trim down the front.

Medieval Costume: Men

Cotton tunic with decorative trim in various colors on sleeves, neck, and bottom of tunic.

Regency Costume: Women

High-wasted bodice with pull sleeves over long sleeves with ruffled cuffs, skirt with sash tie and slight train, and three bands of trim.

Regency Costume: Men

Double-breasted waistcoat with high collar and white linen cravat with rolled hem.

PowerPoint® SECTION 2
Editing and Enhancing Slides

Skills

- Open a presentation and save it with a new name
- Increase and decrease the indent of text
- Select, cut, copy, and paste text
- Apply font and font effects
- Find and replace fonts
- Apply formatting with Format Painter
- Change alignment and line and paragraph spacing
- Change the slide size and format slide elements and background
- Insert, size, and move images
- Insert and format clip art images
- Insert and format a SmartArt organizational chart
- Insert and format a SmartArt graphic
- Apply animation to an object in a slide

Projects Overview

Open an existing project presentation for Marquee Productions, save the presentation with a new name, and then edit and format the presentation. Open an existing annual meeting presentation for Marquee Productions and then save, edit, and format the presentation.

Open an existing presentation for the Theatre Arts Division of Niagara Peninsula College and then save, edit, and format the presentation.

Open an existing presentation containing information on vacation specials offered by First Choice Travel and then save, edit, and format the presentation.

Prepare and format a presentation on the services offered by The Waterfront Bistro.

Prepare and format a presentation on the company structure, policies, and benefits.

Prepare and format a presentation for a planning meeting of the distribution department.

Model Answers for Projects

These model answers for the projects you complete in Section 2 provide a preview of the finished projects before you begin working and also allow you to compare your own results with these models to ensure you have created the materials accurately.

PS2-MPProj.pptx (a two-page document) is the project in Activities 2.1 to 2.11.

10/6/2015

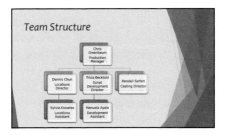

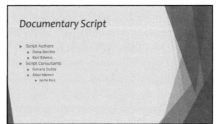

1

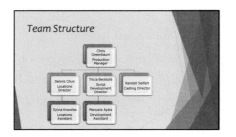

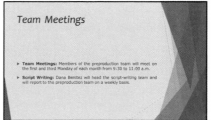

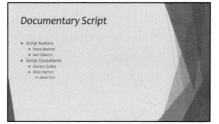

1

Activity 2.1

Increasing and Decreasing Indent; Cutting, Copying, and Pasting Text

If you open an existing presentation and make changes to it, you can then save it with the same name or a different name. Save an existing presentation with a new name at the Save As dialog box. In Outline view, you can organize and develop the content of the presentation by rearranging points within a slide, moving slides, or increasing and decreasing text level indent. Click the Decrease List Level button in the Paragraph group on the HOME tab or press Shift + Tab to decrease text to the previous level. Click the Increase List Level button or press the Tab key to increase text to the next level. You can also increase and/or decrease the indent of text in the slide in the slide pane. You can select text in a slide and then delete the text from the slide, cut text from one location and paste it into another, or copy and paste the text. Use buttons in the Clipboard group on the HOME tab to cut, copy, and paste text.

Project

Tutorial 2.1
Cutting, Copying, Pasting, and Aligning Text

Chris Greenbaum, production manager for Marquee Productions, has prepared a documentary project presentation and has asked you to edit the presentation by increasing and decreasing text levels and selecting, deleting, moving, copying, and pasting text in slides.

1. Open PowerPoint and then click the Open Other Presentations hyperlink located in the lower left corner of the PowerPoint 2013 opening screen. (If PowerPoint is already open, click the FILE tab and then click the *Open* option.)

2. At the Open backstage area, click the *Computer* option or your SkyDrive, and then click the Browse button.

3. At the Open dialog box, navigate to the PowerPointS2 folder and then double-click *MPProj.pptx* in the list box.

4. Click the FILE tab, click the *Save As* option, and then click the PowerPointS2 folder in the *Current Folder* section of the Save As backstage area.

5. At the Save As dialog box, press the Home key to move the insertion point to the beginning of the file name, type **PS2-** in the *File name* text box, and then press the Enter key. (The file name in the *File name* text box should display as *PS2-MPProj.pptx*.)

    Pressing the Home key saves you from having to type the entire file name.

6. Display Slide 5 in the slide pane.

7. You decide to promote the names below *Script Authors* so that they display as first-level bullets. To do this, position the mouse pointer immediately left of the *D* in *Dana*, click the left mouse button, and then click the Decrease List Level button in the Paragraph group on the HOME tab.

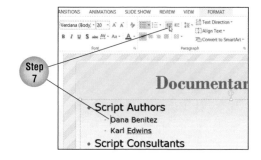

    Clicking the Decrease List Level button will promote text to the previous tab, while clicking the Increase List Level button will demote text to the next tab.

8. Position the insertion point immediately left of the *K* in *Karl* in Slide 5 and then promote the text to the previous level by pressing Shift + Tab.

9 Demote two of the names below *Script Consultants* by clicking immediately left of the *J* in *Jaime* and then clicking the Increase List Level button in the Paragraph group on the HOME tab.

10 Position the insertion point immediately left of the *G* in *Genaro* and then press the Tab key.

11 Display Slide 6 in the slide pane.

12 Position the mouse pointer on the bullet that displays before *Script Rewriting* until the mouse pointer turns into a four-headed arrow and then click the left mouse button.

> This selects the text *Script Rewriting*. Refer to Table 2.1 for additional information on selecting text.

13 Press the Delete key.

> This deletes the selected text.

14 Display Slide 5 in the slide pane, position the mouse pointer on the bullet that displays before *Genaro Dufoe* until the mouse pointer turns into a four-headed arrow, and then click the left mouse button.

15 Click the Cut button in the Clipboard group on the HOME tab.

> The keyboard shortcut to cut text is Ctrl + X.

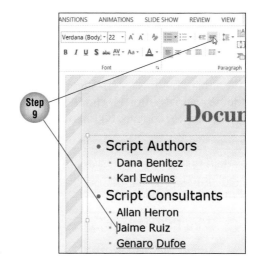

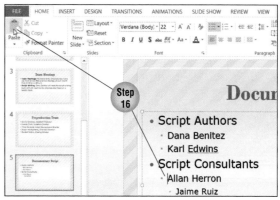

16 Position the mouse pointer immediately left of the *A* in *Allan Herron*, click the left mouse button, and then click the Paste button in the Clipboard group.

> The keyboard shortcut to paste text is Ctrl + V.

17 Using the mouse, drag to select the text *Script Authors* and then click the Copy button in the Clipboard group.

> The keyboard shortcut to copy text is Ctrl + C.

18 Make Slide 2 active, position the insertion point immediately left of the *S* in *Scouting*, and then click the Paste button in the Clipboard group.

> If *Script Authors* and *Scouting* display on the same line, press the Enter key.

19 Save **PS2-MPProj.pptx**.

In Brief

Save Presentation with New Name
1. Click FILE tab.
2. Click *Save As* option.
3. Click the PowerPointS2 folder.
4. Type presentation name.
5. Click Save or press Enter.

Decrease Text Level Indent
Click Decrease List Level button or press Shift + Tab.

Increase Text Level Indent
Click Increase List Level button or press Tab.

Cut and Paste Text
1. Select text.
2. Click Cut button.
3. Position insertion point.
4. Click Paste button.

Copy and Paste Text
1. Select text.
2. Click Copy button.
3. Position insertion point.
4. Click Paste button.

TABLE 2.1 Selecting Text

To select	Perform this action
entire word	Double-click word.
entire paragraph	Triple-click anywhere in paragraph.
text mouse pointer passes through	Click and drag with mouse.
all text in selected object box	Click Select button in Editing group and then click Select All; or press Ctrl + A.

Activity 2.2

Applying Fonts and Font Effects

The Font group on the HOME tab contains two rows of buttons. The top row contains buttons for changing the font and font size and a button for clearing formatting. The bottom row contains buttons for applying font effects such as bold, italics, underlining, text shadow, strikethrough, and character spacing, as well as buttons for changing the case and/or font color of selected text.

Project

Tutorial 2.2
Applying Fonts
Using the Font
Group

Certain text elements on slides in the documentary project presentation need to be highlighted to make them stand out. You decide to apply font effects to and change the font size of specific text.

1. With **PS2-MPProj.pptx** open, display Slide 1 in the slide pane.

2. Select the title *Marquee Productions* and then click the Italic button I in the Font group on the HOME tab.

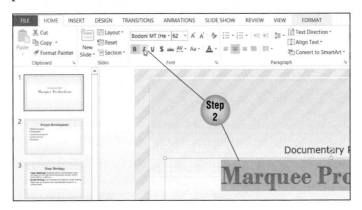

3. Select the subtitle *Documentary Project*, click the Increase Font Size button $A^\uparrow$, and then click the Bold button B in the Font group.

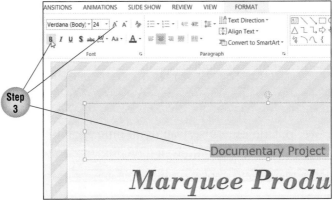

4. Make Slide 6 active in the slide pane, select the text *Phase 1*, and then click the Underline button $\underline{U}$ in the Font group.

5. Select and then underline the text *Phase 2*.

6. Select and then underline the text *Phase 3*.

7. Make Slide 1 active.

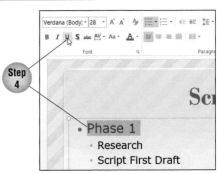

8 Select the title *Marquee Productions*, click the Font button arrow in the Font group, scroll down the drop-down gallery (fonts display in alphabetical order), and then click *Calibri*.

In Brief

Apply Font Effects with Font Group
1. Select text.
2. Click appropriate button in Font group.

9 Select the subtitle *Documentary Project*, click the Font button arrow, and then click *Calibri* at the drop-down gallery.

> The drop-down gallery displays the most recently used fonts toward the top of the gallery.

10 Make Slide 6 active, select the text *Phase 1*, click the Underline button to remove underlining, and then click the Bold button to apply bold formatting.

11 With *Phase 1* still selected, click the Font button arrow and then click *Calibri* at the drop-down gallery.

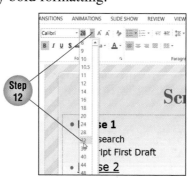

12 Click the Font Size button arrow, scroll down the drop-down gallery, and then click *32*.

13 Select the text *Phase 2*, remove the underlining, turn on bold formatting, change the font to Calibri, and change the font size to 32 points.

14 Select the text *Phase 3*, remove the underlining, turn on bold formatting, change the font to Calibri, and change the font size to 32 points.

15 Print Slides 1 and 6. Begin by clicking the FILE tab and then clicking the *Print* option.

16 At the Print backstage area, click in the *Slides* text box (located below the first gallery in the *Settings* category) and then type **1,6**.

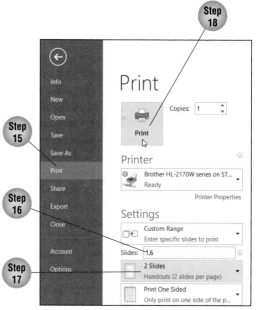

17 Click the second gallery in the *Settings* category (contains the text *Full Page Slides*) and then click *2 Slides* in the *Handouts* section of the drop-down list.

18 Click the Print button in the *Print* category.

> The two slides print on the same page.

19 Save **PS2-MPProj.pptx**.

In Addition

Choosing Typefaces

A typeface is a set of characters with a common design and shape. PowerPoint refers to a typeface as a *font*. Typefaces can be decorative or plain and are either monospaced or proportional. A monospaced typeface allots the same amount of horizontal space for each character, while a proportional typeface allots a different amount of space for each character. Proportional typefaces are divided into two main categories: serif and sans serif. A serif is a small line at the end of a character stroke. Consider using a serif typeface for text-intensive slides, because the serifs can help move the reader's eyes across the text. Use a sans serif typeface for titles, subtitles, headings, and short text lines.

Activity 2.3

Changing the Font at the Font Dialog Box; Replacing Fonts

In addition to buttons in the Font group on the HOME tab, you can apply font formatting with options at the Font dialog box. With options at this dialog box, you can change the font, as well as its style and size; change the font color; and apply formatting effects such as underline, strikethrough, superscript, subscript, and all caps. If you decide to change the font for all slides in a presentation, use the Replace Font dialog box to replace all occurrences of a specific font in the presentation.

Project You are still not satisfied with the fonts in the documentary project presentation, so you decide to change the font for the title and subtitle and replace the Verdana font on the remaining slides.

Tutorial 2.3
Apply Formatting
Using the Font
Dialog Box

1. With **PS2-MPProj.pptx** open, make Slide 1 active.

2. Select the title *Marquee Productions*.

3. Display the Font dialog box by clicking the Font group dialog box launcher on the HOME tab.

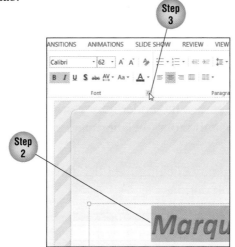

4. At the Font dialog box, click the down-pointing arrow at the right side of the *Latin text font* option box and then click *Candara* at the drop-down list.

5. Select the current measurement in the *Size* measurement box and then type **55**.

6. Click the Font color button in the *All text* section and then click the *Turquoise, Accent 3, Darker 25%* option (seventh column, fifth row in the *Theme Colors* section).

7. Click OK to close the Font dialog box.

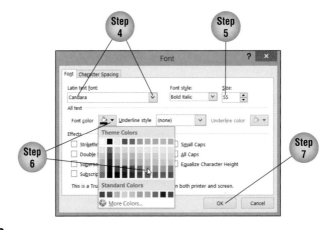

8 Select the subtitle *Documentary Project*.

9 Click the Font group dialog box launcher.

10 At the Font dialog box, click the down-pointing arrow at the right side of the *Latin text font* option box and then click *Candara* at the drop-down list.

11 Click the down-pointing arrow at the right side of the *Font style* option box and then click *Bold Italic* at the drop-down list.

12 Select the current measurement in the *Size* measurement box and then type **30**.

13 Click the Font color button in the *All text* section and then click the *Dark Blue* color (ninth color option in the *Standard Colors* section).

14 Click OK to close the Font dialog box.

15 Make Slide 2 active.

16 You decide to replace all occurrences of the Verdana font in the presentation with the Cambria font. To begin, click the Replace button arrow in the Editing group on the HOME tab and then click *Replace Fonts* at the drop-down list.

17 At the Replace Font dialog box, click the down-pointing arrow at the right side of the *Replace* option box and then click *Verdana* at the drop-down list.

18 Click the down-pointing arrow at the right side of the *With* option box and then click *Cambria* at the drop-down list. (You will need to scroll down the list box to display *Cambria*.)

19 Click the Replace button and then click the Close button.

20 Save **PS2-MPProj.pptx**.

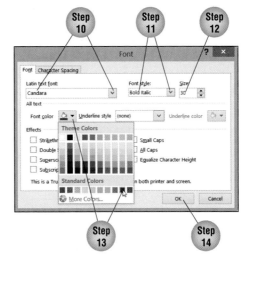

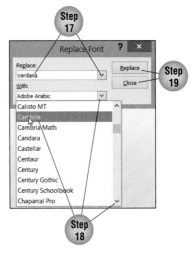

In Brief

Change Font at Font Dialog Box
1. Select text.
2. Click Font group dialog box launcher.
3. Click desired options at Font dialog box.
4. Click OK.

Change All Occurrences of Font
1. Click Replace button arrow, then click *Replace Fonts*.
2. At Replace Font dialog box, make sure desired font displays in *Replace* text box.
3. Press Tab.
4. Click down-pointing arrow at right of *With* and click desired font.
5. Click Replace button.
6. Click Close button.

In Addition

Choosing Typefaces for a Presentation

Choose a typeface for a presentation based on the tone and message you want the presentation to convey. For example, choose a more serious typeface such as Constantia or Times New Roman for a conservative audience and choose a less formal typeface such as Comic Sans MS, Lucida Handwriting, or Mistral for a more informal or lighthearted audience. For text-intensive slides, choose a serif typeface such as Cambria, Candara, Times New Roman, or Bookman Old Style. For titles, subtitles, headings, and short text items, consider a sans serif typeface such as Calibri, Arial, Tahoma, or Univers. Use no more than two or three different typefaces in each presentation. To ensure text readability in a slide, choose a font color that contrasts with the slide background.

Activity 2.4

Formatting with Format Painter

Use the Format Painter feature to apply the same formatting in more than one location in a slide or slides. To use the Format Painter, apply the desired formatting to text, position the insertion point anywhere in the formatted text, and then double-click the Format Painter button in the Clipboard group on the HOME tab. Using the mouse, select the additional text to which you want the formatting applied. After applying the formatting in the desired locations, click the Format Painter button to deactivate it. If you only need to apply formatting in one other location, click the Format Painter button just once. The first time you select text, the formatting will be applied and the Format Painter button will be deactivated.

Project

Improve the appearance of slides in the documentary project presentation by applying a font and then using the Format Painter to apply the formatting to other text.

Tutorial 2.4
Formatting with
Format Painter

1. With **PS2-MPProj.pptx** open, make sure Slide 2 is active.

2. Select the title *Project Development*.

3. Click the Font group dialog box launcher.

4. At the Font dialog box, click the down-pointing arrow in the *Latin text font* option box and then click *Candara* at the drop-down list.

   You will need to scroll down the list to display *Candara*.

5. Click the down-pointing arrow at the right side of the *Font style* option box and then click *Bold Italic* at the drop-down list.

6. Select the current measurement in the *Size* measurement box and then type **50**.

7. Click the Font color button in the *All text* section and then click the *Dark Blue* option (ninth color option in the *Standard Colors* section).

8. Click OK to close the Font dialog box.

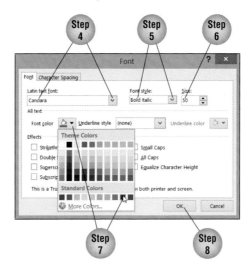

9. Deselect the text by clicking in the slide in the slide pane.

10 Click anywhere in the title *Project Development*.

11 Double-click the Format Painter button in the Clipboard group on the HOME tab.

12 Click the Next Slide button to display Slide 3.

13 Click in the word *Team* and then click in the word *Meetings* in the title placeholder.

> The mouse pointer displays with a paintbrush attached. This indicates that the Format Painter feature is active. You can also apply the formatting by selecting the title.

Need Help?
If the paintbrush is no longer attached to the mouse pointer, Format Painter has been turned off. Turn it back on by clicking in a slide title with the desired formatting and then double-clicking the Format Painter button.

14 Click the Next Slide button to display Slide 4.

15 Using the mouse, select the title *Preproduction Team*.

16 Apply formatting to the titles in the remaining three slides.

17 When formatting has been applied to all slide titles, click the Format Painter button in the Clipboard group on the HOME tab.

> Clicking the Format Painter button turns off the feature.

18 Save **PS2-MPProj.pptx**.

In Brief

Format with Format Painter
1. Position insertion point on text containing desired formatting.
2. Double-click Format Painter button.
3. Select text to which you want to apply formatting.
4. Click Format Painter button.

In Addition

Choosing a Custom Color

Click the Font Color button at the Font dialog box and a palette of color choices displays. Click the *More Colors* option and the Colors dialog box with the Standard tab selected displays with a honeycomb of color options. Click the Custom tab and the dialog box displays as shown at the right. Use options at this dialog box to mix your own color. Click the desired color in the *Colors* palette or enter the values for the color in the *Red*, *Green*, and *Blue* text boxes. Adjust the luminosity of the current color by dragging the slider located at the right side of the color palette.

Activity 2.5

Changing Alignment and Line and Paragraph Spacing

The slide design template generally determines the horizontal and vertical alignment of text in placeholders. Text may be left-aligned, center-aligned, or right-aligned in a placeholder as well as aligned at the top, middle, or bottom of the placeholder. You can change alignment for specific text with buttons in the Paragraph group on the HOME tab or with options from the Align Text button drop-down list. Use options at the Line Spacing button drop-down list or the *Line Spacing* option at the Paragraph dialog box to change line spacing. The Paragraph dialog box also contains options for changing text alignment and indentation as well as spacing before and after text.

Project Change the alignment and improve the appearance of specific text in slides by adjusting the vertical alignment and paragraph spacing of text.

Tutorial 2.5
Changing Paragraph
Formatting

1. With **PS2-MPProj.pptx** open, make Slide 1 active.

2. Click anywhere in the text *Documentary Project* and then click the Align Right button ☰ in the Paragraph group on the HOME tab.

   You can also change text alignment with the keyboard shortcuts shown in Table 2.2.

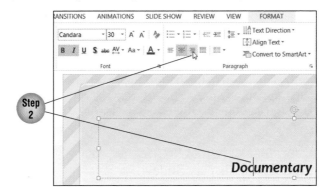

3. Click anywhere in the text *Marquee Productions* and then click the Align Right button.

4. Make Slide 3 active (contains the title *Team Meetings*), click once in the bulleted text, and then press Ctrl + A to select all of the bulleted text.

   Ctrl + A is the keyboard shortcut for selecting all text in a placeholder.

5. Justify the text by clicking the Justify button ☰ in the Paragraph group.

6. Click the Align Text button 🔲 in the Paragraph group and then click *Middle* at the drop-down gallery.

   This aligns the bulleted text in the middle of the placeholder.

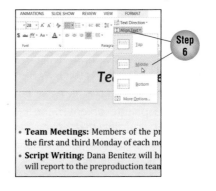

7 With the bulleted text still selected, click the Line Spacing button 📇 and then click *Line Spacing Options* at the drop-down list.

8 At the Paragraph dialog box, click twice on the up-pointing arrow at the right side of the *After* measurement box in the *Spacing* section.

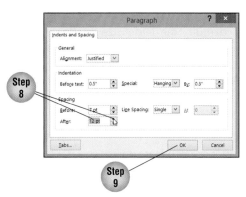

> This inserts *12 pt* in the *After* measurement box.

9 Click OK to close the dialog box.

10 Make Slide 4 active (contains the title *Preproduction Team*).

11 Click once in the bulleted text and then select all of the bulleted text by clicking the Select button 📍 in the Editing group on the HOME tab and then clicking *Select All* at the drop-down list.

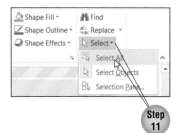

12 Click the Line Spacing button and then click *1.5* at the drop-down list.

13 Make Slide 7 active (contains the title *Preproduction Assignments*).

14 Click once in the bulleted text and then press Ctrl + A.

15 Click the Line Spacing button in the Paragraph group and then click *Line Spacing Options* at the drop-down list.

16 At the Paragraph dialog box, click twice on the up-pointing arrow at the right side of the *After* measurement box in the *Spacing* section.

> This inserts *12 pt* in the *After* measurement box.

17 Click OK to close the dialog box.

18 Print only Slide 1 of the presentation as a handout.

19 Save **PS2-MPProj.pptx**.

In Brief

Change Horizontal Text Alignment
1. Select text or click in text paragraph.
2. Click desired alignment button in bottom row of Paragraph group.

Change Vertical Text Alignment
1. Click Align Text button.
2. Click desired alignment at drop-down list.

Change Line Spacing
1. Click Line Spacing button.
2. Click desired spacing at drop-down list.
OR
1. Click Line Spacing button.
2. Click *Line Spacing Options* at drop-down list.
3. At Paragraph dialog box, specify desired spacing.
4. Click OK.

TABLE 2.2 Alignment Shortcut Keys

Alignment	Keyboard Shortcut
left	Ctrl + L
center	Ctrl + E
right	Ctrl + R
justify	Ctrl + J

In Addition

Inserting a New Line

When creating bulleted text in a slide, pressing the Enter key causes the insertion point to move to the next line, inserting another bullet. Situations may occur wherein you want to create a blank line between bulleted items without creating another bullet. One method for doing this is to use the New Line command, Shift + Enter. Pressing Shift + Enter inserts a new line that is considered part of the previous paragraph.

Activity 2.6

Changing Slide Size, Design Theme, Theme Colors, Theme Fonts, and Slide Background

By default, the slide size in PowerPoint 2013 is Widescreen (16:9), but you can change the slide size with options in the Slide Size button drop-down list in the Customize group on the DESIGN tab. Change the design theme applied to slides in a presentation or change the color, font, or effects of a theme with options on the DESIGN tab. Format the slide background with options in the Format Background task pane. Display this task pane by clicking the Format Background button in the Customize group on the DESIGN tab.

Project You are not pleased with the design theme for the documentary project presentation and decide to apply a different theme and then change the color and font for the theme.

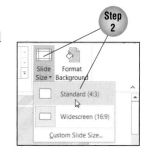

1 With **PS2-MPProj.pptx** open, click the DESIGN tab.

2 Click the Slide Size button 🔲 in the Customize group and then click *Standard (4:3)* at the drop-down list.

3 At the Microsoft PowerPoint dialog box, click the Ensure Fit button.

> Click the Ensure Fit button to scale down the contents of the slide to fit on the new slide. Click the Maximize button to maximize the size of the content on the new slide.

Tutorial 2.6
Changing Slide Size, Design Themes, and Background Styles

4 Run the presentation beginning with Slide 1 and notice any changes to the layout of the slides.

5 Click the Undo button on the Quick Access toolbar to return the presentation to the original slide size (Widescreen).

6 Click *Facet* in the Themes group (third thumbnail from the left).

7 Click the More button located in the Variants group, point to *Colors*, and then click *Violet II* at the side menu.

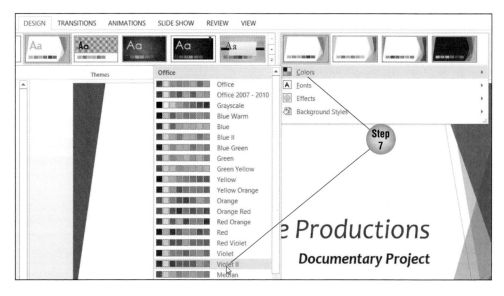

8 Make Slide 2 active.

9 Click the More button located in the Variants group, point to *Fonts*, scroll down the side menu, and then click *Consolas-Verdana*.

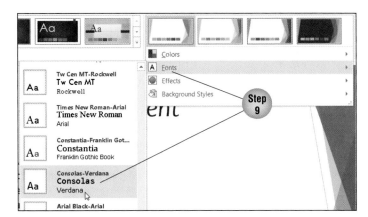

10 Apply a background style by clicking the More button in the Variants group, pointing to *Background Styles*, and then clicking *Style 9* at the side menu (first column, third row).

11 Run the presentation beginning with Slide 1.

12 Customize the background format by clicking the Format Background button [icon] in the Customize group on the DESIGN tab.

> This displays the Format Background task pane with a number of options for customizing slide backgrounds.

13 At the Format Background task pane that displays at the right side of the screen, if necessary, click *FILL* to display fill options.

14 Click the *Solid fill* option, click the Color button, and then click *Lavender, Background 2* (third column, first row in the *Theme Colors* section).

15 Click the Apply to All button located toward the bottom of the task pane.

16 Close the task pane by clicking the close button located in the upper right corner.

17 Save **PS2-MPProj.pptx** and then print Slide 1 of the presentation.

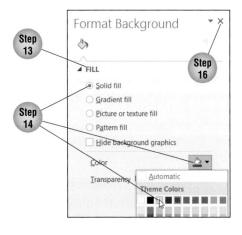

In Brief

Change Slide Size
1. Click DESIGN tab.
2. Click Slide Size button.
3. Click desired slide size at drop-down list.

Format Slide Background
1. Click DESIGN tab.
2. Click Format Background button.
3. Make desired changes in task pane.

Change Design Theme
1. Click DESIGN tab.
2. Click More button at right side of theme thumbnails.
3. Click desired theme at drop-down gallery.

Change Theme Colors
1. Click DESIGN tab.
2. Click More button in Variants group.
3. Point to *Colors*.
4. Click desired option at side menu.

Change Theme Fonts
1. Click DESIGN tab.
2. Click More button in Variants group.
3. Point to *Fonts*.
4. Click desired option at side menu.

In Addition

Insert a Picture as a Slide Background

Insert a picture as the background of an entire slide by clicking the DESIGN tab and then clicking the Format Background button in the Customize group. At the Format Background task pane, click the Fill icon, click *FILL* to display fill options, and then click the *Picture or texture fill* option. Click the File button in the *Insert picture from* section, navigate to the desired folder containing the picture, and then double-click the picture. The picture will automatically be inserted as the current slide's background.

Activity 2.7

Inserting, Sizing, and Moving an Image and Screenshot

Add visual appeal to a presentation by inserting an image such as a logo, picture, or clip art in a slide. Insert an image from a drive or folder with the Pictures button on the INSERT tab or by choosing a slide layout containing a content placeholder. Click the Pictures button on the INSERT tab or click the picture image in the content placeholder and the Insert Picture dialog box displays. At this dialog box, navigate to the desired drive or folder and then double-click the image.

Use buttons on the PICTURE TOOLS FORMAT tab to recolor the picture, apply a picture style, arrange the picture in the slide, and size the image. You can also size an image using the sizing handles that display around the selected image and you can move the image using the mouse. The Images group contains the Screenshot button, which you can use to capture all or part of the contents of a screen as an image. Format a screenshot with options on the PICTURE TOOLS FORMAT tab.

Project Chris Greenbaum has asked you to insert the company logo on the first slide of the presentation and a screenshot of the first page of the script on Slide 6.

Tutorial 2.7A
Inserting and Formatting Images

Tutorial 2.7B
Creating and Inserting Screenshots

① With **PS2-MPProj.pptx** open, make sure Slide 1 is active.

② Click in the title *Marquee Productions*, click the title placeholder border (border turns into a solid line when selected), and then press the Delete key.

> The title text will be deleted but the placeholder will not.

③ Click the title placeholder border again and then press the Delete key.

④ Complete steps similar to those in Steps 2 and 3 to delete the subtitle text and placeholder.

⑤ Insert the company logo in the new slide as shown in Figure 2.1 on the next page. To begin, click the INSERT tab and then click the Pictures button in the Images group.

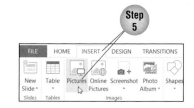
Step 2

Marquee Productions

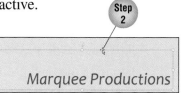
Step 5

⑥ At the Insert Picture dialog box, navigate to the PowerPointS2 folder on your storage medium and then double-click *MPLogo.jpg*.

> The image is inserted in the slide, selection handles display around the image, and the PICTURE TOOLS FORMAT tab is selected.

⑦ Increase the size of the logo by clicking in the *Shape Width* measurement box in the Size group, typing **7**, and then pressing Enter.

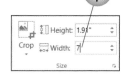
Step 7

> When you change the width of the logo, the height automatically adjusts to maintain the proportions of the logo. You can also size an image using the sizing handles that display around the selected image. Use the middle sizing handles to change the width of an image. Use the top and bottom handles to change the height, and use the corner sizing handles to adjust both the width and height of the image at the same time.

⑧ Move the logo so it is positioned as shown in Figure 2.1. To do this, position the mouse pointer on the image until the pointer displays with a four-headed arrow attached, drag the image to the position shown in the figure, and then release the mouse button.

9 With the image selected, click the Color button 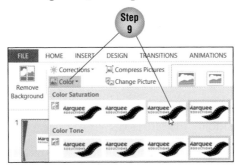 in the Adjust group and then click the *Saturation 66%* option (third option in the *Color Saturation* section).

10 Click the Corrections button ☀ in the Adjust group and then click the *Sharpen: 50%* option (last option in the *Sharpen/ Soften* section).

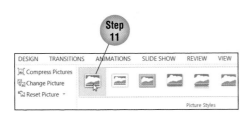

11 Click the *Simple Frame, White* option in the Picture Styles group (first option).

12 Click the Picture Effects button 🖾 in the Picture Styles group, point to *Shadow*, and then click the *Offset Diagonal Bottom Right* option (first column, first row in the *Outer* section).

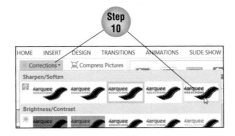

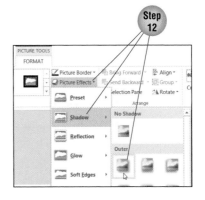

FIGURE 2.1 Slide 1

continues

13 Click outside the logo to deselect it.

14 Make Slide 6 active.

15 Insert a screen capture image from a Word document into the slide. Begin by opening Word and then opening the document named **MPScript.docx**.

> Make sure PS2-MPProj.pptx and MPScript.docx are the only open files on your desktop.

16 Click the Zoom Out button at the left side of the Zoom slider bar until *40%* displays at the right side of the slider bar.

17 Click the button on the Taskbar representing the PowerPoint presentation **PS2-MPProj.pptx**.

18 Click the INSERT tab, click the Screenshot button ⬚ in the Images group, and then click *Screen Clipping* at the drop-down list.

> When you click the *Screen Clipping* option, the Word document will automatically display in a dimmed manner and the insertion point will display as a + symbol.

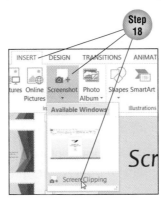

19 With the Word document displayed in a dimmed manner, position the insertion point in the top left corner of the Word document and drag down and to the right to select the entire document.

> Once you have created a screenshot of the Word document, the image will automatically be inserted into Slide 6 of PS2-MPProj.pptx.

20 With the screenshot selected, click in the *Shape Height* measurement box in the Size group on the PICTURE TOOLS FORMAT tab, type **5**, and then press Enter.

21 Click the Picture Border button arrow 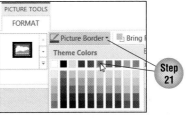 in the Picture Styles group and then click *Purple, Accent 2* at the drop-down list (sixth column, first row in the *Theme Colors* section).

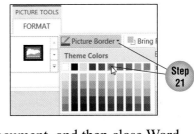

22 Position the screenshot in the slide as shown in Figure 2.2.

23 Click the Word button on the Taskbar, close the document, and then close Word.

> If a message displays asking if you want to save changes made in the document, click the Don't Save button.

24 Save **PS2-MPProj.pptx**.

In Brief

Insert Image
1. Click INSERT tab.
2. Click Pictures button.
3. At Insert Picture dialog box, navigate to desired folder.
4. Double-click desired picture file.

Insert Screenshot
1. Click INSERT tab.
2. Click Screenshot button.
3. Click *Screen Clipping*.
4. Select desired image or text.

FIGURE 2.2 Slide 6

Script Schedule

▶ **Phase 1**
  ▶ Research
  ▶ Script First Draft
▶ **Phase 2**
  ▶ Documenting
  ▶ Editing
  ▶ Rewriting
▶ **Phase 3**
  ▶ Final Draft
  ▶ Script Approval

Marquee
PRODUCTIONS

Raising the Bar

SCRIPT

Dana Benitez
Karl Edwins

September 2015

In Addition

Formatting with Buttons on the PICTURE TOOLS FORMAT Tab

Format images in a slide with buttons and options on the PICTURE TOOLS FORMAT tab, shown below. Use buttons in the Adjust group to adjust the brightness and contrast of the image; change the image color or change to a different image; reset the image to its original size, position, and color; and compress the picture. (Compress a picture to reduce the resolution or discard extra information to save room on a hard drive or to reduce download time.) Use buttons in the Picture Styles group to apply a predesigned style, insert a picture border, or apply a picture effect. The Arrange group contains buttons for positioning the image and aligning and rotating the image. Use options in the Size group to crop the image and specify the height and width of the image.

Activity 2.8

Inserting and Formatting Clip Art Images

Microsoft Office includes a gallery of media images you can insert in a presentation, such as clip art, photographs, and illustrations. Click the Online Pictures button on the INSERT tab and the Insert Pictures window displays. Use options in this window to search for and insert images from Office.com. At the window, type a category in the search text box to the right of the *Office.com Clip Art* option and then press Enter. In the list of clip art images and pictures that displays, double-click the desired image. The image is inserted in the slide and the PICTURE TOOLS FORMAT tab is selected. Use buttons and options on this tab to format and customize the clip art image.

Project

Chris Greenbaum has asked you to include an additional slide containing information on travel arrangements. You decide to enhance the visual appeal of the slide by inserting and formatting a clip art image.

1. With **PS2-MPProj.pptx** open, make Slide 7 active.

   This is the last slide in the presentation.

2. Insert a new slide by clicking the New Slide button in the Slides group on the HOME tab.

Tutorial 2.8
Inserting and Formatting Clip Art Images

3. Click the *Click to add title* placeholder and then type **Travel Arrangements**.

4. Click the *Click to add text* placeholder and then type the bulleted text shown in Figure 2.3.

5. Click the INSERT tab and then click the Online Pictures button in the Images group.

6. At the Insert Pictures window, click in the search text box located to the right of *Office.com Clip Art*; type **airplanes, symbols, transportation**; and then press Enter.

7. Double-click the image shown at the right.

8. Recolor the image so it complements the slide design color scheme. To do this, click the Color button in the Adjust group on the PICTURE TOOLS FORMAT tab and then click the *Purple, Accent color 2 Dark* option (third column, second row).

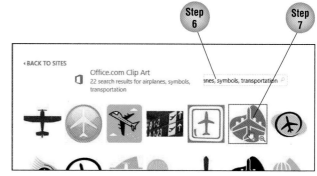

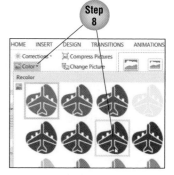

Need Help?

If the jet image is not available, check with your instructor to determine which clip art image you should substitute.

9 Click the Corrections button in the Adjust group and then click *Brightness: 0% (Normal) Contrast: +20%* at the drop-down gallery (third column, fourth row).

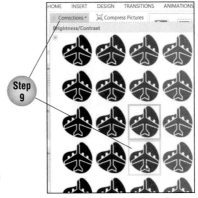

Step 9

10 Click the Picture Effects button in the Picture Styles group, point to *Shadow*, and then click the *Offset Diagonal Top Right* option (first column, third row in the *Outer* section).

11 Click in the *Shape Height* measurement box, type **3.5**, and then press Enter.

> When you change the height measurement, the width measurement changes automatically to maintain the proportion of the image.

12 Using the mouse, drag the image so it is positioned as shown in Figure 2.3.

13 Make Slide 7 active and then click the HOME tab.

14 Click on any character in the title *Preproduction Assignments* and then click the Format Painter button in the Clipboard group.

15 Make Slide 8 active and then select the entire title *Travel Arrangements*.

> This applies 50-point Candara italic dark blue formatting.

16 Save **PS2-MPProj.pptx**.

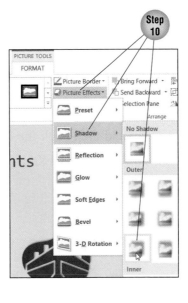

Step 10

FIGURE 2.3 Slide 8

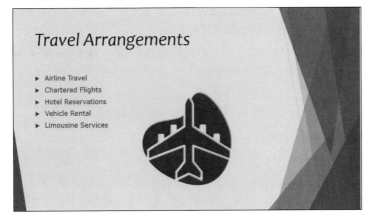

In Addition

Searching and Browsing for Images

At the Insert Pictures window, you can use the Bing Image Search text box to use the Bing search engine to find images online. The Insert Pictures window also includes a Browse button you can click to browse your SkyDrive for any images you have saved in your SkyDrive folders.

Inserting and Formatting an Organizational Chart with SmartArt

If you need to visually illustrate hierarchical data, consider creating an organizational chart with SmartArt. To display a menu of SmartArt choices, click the INSERT tab and then click the SmartArt button in the Illustrations group. This displays the Choose a SmartArt Graphic dialog box. At this dialog box, click *Hierarchy* in the left panel and then double-click the desired organizational chart in the middle panel. This inserts the organizational chart in the slide. Some SmartArt graphics are designed to include text. Type text in a graphic shape by selecting the shape and then typing text in the shape. Or, click the Text Pane button in the Create Graphic group to display the *Type your text here* window and then type the text in the window.

Project

Chris Greenbaum has asked you to create a slide containing an organizational chart that illustrates the hierarchy of the people involved in production.

Tutorial 2.9
Inserting and
Formatting SmartArt

1. With **PS2-MPProj.pptx** open, make Slide 2 active and then click the New Slide button in the Slides group on the INSERT tab.

2. Create the organizational chart shown in Figure 2.4. To begin, click the INSERT tab and then click the SmartArt button in the Illustrations group.

3. At the Choose a SmartArt Graphic dialog box, click *Hierarchy* in the left panel of the dialog box and then double-click the *Hierarchy* option in the middle panel.

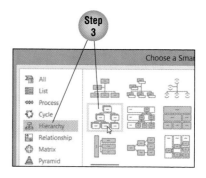

   This displays the organizational chart in the slide with the SMARTART TOOLS DESIGN tab selected. Use buttons on this tab to add additional boxes, change the order of the shapes, choose a different layout, apply formatting with a SmartArt style, and reset the formatting of the organizational chart.

4. If a *Type your text here* window displays at the left side of the organizational chart, close it by clicking the Text Pane button in the Create Graphic group.

   You can also close the window by clicking the Close button that displays in the upper right corner of the window.

5. Delete one of the boxes in the organizational chart. Begin by clicking the border of the second text box from the top at the left side of the chart.

   Make sure *[Text]* displays in the box.

6. Press the Delete key.

7. Click the second box from the top at the right side to select it and then click the Add Shape button in the Create Graphic group.

   This inserts a box to the right of the selected box. Your organizational chart should contain the same boxes shown in Figure 2.4. (The new box does not contain a [Text] placeholder, but you can still type text in the box.)

8. Click *[Text]* in the top box, type **Chris Greenbaum**, press the Enter key, and then type **Production Manager**. Click in each of the remaining boxes and type the text as shown in Figure 2.4.

FIGURE 2.4 Organizational Chart

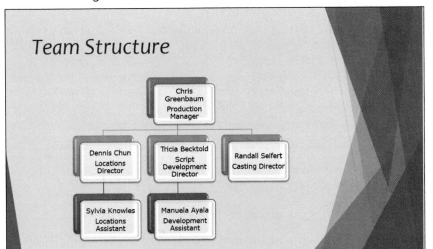

⑨ Click the Change Colors button ⬚ in the SmartArt Styles group on the SMARTART TOOLS DESIGN tab and then click the *Colorful - Accent Colors 5 to 6* option (fifth option in the *Colorful* section).

⑩ Click the More button located at the right side of the SmartArt Styles group.

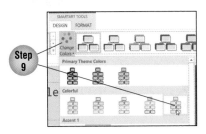
Step 9

⑪ Click the *Inset* option at the drop-down gallery (second column, first row in the *3-D* section).

⑫ Click the SMARTART TOOLS FORMAT tab.

⑬ Click inside the SmartArt graphic border but outside any shape.

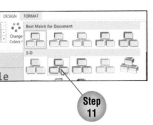
Step 11

⑭ Click in the *Shape Height* measurement box in the Size group, type **5**, click in the *Shape Width* measurement box, type **10**, and then press Enter.

⑮ Move the graphic so it is positioned in the slide as shown in Figure 2.4. Do this by positioning the arrow pointer on the graphic border until the pointer displays with a four-headed arrow attached, holding down the left mouse button, and then dragging the graphic to the desired location.

⑯ Click the *Click to add title* placeholder and then type **Team Structure**.

⑰ Make Slide 2 active and then click the HOME tab.

⑱ Click on any character in the title *Project Development* and then click the Format Painter button in the Clipboard group.

⑲ Make Slide 3 active and then select the entire title *Team Structure*.

⑳ Save **PS2-MPProj.pptx**.

In Addition

Resizing a SmartArt Graphic

Increase or decrease the size of a graphic with the *Shape Height* and *Shape Width* measurement boxes or by dragging a corner of the graphic border. If you want to maintain the proportions of the graphic, hold down the Shift key while dragging the border.

Inserting and Formatting a SmartArt Graphic

Use the SmartArt feature to create a variety of graphic diagrams, including process, cycle, relationship, matrix, and pyramid diagrams. Click the INSERT tab and then click the SmartArt button to display the Choose a SmartArt Graphic dialog box. Click the desired graphic type in the left panel of the dialog box and then use the scroll bar at the right side of the middle panel to scroll down the list of graphic choices. Double-click a graphic in the middle panel of the dialog box and the graphic is inserted in the slide. Use buttons in the SMARTART TOOLS DESIGN tab and the SMARTART TOOLS FORMAT tab to customize a graphic.

Project The finance director, Shawn Montgomery, has asked you to include a slide containing a SmartArt graphic diagram of travel expenses.

1. With **PS2-MPProj.pptx** open, make Slide 9 active.

2. Click the New Slide button arrow in the Slides group on the INSERT tab and then click the *Blank* layout at the drop-down list.

3. Create the SmartArt graphic diagram shown in Figure 2.5. To begin, click the INSERT tab and then click the SmartArt button in the Illustrations group.

Review Tutorial 2.9
Inserting and
Formatting SmartArt

4. At the Choose a SmartArt Graphic dialog box, click *Relationship* in the left panel of the dialog box and then double-click the *Converging Radial* option. (This option may be the first option from the right in the sixth row or the first

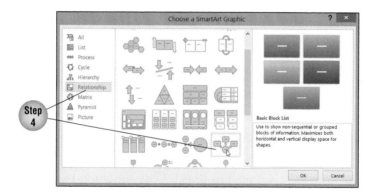

option from the left in the seventh row.)

5. If necessary, close the *Type your text here* window by clicking the Close button that displays in the upper right corner of the window.

6. Click the Add Shape button in the Create Graphic group.

7. Click in each of the shapes and insert the text shown in Figure 2.5.

8. Click the Change Colors button in the SmartArt Styles group and then click the *Colorful Range - Accent Colors 4 to 5* option (fourth option in the *Colorful* section).

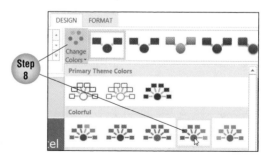

9. Click the More button located at the right side of the thumbnails in the SmartArt Styles group.

10 Click the *Cartoon* option at the drop-down gallery (third option in the *3-D* section).

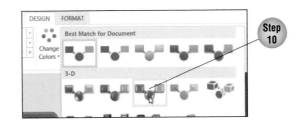

11 Click the SMARTART TOOLS FORMAT tab.

12 Click inside the SmartArt graphic border but outside any shape.

> This deselects the shapes but keeps the graphic selected.

13 Click the More button located at the right side of the thumbnails in the WordArt Styles group and then click the *Fill - White, Outline - Accent 2, Hard Shadow - Accent 2* option (fourth column, third row).

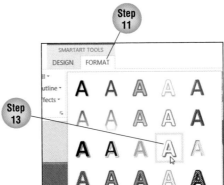

14 Click in the *Shape Width* measurement box in the Size group, type **9.5**, and then press Enter.

15 Click the Align button in the Arrange group and then click *Align Center* at the drop-down list.

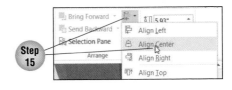

16 Save **PS2-MPProj.pptx**

FIGURE 2.5 SmartArt Graphic

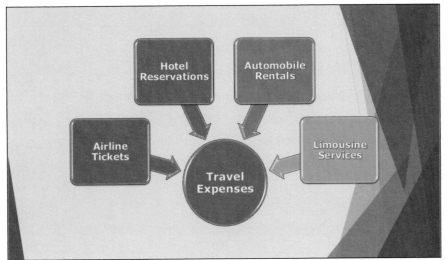

In Addition

Inserting Text in the Text Pane

Enter text in a SmartArt shape by clicking in the shape and then typing the text. You can also insert text in a SmartArt shape by typing text in SmartArt's text pane. Display the text pane by clicking the Text Pane button in the Create Graphic group on the SMARTART TOOLS DESIGN tab.

Activity 2.11

Applying Animation to Objects and Text

Animate individual objects and text in a slide with options on the ANIMATIONS tab. Click the ANIMATIONS tab and the tab displays with a variety of animation styles and options for customizing and applying times to animations in a presentation. Click the More button at the right side of the thumbnails in the Animation group and a gallery of animation styles displays that you can apply to objects and text as they enter a slide, exit a slide, and/or follow a motion path. You can also apply animations to emphasize objects in a slide. If you want the same animation applied to other objects in a presentation, use the Animation Painter button in the Advanced Animation group on the ANIMATIONS tab.

Project

To finalize the presentation, Chris Greenbaum has asked you to apply animation to objects and text in the presentation.

Tutorial 2.11
Applying Animation to Objects and Text

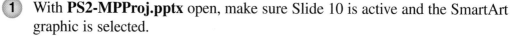

1. With **PS2-MPProj.pptx** open, make sure Slide 10 is active and the SmartArt graphic is selected.

2. Click the ANIMATIONS tab and then click the *Fly In* option in the Animation group.

3. Click the Effect Options button ↑ in the Animation group and then click *One by One* at the drop-down list.

4. Click twice on the up-pointing arrow to the right of the *Duration* measurement box in the Timing group.

    This inserts *01.00* into the measurement box.

5. Click the Preview button ★ in the Preview group to view the animation applied to the SmartArt graphic.

6. Make Slide 3 active and then click the organizational chart to select it.

7. Click the More button located to the right of the thumbnails in the Animation group and then click the *Zoom* option at the drop-down gallery.

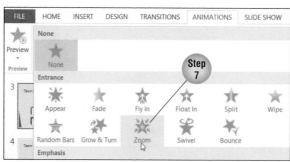

8. Click the Effect Options button in the Animation group and then click *One by One* at the drop-down list.

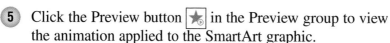

9 Click Slide 2 to make it active and then click in the bulleted text to select the placeholder.

10 Click the *Fly In* option in the Animation group

> Applying this animation creates a **build** for the bulleted items. A build displays important points in a slide one point at a time and is useful for keeping the audience's attention focused on the point being presented rather than reading ahead.

11 Click twice on the up-pointing arrow to the right of the *Duration* measurement box in the Timing group.

> This inserts *01.00* into the measurement box.

12 Apply the same animation to the bulleted text in Slides 4 through 9. To begin, click anywhere in the bulleted text to select the placeholder and then double-click the Animation Painter button 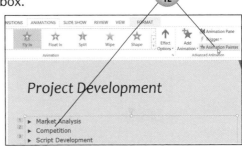 in the Advanced Animation group.

13 Make Slide 4 active and then click anywhere in the bulleted text. (This selects the placeholder and applies the Fly In animation and the duration time.)

14 Make Slide 5 active and then click anywhere in the bulleted text.

15 Make Slide 6 active and then click in the bulleted text. Make Slide 7 active and then click in the bulleted text. Make Slide 8 active and then click in the bulleted text. Make Slide 9 active and then click in the bulleted text.

16 Click the Animation Painter button to turn off the feature.

17 Make Slide 1 active and then run the presentation. Click the mouse button to advance slides and to display the individual organizational chart boxes, bulleted items, and SmartArt graphic boxes.

18 Print the presentation as handouts with six slides per page. To do this, click the FILE tab and then click the *Print* option.

19 At the Print backstage area, click the second gallery (contains the text *Full Page Slides*) in the *Settings* category and then click *6 Slides Horizontal* at the drop-down list.

20 Click the Print button.

21 Save and then close **PS2-MPProj.pptx**.

In Brief

Apply Animation to Object
1. Click desired object.
2. Click ANIMATIONS tab.
3. Click desired animation thumbnail.

In Addition

Applying Custom Animation

Apply custom animation to selected objects in a slide by clicking the Animation Pane button in the Advanced Animation group on the ANIMATIONS tab. This displays the Animation task pane at the right side of the screen. Use options in this task pane to control the order in which objects appear on a slide, choose animation direction and speed, and specify how objects will appear in the slide.

Features Summary

Feature	Ribbon Tab, Group	Button	Keyboard Shortcut
align left	HOME, Paragraph		Ctrl + L
align right	HOME, Paragraph		Ctrl + R
align vertically	HOME, Paragraph		
animation effect options	ANIMATIONS, Animation		
bold	HOME, Font	B	Ctrl + B
center	HOME, Paragraph		Ctrl + E
copy selected text	HOME, Clipboard		Ctrl + C
cut selected text	HOME, Clipboard		Ctrl + X
decrease font size	HOME, Font		Ctrl + Shift + <
decrease list level	HOME, Paragraph		Shift + Tab
font	HOME, Font		
font color	HOME, Font		
Font dialog box	HOME, Font		Ctrl + Shift + F
font size	HOME, Font		
format background	DESIGN, Customize		
Format Painter	HOME, Clipboard		
increase font size	HOME, Font		Ctrl + Shift + >
increase list level	HOME, Paragraph		Tab
insert clip art image	INSERT, Images		
insert picture	INSERT, Images		
insert screenshot	INSERT, Images		
insert SmartArt	INSERT, Illustrations		
italic	HOME, Font	I	Ctrl + I
justify	HOME, Paragraph		Ctrl + J
line spacing	HOME, Paragraph		
paste selected text	HOME, Clipboard		Ctrl + V
preview animation	ANIMATIONS, Preview		
slide size	DESIGN, Customize		
underline	HOME, Font	U	Ctrl + U

Knowledge Check SNAP

Completion: In the space provided at the right, indicate the correct term, command, or option.

1. Save an existing presentation with a new name at this dialog box. _____
2. Increase the text level indent by clicking the Increase List Level button or by pressing this key on the keyboard. _____
3. Decrease the text level indent by clicking the Decrease List Level button or by pressing these keys on the keyboard. _____
4. The Cut button is located in this group on the HOME tab. _____
5. This is the keyboard shortcut to copy selected text. _____
6. Press these keys on the keyboard to select all text in a placeholder. _____
7. Use this feature to apply the same formatting in more than one location in a slide or slides. _____
8. Click this button in the Paragraph group on the HOME tab to change the text alignment to right. _____
9. Change the vertical alignment of text in a placeholder with options from this button drop-down list. _____
10. This dialog box contains options for changing line spacing and text alignment, indentation, and spacing. _____
11. Click this tab to display the Themes group. _____
12. The Format Background button is located in this group on the DESIGN tab. _____
13. Use buttons on this tab to change the color of the selected picture, apply a picture style, arrange the picture, and size the picture. _____
14. Display the Insert Pictures window by clicking the INSERT tab and then clicking this button in the Images group. _____
15. Use this feature to create an organizational chart or a variety of graphic diagrams. _____
16. The Effect Options button is located on this tab. _____

Skills Review

Review 1 Editing and Formatting a Presentation for Marquee Productions

SNAP Grade It

Marquee PRODUCTIONS

1. Open the presentation named **MPMeeting.pptx** located in the PowerPointS2 folder.
2. Save the presentation with Save As in the PowerPointEOS folder on your storage medium and name it **PS2-R-MPMeeting**.
3. Apply the Ion Boardroom design theme to the slides in the presentation, change the theme colors to *Slipstream*, and change the theme fonts to *Arial Black - Arial*.
4. Delete Slide 5 (contains the title *Financial*) in the slide thumbnails pane.
5. Change to Slide Sorter view and move Slide 7 (*Expenses*) immediately after Slide 3 (*Review of Goals*).

6. Move Slide 6 (*Future Goals*) immediately after the new Slide 7 (*Technology*).
7. Change to the Normal view and then make Slide 4 (*Expenses*) the active slide.
8. Decrease the indent of *Payroll* so it displays aligned at the left with *Administration*.
9. Decrease the indent of *Benefits* so it displays aligned at the left with *Payroll* and *Administration*.
10. Make Slide 6 (*Technology*) active and then increase the indent of *Hardware* to the next level, the indent of *Software* to the next level, and the indent of *Technical Support* to the next level.
11. Make Slide 7 (*Future Goals*) active, select the name *Chris Greenbaum*, and then click the Copy button. (Make sure you select only the name and not the space following the name.)
12. Make Slide 3 (*Review of Goals*) active.
13. Move the insertion point immediately to the right of *Overview of Goals*, press the Enter key, press the Tab key, and then click the Paste button. (Clicking the Paste button inserts the name *Chris Greenbaum*.)
14. Move the insertion point immediately to the right of *Completed Goals*, press the Enter key, press the Tab key, and then click the Paste button.
15. Make Slide 7 (*Future Goals*) active, select the name *Shannon Grey* (do not include the space after the name), and then click the Copy button.
16. Make Slide 3 (*Review of Goals*) active and then paste the name *Shannon Grey* below *Goals Remaining* at the same tab location as *Chris Greenbaum*.
17. Paste the name *Shannon Grey* below *Analysis/Discussion* at the same tab location as *Chris Greenbaum*.
18. Make Slide 1 active, select the text *Marquee Productions*, change the font to Candara, change the font size to 60 points, and then turn on bold formatting.
19. Select the text *ANNUAL MEETING*, change the font to Candara, change the font size to 32 points, and then turn on bold formatting.
20. Make Slide 2 (*Agenda*) active, select the title *Agenda*, change the font to Candara, change the font size to 48 points, and then turn on bold formatting.
21. Using Format Painter, apply the same formatting to the title in each of the remaining slides.
22. Make Slide 6 active, select all of the bulleted text, and then change the line spacing to 1.5.
23. Make Slide 8 active, select all of the bulleted text, and then change the spacing before paragraphs to 24 points.
24. Make Slide 2 active and then insert the clip art image shown in Figure 2.6 with the following specifications:
    • At the Insert Pictures window, type **archery, arrows, bull's eyes** in the search text box and then insert the image shown in Figure 2.6.
    • Apply the Blue, Accent color 1 Light color to the clip art image (second column, third row).
    • Change the height of the image to 4 inches.
    • Position the image as shown in the figure.
25. Make Slide 4 active and then insert the clip art image shown in Figure 2.7 on the next page. Use the words *money symbol icon button* in the Insert Pictures window to find the clip art. Apply the Blue, Accent color 1 Light color to the clip art and change the height of the image to 3.5 inches. Position the clip art image as shown in Figure 2.7.
26. Apply a transition, sound, and transition duration time to all slides in the presentation.
27. Run the presentation.
28. Print the presentation as handouts with four slides printed horizontally on each page.
29. Save and then close **PS2-R-MPMeeting.pptx**.

FIGURE 2.6 Review 1, Slide 2

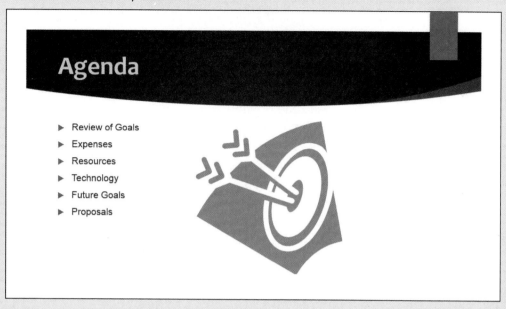

FIGURE 2.7 Review 1, Slide 4

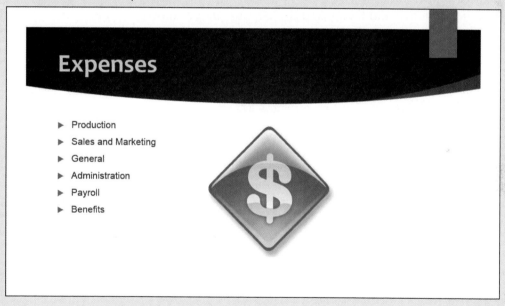

Review 2 **Formatting a Presentation for Performance Threads**

1. Open **PTPres.pptx** and then save the presentation in the PowerPointEOS folder and name it **PS2-R-PTPres**.
2. Change the design theme to *Organic*.
3. Change the slide size to *Standard (4:3)* and ensure the fit.
4. With Slide 1 active, insert the **PTLogo.jpg** file from the PowerPointS2 folder. (Use the Pictures button in the Images group on the INSERT tab.) Change the height of the logo to 3.7 inches and then position the logo in the middle of the slide.

5. Make the background of the logo transparent by clicking the Color button on the PICTURE TOOLS FORMAT tab, clicking the *Set Transparent Color* option at the drop-down gallery, and then clicking anywhere in the white background of the logo.

6. Make Slide 3 active, select the bulleted text, and then change the line spacing to 1.5.

7. Make Slide 4 active, select the bulleted text, and then change the spacing after paragraphs to 18 points.

8. Make Slide 2 active and then insert the organizational chart shown in Figure 2.8 on the next page with the following specifications:
   - Click the *Hierarchy* option in the left panel at the Choose a SmartArt Graphic dialog box and then double-click *Organization Chart*.
   - Delete and add boxes so your organization chart has the same boxes as the organization chart in Figure 2.8. ***Hint: Delete the single box in the middle row, delete one of the boxes in the bottom row, and then use the Add Shape button arrow and click* Add Shape Below *to add the boxes in the bottom row of the organization chart.***
   - Type the text in the boxes. (Press Shift + Enter after entering the names.)
   - Apply the Colorful Range - Accent Colors 5 to 6 color to the organizational chart.
   - Apply the Cartoon SmartArt style to the organizational chart.
   - Apply the Fill - Black, Text 1, Shadow WordArt style to the text in the shapes (first column, first row in the WordArt styles drop-down gallery).

9. Make Slide 3 active and then insert the clip art image shown in Figure 2.9 on the next page with the following specifications:
   - At the Insert Pictures window, use the words *healthcare insurance* to search for the clip art image shown in Figure 2.9.
   - Change the height of the clip art image to 2.9 inches.
   - Apply the Brightness: -20% Contrast: +20% brightness and contrast (second column, fourth row).
   - Position the clip art as shown in Figure 2.9.

10. Make Slide 5 active and then insert the SmartArt graphic shown in Figure 2.10 on the next page with the following specifications:
    - Click the *Process* option in the left panel at the Choose a SmartArt Graphic dialog box and then double-click *Alternating Flow*.
    - Apply the Colorful Range - Accent Colors 4 to 5 color to the graphic.
    - Apply the Cartoon SmartArt style to the graphic.
    - Type the text in the boxes as shown in Figure 2.10.

11. Make Slide 2 active, click the organizational chart, and then animate the organizational chart using options on the ANIMATIONS tab. (You determine the type of animation.)

12. Make Slide 5 active, click the SmartArt graphic, and then animate the graphic using options on the ANIMATIONS tab. (You determine the type of animation.)

13. Make Slide 3 active, click the bulleted text, and then apply the Split animation.

14. Make Slide 4 active, click the bulleted text, and then apply the Split animation.

15. Run the presentation.

16. Print the presentation as handouts with all five slides printed horizontally on one page.

17. Save and then close **PS2-R-PTPres.pptx**.

FIGURE 2.8 Review 2, Slide 2

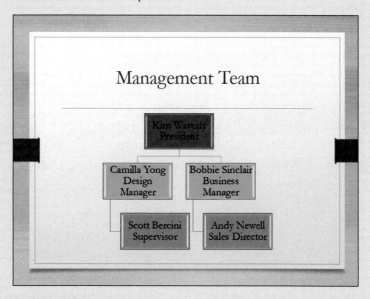

FIGURE 2.9 Review 2, Slide 3

FIGURE 2.10 Review 2, Slide 5

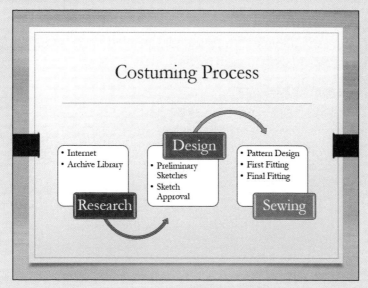

Skills Assessment

Assessment 1 Formatting a Presentation for Niagara Peninsula College, Theatre Arts Division

1. Open **NPCTheatreArts.pptx** and then save the presentation in the PowerPointEOS folder and name it **PS2-A1-NPCTheatreArts**.
2. Move Slide 7 (*Associate Degrees*) immediately after Slide 2 (*Mission Statement*).
3. Move Slide 6 (*Semester Costs*) immediately after the new Slide 7 (*Fall Semester Classes*).
4. Make Slide 2 (*Mission Statement*) active, click in the paragraph below the title *Mission Statement*, and then justify the text alignment.
5. Change the line spacing to 1.5 for the bulleted text in Slides 5 and 7.
6. Make Slide 5 active, select the bulleted text, and then apply italics formatting.
7. Make Slide 1 active and then insert the logo file named **NPCLogo.jpg** into the slide. Increase the size of the logo and then center it in the dark blue portion of the slide.
8. Make Slide 3 active and then insert a *Radial Cycle* SmartArt graphic (located in the *Cycle* category in the Choose a SmartArt Graphic dialog box) in the slide. Insert the text *Theatre Arts Division* in the middle circle and then insert the following text in the remaining four circles: *Production, Acting, Set Design,* and *Interactive Media*. Apply a color and SmartArt style of your choosing to the graphic. Apply any other formatting you desire to enhance the visual display of the graphic. Position the graphic attractively on the slide.
9. Make Slide 4 active and then insert the Organization Chart SmartArt graphic (located in the *Hierarchy* category in the Choose a SmartArt Graphic dialog box) in the slide with the boxes and text shown in Figure 2.11. ***Hint: To add the extra box along the bottom, click the left box at the bottom, click the Add Shape button arrow, and then click* Add Shape Before.** Apply a color and SmartArt style of your choosing to the organizational chart. Apply any other formatting you desire to enhance the visual display of the organizational chart. Position the chart attractively on the slide.
10. Make Slide 7 active and then insert a clip art image related to *money*. Size, position, and recolor the image so it enhances the slide.
11. Make Slide 3 active and then apply an animation of your choosing to the SmartArt graphic.
12. Make Slide 4 active and then apply an animation of your choosing to the organizational chart.
13. Apply a transition, sound, and transition duration time of your choosing to all slides in the presentation.
14. Run the presentation.
15. Print the presentation as handouts with four slides printed horizontally on one page.
16. Save and then close **PS2-A1-NPCTheatreArts.pptx**.

FIGURE 2.11 Assessment 1, Organizational Chart

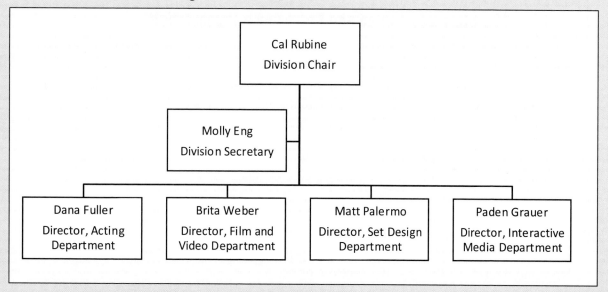

Assessment 2 Formatting a Presentation for First Choice Travel

1. Open **FCTVacations.pptx** and then save the presentation in the PowerPointEOS folder and name it **PS2-A2-FCTVacations**.
2. Display the Format Background task pane and make sure the FILL options display. Apply the Medium Gradient - Accent 3 gradient fill color and then apply the gradient fill to all slides in the presentation.
3. Increase the font size of the subtitle *Vacation Specials* located in Slide 1. (You determine the size.)
4. Apply bold formatting, apply the Blue font color, and change to left alignment for each heading in Slides 2 through 6.
5. Make Slide 1 active and then insert the **FCTLogo.jpg** file into the slide. Make the background of the logo transparent. You determine the size and position of the logo.
6. Apply any formatting you feel is necessary to improve the appearance of each slide.
7. Apply a transition and sound to each slide in the presentation.
8. Run the presentation.
9. Print the presentation as handouts with all six slides printed horizontally on one page.
10. Save and then close **PS2-A2-FCTVacations.pptx**.

Assessment 3 Finding Information on Converting Text to a SmartArt Graphic

1. Open **PS2-A2-FCTVacations.pptx** and then save the presentation in the PowerPointEOS folder and name it **PS2-A3-FCTVacations**.
2. Use the Help feature to learn how to convert text in a slide to a SmartArt graphic.
3. After learning how to convert text, make Slide 4 active and then convert the bulleted text to a SmartArt graphic of your choosing.
4. Apply formatting to enhance the visual display of the SmartArt graphic.
5. Print only Slide 4.
6. Save and then close **PS2-A3-FCTVacations.pptx**.

HELP

Assessment 4 Individual Challenge
Locating Information and Preparing a Presentation

1. Connect to the Internet and search for information on your favorite author, historical figure, or someone in the entertainment business.
2. Using PowerPoint, create a presentation with a minimum of four slides on the person you chose that contains a title slide that includes the person's name and your name, and additional slides that includes information such as personal statistics, achievements, and awards.
3. Insert an appropriate screenshot image of the person or something related to the person and insert it into any slide where it seems appropriate.
4. Apply a transition and sound to each slide in the presentation.
5. Save the presentation in the PowerPointEOS folder and name it **PS2-A4-IC-PerPres**.
6. Run the presentation.
7. Print the slides as handouts with six slides printed horizontally per page.
8. Save and then close **PS2-A4-IC-PerPres.pptx**.

Marquee Challenge

Challenge 1 Preparing a Presentation for Worldwide Enterprises

1. Create the presentation shown in Figure 2.12. Apply the Retrospect design theme. Insert the logo file named **WELogo.jpg** in Slide 1. In Slide 2, apply the *Brown, Accent 3* font color to the title text and the *Orange, Accent 2* font color to the subtitle text. Insert the clip art image in Slide 3 using *businesses, finances, graphs* as the search text and insert the clip art image in Slide 6 using *business, distribution* as the search text. Format, size, and position the clip art images as shown. Create and format the SmartArt graphic shown in Slide 5.
2. Save the completed presentation in the PowerPointEOS folder and name it **PS2-C1-WEDist**.
3. Print the presentation as a handout with all six slides on the same page and then close the presentation.

Challenge 2 Preparing a Presentation for The Waterfront Bistro

1. Create the presentation shown in Figure 2.13 on page 80. Apply the Dividend theme and the blue variant (second option in the Variants group). Change the slide size to *Standard (4:3)* and ensure fit. Insert the logo file named **TWBLogo.jpg** in Slides 1 and 2 and then apply the Drop Shadow Rectangle picture style to the logo on both slides. Create and format the SmartArt organizational chart in Slide 3 using the Hierarchy SmartArt graphic. Create and format the SmartArt graphic shown in Slide 4. Insert the clip art image as shown in Slide 6 using *catering* as the search text.
2. Save the completed presentation in the PowerPointEOS folder and name it **PS2-C2-TWBInfo**.
3. Print the presentation as a handout with all six slides on the same page and then close the presentation.

FIGURE 2.12 Challenge 1

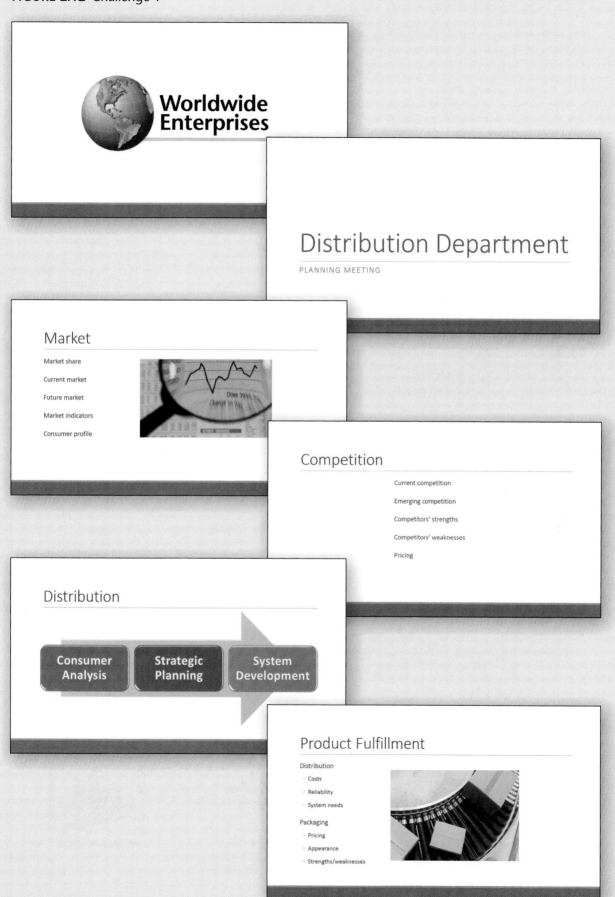

FIGURE 2.13 Challenge 2

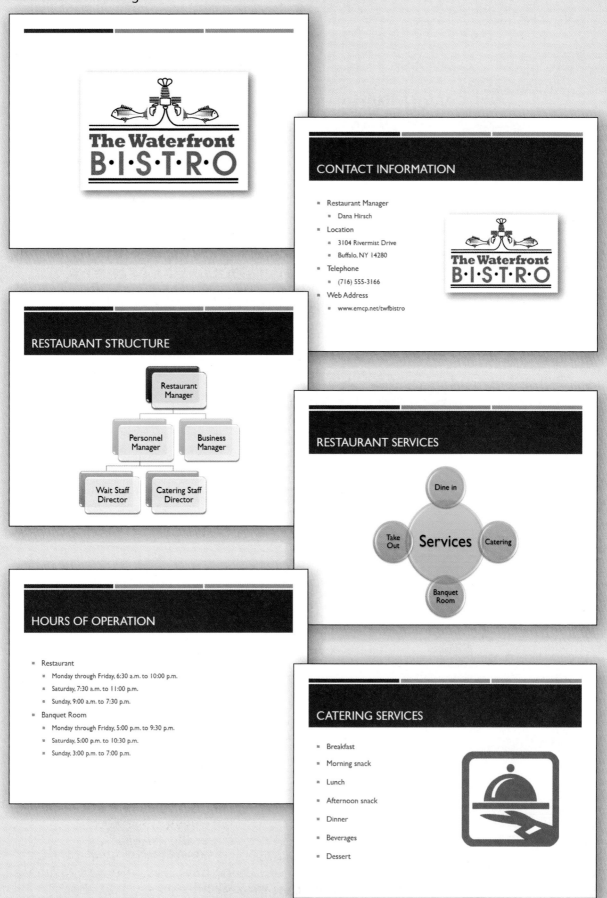

PowerPoint® SECTION 3

Customizing a Presentation

Skills

- Copy and paste items using the Clipboard task pane
- Find and replace text
- Insert and format WordArt
- Draw and customize objects
- Display gridlines
- Insert a text box
- Copy and rotate shapes
- Create and format a table
- Insert action buttons
- Insert a hyperlink
- Format with a slide master
- Insert headers and footers
- Add audio and video
- Set and rehearse timings for a presentation

Projects Overview

Open a presentation on filming in Toronto, save the presentation with a new name, and then format the presentation and add visual appeal by inserting WordArt, shapes, text boxes, and a table. Open an existing presentation on a biography project, save the presentation with a new name, and then format and add visual appeal by inserting WordArt, shapes, text boxes, clip art, a logo, and a footer. Open an existing presentation on the annual meeting, apply a design theme, theme colors, and theme fonts and format using a slide master. Prepare and format a project schedule presentation.

Open a presentation on costume designs for Marquee Productions, save the presentation with a new name, and then format the presentation and add visual appeal by inserting a logo, WordArt, shapes, text boxes, a table, and a footer.

Open a presentation on eco-tour adventures and add a video clip and audio file. Open a presentation on a vacation cruise, save the presentation with a new name, and then format the presentation and add visual appeal by inserting a logo and audio clip, setting and rehearsing timings, and setting up the presentation to run continuously. Open a presentation on tours in Australia and New Zealand and then enhance the presentation by inserting WordArt, a footer, and an audio clip; setting and rehearsing timings; and setting up the presentation to run continuously. Prepare a presentation on a Moroccan tour.

Model Answers for Projects

These model answers for the projects you complete in Section 3 provide a preview of the finished projects before you begin working and also allow you to compare your own results with these models to ensure you have created the materials accurately.

PS3-MPToronto.pptx (a two-page document) is the project in Activities 3.1 to 3.7.

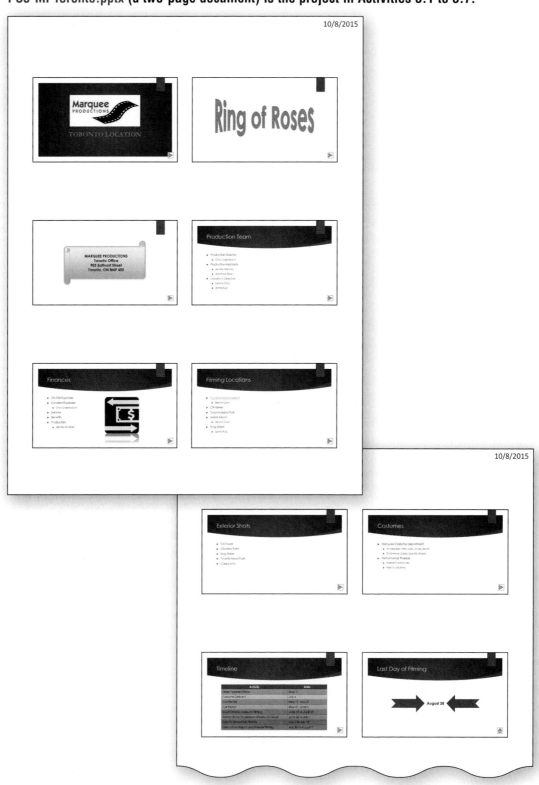

PS3-FCTEcoTours.pptx is the project in Activities 3.8 and 3.9.

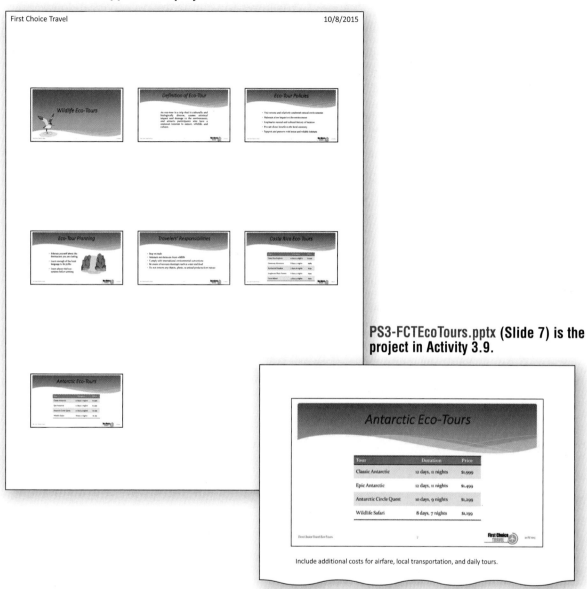

PS3-FCTEcoTours.pptx (Slide 7) is the project in Activity 3.9.

PS3-FCTEcoTours-Rehearsed.pptx (Slides 1–6 appear exactly as above) is the project in Activity 3.11.

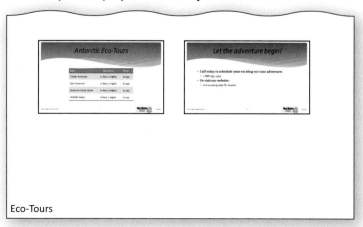

Activity 3.1

Using the Clipboard Task Pane

Using the Clipboard task pane, you can collect up to 24 different items and then paste them in various locations. To display the Clipboard task pane, click the Clipboard task pane launcher in the Clipboard group on the HOME tab. The Clipboard task pane displays at the left side of the screen. Select text or an object you want to copy and then click the Copy button in the Clipboard group. Continue selecting text or items and clicking the Copy button. To paste an item into a presentation, position the insertion point in the desired location and then click the item in the Clipboard task pane. (If the copied item is text, the first 50 characters display in the Clipboard task pane.) After inserting all desired items into the presentation, click the Clear All button to remove any remaining items from the Clipboard task pane.

Project

In preparation for a meeting about the Toronto location shoot, you will open the presentation **MPToronto.pptx** and then copy and paste multiple items into the appropriate slides.

Tutorial 3.1
Using the Clipboard Task Pane

1. Open **MPToronto.pptx** from the PowerPointS3 folder on your storage medium and then save the presentation and name it **PS3-MPToronto**.

2. Display the Clipboard task pane by clicking the Clipboard task pane launcher 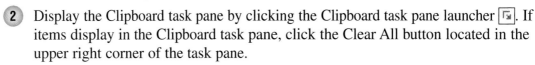. If items display in the Clipboard task pane, click the Clear All button located in the upper right corner of the task pane.

3. Make Slide 2 active and then select the name *Chris Greenbaum*. (Do not include the space after the name.)

4. With *Chris Greenbaum* selected, click the Copy button in the Clipboard group.

   When you click the Copy button, the name *Chris Greenbaum* is inserted as an item in the Clipboard task pane.

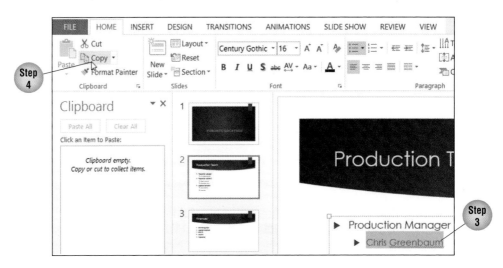

5. Select the name *Camille Matsui* (do not include the space after the name) and then click the Copy button. Select the name *Dennis Chun* (without the space after) and then click the Copy button. Select the name *Josh Hart* (without the space after) and then click the Copy button.

6. Make Slide 3 active, position the insertion point immediately to the right of *Location Expenses*, press the Enter key, and then press the Tab key.

7 Click *Chris Greenbaum* in the Clipboard task pane.

In Brief

Use Clipboard Task Pane
1. Click Clipboard task pane launcher.
2. Select text, click Copy button.
3. Continue selecting text and clicking Copy button.
4. Position insertion point.
5. Click desired item in Clipboard task pane.
6. Insert additional items.
7. Click Clear All button.
8. Close Clipboard task pane.

8 Position the insertion point immediately right of *Production*, press the Enter key, press the Tab key, and then click *Camille Matsui* in the Clipboard task pane.

9 Make Slide 4 active, position the insertion point immediately right of *Royal Ontario Museum*, press the Enter key, press the Tab key, and then click *Dennis Chun* in the Clipboard task pane.

10 Position the insertion point immediately to the right of *Island Airport*, press the Enter key, press the Tab key, and then click *Dennis Chun* in the Clipboard task pane.

11 Position the insertion point immediately to the right of *King Street*, press the Enter key, press the Tab key, and then click *Josh Hart* in the Clipboard task pane.

12 Click the Clear All button in the Clipboard task pane and then click the Close button ☒ located in the upper right corner of the task pane.

13 Make Slide 1 active and then insert the **MPLogo.jpg** file. To begin, click the INSERT tab and then click the Pictures button in the Images group. Make the PowerPointS3 folder active and then double-click *MPLogo.jpg*.

14 Size and move the logo so it better fills the slide.

15 Save **PS3-MPToronto.pptx**.

In Addition

Clipboard Task Pane Options

Click the Options button located toward the bottom of the Clipboard task pane and a drop-down list displays with five options, as shown at the right. Insert a check mark before those options you want active. For example, you can choose to display the Clipboard task pane automatically when you cut or copy text, cut and copy text without displaying the Clipboard task pane, display the Clipboard task pane by pressing Ctrl + C twice, display the Office Clipboard icon on the Taskbar when the clipboard is active, and display the item message near the Taskbar when copying items to the Clipboard.

Activity 3.2

Finding and Replacing Text

Use the Find and Replace feature to search for specific text or formatting in slides in a presentation and replace it with other text or formatting. Display the Find dialog box if you want to find something specific in a presentation. Display the Replace dialog box if you want to find something in a presentation and replace it with another item.

Project A couple of people have been replaced on the Toronto location shoot. Use the Replace feature to find names and replace them with new names in the Toronto presentation.

① With **PS3-MPToronto.pptx** open, make sure Slide 1 is active.

② Camille Matsui has been replaced by Jennie Almonzo. Begin the find and replace by clicking the Replace button in the Editing group on the HOME tab.

> This displays the Replace dialog box with the insertion point positioned in the *Find what* text box.

Tutorial 3.2
Finding and
Replacing Text

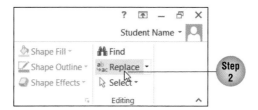

③ Type **Camille Matsui** in the *Find what* text box.

④ Press the Tab key and then type **Jennie Almonzo** in the *Replace with* text box.

⑤ Click the Replace All button.

> Clicking the Replace All button replaces all occurrences of the *Find what* text in the presentation. If you want control over which occurrences are replaced in a presentation, click the Find Next button to move to the next occurrence of the text. Click the Replace button if you want to replace the text, or click the Find Next button if you want to leave the text as written and move to the next occurrence.

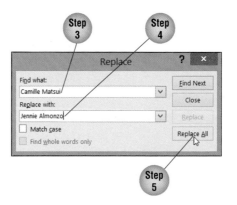

⑥ At the message telling you that two replacements were made, click OK.

> The Replace dialog box remains on the screen.

7 Josh Hart had to leave the project and is being replaced by Jaime Ruiz. At the Replace dialog box, type **Josh Hart** in the *Find what* text box.

> When you begin typing the name *Josh Hart*, the previous name, *Camille Matsui*, is deleted.

8 Press the Tab key, type **Jaime Ruiz** in the *Replace with* text box, and then click the Replace All button.

In Brief

Find and Replace Text
1. Click Replace button.
2. At Replace dialog box, type find text.
3. Press Tab and then type replace text.
4. Click Replace All button.
5. Click Close button.

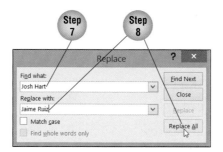

9 At the message telling you that two replacements were made, click OK.

> The Replace dialog box remains on the screen.

10 The title *Manager* has been changed to *Director*. At the Replace dialog box, type **Manager** in the *Find what* text box.

11 Press the Tab key, type **Director** in the *Replace with* text box, and then click the Replace All button.

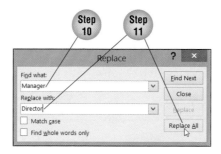

12 At the message telling you that one replacement was made, click OK.

13 Close the Replace dialog box by clicking the Close button located at the right side of the dialog box.

14 Save **PS3-MPToronto.pptx**.

In Addition

Using Replace Dialog Box Options
The Replace dialog box shown at the right contains two options for completing a find and replace. Choose the *Match case* option if you want to exactly match the case of the find text. For example, if you look for *Company*, PowerPoint will stop at *Company* but not *company* or *COMPANY*. Choose the *Find whole words only* option if you want to find a whole word, not a part of a word. For example, if you search for *his* and do not select *Find whole words only*, PowerPoint will stop at t*his*, *his*tory, c*his*el, etc.

Activity 3.3

Inserting and Formatting WordArt

Use the WordArt feature to create text with special formatting that makes it stand out. You can format WordArt in a variety of ways, including conforming it to a shape. To insert WordArt, click the INSERT tab, click the WordArt button in the Text group, and then click the desired WordArt style at the drop-down gallery. When WordArt is selected, the DRAWING TOOLS FORMAT tab displays. Use options and buttons on this tab to modify and customize WordArt.

Project

You want to improve the visual appeal of the slide containing information on exterior shots by changing text to WordArt. You also want to insert a new slide with the title of the film formatted as WordArt.

Tutorial 3.3
Inserting and Formatting WordArt

① With **PS3-MPToronto.pptx** open, make sure Slide 1 is active.

② Click the New Slide button arrow in the Slides group on the HOME tab and then click the *Blank* layout (first column, third row).

③ Insert WordArt by clicking the INSERT tab, clicking the WordArt button 🅰 in the Text group, and then clicking *Fill - Lavender, Accent 1, Outline - Background 1, Hard Shadow - Accent 1* (third column, third row).

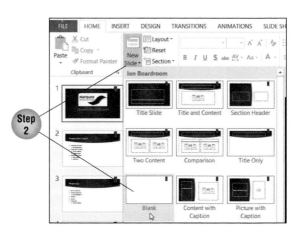

This inserts a text box with *Your text here* inside and makes the DRAWING TOOLS FORMAT tab active.

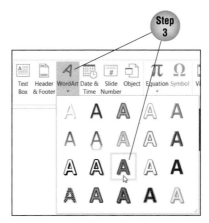

④ Type **Ring of Roses**.

⑤ Click in the *Shape Height* measurement box in the Size group, type **4**, and then press Enter.

⑥ Click in the *Shape Width* measurement box in the Size group, type **9**, and then press Enter.

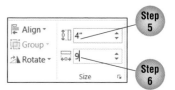

7 Click the Text Effects button in the WordArt Styles group, point to *Transform* at the drop-down list, scroll down the side menu, and then click *Deflate* at the drop-down gallery (second column, sixth row in the *Warp* section).

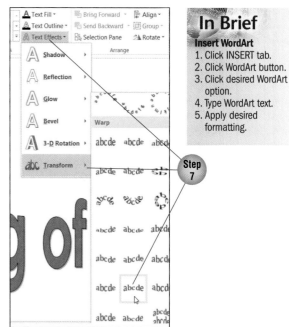

8 Click the border of the WordArt (border will display as a solid line), click the Text Outline button arrow, and then click *Plum, Accent 1* at the drop-down gallery (fifth column, first row in *Theme Colors* section).

9 Position the WordArt in the middle of the slide as shown in Figure 3.1 by clicking the Align button in the Arrange group and then clicking *Distribute Horizontally* at the drop-down list. Click the Align button again and then click *Distribute Vertically* at the drop-down list.

10 Make Slide 4 active and then insert a clip art image related to finance or money. You determine the size, position, and coloring of the clip art image.

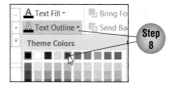

11 Save **PS3-MPToronto.pptx**.

In Brief

Insert WordArt
1. Click INSERT tab.
2. Click WordArt button.
3. Click desired WordArt option.
4. Type WordArt text.
5. Apply desired formatting.

FIGURE 3.1 Slide 2

In Addition

Using Buttons and Options on the DRAWING TOOLS FORMAT Tab

When WordArt is selected in a slide, the DRAWING TOOLS FORMAT tab displays as shown below. You can draw a shape or text box with buttons in the Insert Shapes group. Apply a style, fill, outline, and/or effects to the WordArt text box with options in the Shape Styles group. Change the style of the WordArt text with options in the WordArt Styles group, specify the layering of the WordArt text with options in the Arrange group, and identify the height and width of the WordArt text box with measurement boxes in the Size group.

Activity 3.4

Drawing and Customizing Shapes

Use the Shapes button on the HOME and INSERT tabs to draw shapes in a slide including lines, rectangles, basic shapes, block arrows, equation shapes, flowchart shapes, stars, banners, and callout shapes. Click a shape and the mouse pointer displays as crosshairs (plus sign). Position the crosshairs where you want the image to begin, hold down the left mouse button, drag to create the shape, and then release the mouse button. This inserts the shape in the slide and also displays the DRAWING TOOLS FORMAT tab. Use buttons on this tab to change the shape, apply a style to the shape, arrange the shape, and change the size of the shape. You can type text directly into a shape or you can use the Text Box button in the Text group on the INSERT tab to draw a text box inside a shape and then type text in the box. The DRAWING TOOLS FORMAT tab also provides a Text Box button you can use to draw a text box in a slide.

Project

You will create a new slide for the Toronto site presentation that includes the Toronto office address inside a shape.

Tutorial 3.4
Drawing and Customizing Shapes

1 With **PS3-MPToronto.pptx** open, make Slide 2 active.

2 Click the New Slide button in the Slides group on the HOME tab. (Make sure the slide layout is *Blank*.)

3 Click the More button at the right side of the shapes in the Drawing group on the HOME tab.

4 Click *Horizontal Scroll* at the drop-down list (sixth column, bottom row in the *Stars and Banners* section).

5 Position the mouse pointer in the slide, hold down the left mouse button, drag to create the shape as shown below, and then release the mouse button.

> If you are not satisfied with the size and shape of the image, press the Delete key to remove the image, select the desired shape, and then draw the image again.

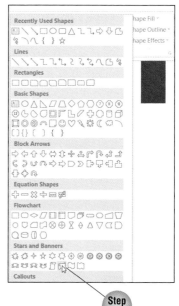

Step 4

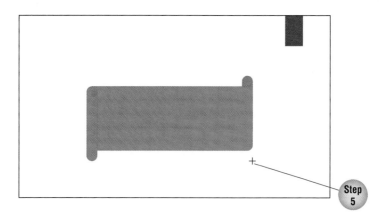

Step 5

6 With the image selected, click the DRAWING TOOLS FORMAT tab and then change the shape style by clicking the More button at the right side of the shape style thumbnails in the Shape Styles group and then clicking *Subtle Effect - Lavender, Accent 5* at the drop-down gallery (sixth column, fourth row).

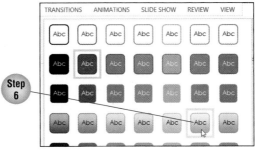

Step 6

7 Click the Shape Effects button 🔲 in the Shape Styles group, point to *Glow*, and then click the *Plum, 11 pt glow, Accent color 1* option (first column, third row in the *Glow Variations* section).

Step 7

8 Click the HOME tab.

9 Click the Font Size button arrow and then click *24* at the drop-down gallery.

10 Click the Bold button in the Font group.

11 Click the Font Color button in the Font group and then click *Plum, Accent 1, Darker 50%* at the drop-down gallery (fifth column, last row in the *Theme Colors* section).

12 Make sure paragraph alignment is set to center. If not, click the Center button in the Paragraph group.

13 Type the following text in the text box:

MARQUEE PRODUCTIONS
Toronto Office
905 Bathurst Street
Toronto, ON M4P 4E5

14 Distrubute the shape horizontally and vertically on the slide using options in the Arrange button drop-down list in the Drawing group on the HOME tab.

15 Save **PS3-MPToronto.pptx**.

In Addition

Displaying the Selection Task Pane

If you want to select an object or multiple objects in a slide, consider turning on the display of the Selection task pane. Turn on the display of this task pane by clicking the Selection Pane button in the Arrange group on the DRAWING TOOLS FORMAT tab (see example at right). Select an object by clicking the object name in the Selection task pane list box. Select multiple objects by holding down the Ctrl key as you click objects. Click the button that displays at the right side of the object name to turn on/off the display of the object.

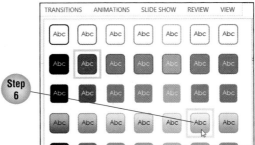

Activity 3.5

Displaying Gridlines; Inserting a Text Box; Copying and Rotating Shapes

To help position elements such as shapes and images on a slide, consider displaying gridlines. *Gridlines* are intersecting horizontal and vertical dashed lines that display on the slide in the slide pane. Display gridlines by clicking the VIEW tab and then clicking the *Gridlines* check box in the Show group to insert a check mark. Create a text box in a slide by clicking the Text Box button in the Text group on the INSERT tab. Click or drag in the slide to create the text box. Draw a shape in a slide and the selected shape displays with an adjustment handle and a rotation handle. Rotate a shape with the rotation handle or with the Rotate button in the Arrange group on the DRAWING TOOLS FORMAT tab. If you draw more than one object in a slide, you can select multiple objects at once so you can work with them as if they were a single object. You can format, size, move, flip, and/ or rotate selected objects as a single unit.

Project

You need to create a new slide for the Toronto presentation that displays the date for the last day of filming in Toronto. To highlight this important information, you will insert an arrow shape and then copy and rotate the shape.

Tutorial 3.5
Displaying Gridlines; Inserting a Text Box; Copying and Rotating Shapes

1. With **PS3-MPToronto.pptx** open, make Slide 8 active and then click the INSERT tab.

2. Click the New Slide button arrow and then click *Title Only* at the drop-down list.

3. Click in the *Click to add title* placeholder and then type **Last Day of Filming**.

4. Turn on the display of gridlines by clicking the VIEW tab and then clicking the *Gridlines* check box in the Show group to insert a check mark.

5. Click the INSERT tab and then click the Text Box button in the Text group.

6. Position the mouse pointer in the slide and then draw a text box similar to what you see below. Use the gridlines to help you position the mouse when drawing the text box.

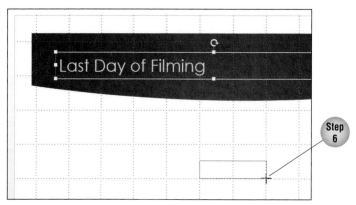

7. Change the font size to 24 points, turn on bold formatting, apply the Plum, Accent 1, Darker 50% font color, change the alignment to center, and then type **August 28**. Click outside the text box to deselect it.

8. Click the INSERT tab, click the Shapes button in the Illustrations group, and then click the *Notched Right Arrow* shape (sixth column, second row in the *Block Arrows* section).

9 Position the mouse pointer at the left side of the slide, hold down the left mouse button, drag to create the arrow shape as shown at the right, and then release the mouse button.

> Use the gridlines to help position the arrow.

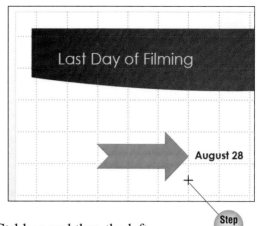

In Brief

Display Gridlines
1. Click VIEW tab.
2. Click *Gridlines* check box.

Insert Text Box
1. Click INSERT tab.
2. Click Text Box button.
3. Click in slide or drag to create text box.

10 With the arrow shape selected, copy the arrow by positioning the mouse pointer inside the shape until the mouse pointer displays with a four-headed arrow attached. Hold down the Ctrl key and then the left mouse button. Drag the arrow to the right side of the date, release the left mouse button, and then release the Ctrl key.

11 Click the DRAWING TOOLS FORMAT tab and then flip the copied arrow by clicking the Rotate button in the Arrange group and then clicking *Flip Horizontal* at the drop-down list.

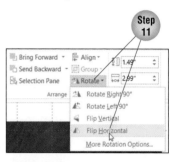

12 Using the mouse pointer, draw a border around the three objects.

> When you release the mouse button, the three objects are selected.

13 With the DRAWING TOOLS FORMAT tab active, center-align the three grouped objects by clicking the Align button in the Arrange group and then clicking *Align Middle* at the drop-down list.

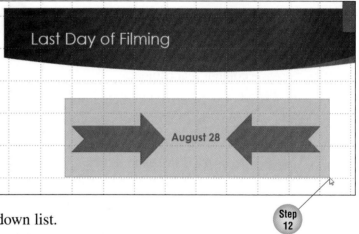

14 With the three objects still selected, horizontally distribute the objects by clicking the Align button and then clicking *Distribute Horizontally* at the drop-down list.

15 Turn off the display of the gridlines by clicking the VIEW tab and then clicking the *Gridlines* check box to remove the check mark.

16 Click outside the objects to deselect them.

17 Save **PS3-MPToronto.pptx**.

In Addition

Rotating Objects

Use the rotation handle that displays near a selected object to rotate the object. Position the mouse pointer on the rotation handle until the pointer displays as a circular arrow, as shown at the right. Hold down the left mouse button, drag in the desired direction, and then release the mouse button.

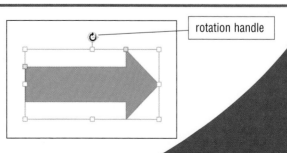

rotation handle

Activity 3.6

Creating a Table in a Slide

PowerPoint includes a Table feature you can use for displaying columns and rows of data. Insert a table in a slide with the Table button on the INSERT tab or with the Insert Table button in a content placeholder. When you insert a table in a slide, the TABLE TOOLS DESIGN tab is selected. Use buttons on this tab to enhance the appearance of the table. With options in the Table Styles group, apply pre-designed colors and border lines to a table. Maintain further control over the predesigned style format-

ting applied to columns and rows with options in the Table Style Options group. Apply additional design formatting to cells in a table with the Shading and Borders buttons in the Table Styles group. Draw a table or draw additional rows and/or columns in a table with options in the Draw Borders group. Click the TABLE TOOLS FORMAT tab and display options and buttons for inserting and deleting columns and rows; changing cell size, alignment, direction, and margins; changing the table size; and arranging the table in the slide.

Project

After reviewing the slides, you decide to include additional information on the location timeline. To do this, you will insert a new slide and then create a table with specific dates.

Tutorial 3.6
Creating a Table in a Slide

1. With **PS3-MPToronto.pptx** open, make Slide 8 active and then click the INSERT tab.

2. Click the New Slide button arrow and then click the *Title and Content* layout at the drop-down list.

3. Click the *Click to add title* placeholder in the new slide and then type **Timeline**.

4. Click the Insert Table button ⊞ that displays in the content placeholder.

5. At the Insert Table dialog box, type **2** in the *Number of columns* measurement box.

6. Press the Tab key and then type **9** in the *Number of rows* measurement box.

7. Click OK to close the Insert Table dialog box.

8. Turn on the display of the horizontal and vertical rulers. To do this, click the VIEW tab and then click the *Ruler* check box in the Show group to insert a check mark.

9. Column 1 needs to be widened to accommodate the project tasks. To do this, position the mouse pointer on the middle gridline in the table until the pointer turns into a left-and-right-pointing arrow with two short lines in the middle.. Hold down the left mouse button, drag to approximately the 6-inch mark on the horizontal ruler, and then release the mouse button.

Step 3

Step 4

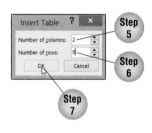

Step 5

Step 6

Step 7

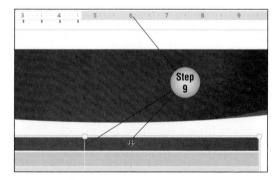

Step 9

10 Starting with the insertion point positioned in the first cell, type all of the text shown in Figure 3.2. Press the Tab key to move the insertion point to the next cell. Press Shift + Tab to move the insertion point to the previous cell.

11 Click the More button at the right side of the Table Styles group on the TABLE TOOLS DESIGN tab.

12 Click the *Themed Style 1 - Accent 1* option in the drop-down gallery (second column, first row in the *Best Match for Document* group).

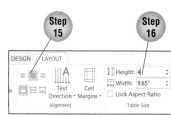

13 Click the TABLE TOOLS LAYOUT tab.

14 Select the first row in the table by positioning the mouse pointer at the left side of the first row in the table until the pointer turns into a black, right-pointing arrow and then clicking the left mouse button.

15 Click the Center button ≣ in the Alignment group.

16 Click in the *Height* measurement box in the Table Size group, type **4**, and then press Enter.

17 Distribute the table horizontally on the slide.

18 Save **PS3-MPToronto.pptx**.

FIGURE 3.2 Slide Table

In Addition

Moving and Sizing a Table

Increase or decrease the size of a table by typing the desired measurements in the *Height* and *Width* measurement boxes in the Table Size group on the TABLE TOOLS LAYOUT tab. You can also drag the sizing handles that display around a table border to increase or decrease the size. When the insertion point is positioned in a table, a border containing sizing handles that display as small white squares surrounds the table. Position the mouse pointer on one of the sizing handles until the pointer displays as a two-headed arrow, hold down the left mouse button, and then drag to increase or decrease the size. Drag a corner sizing handle to change the size of the table proportionally. To move the table, position the mouse pointer on the table border until the pointer displays with a four-headed arrow attached and then drag to the desired position.

Activity 3.7

Inserting Action Buttons and Hyperlinks

Action buttons are drawn objects on a slide that have a routine attached to them. The routine is activated when the presenter clicks the action button. For example, you can insert an action button that displays a specific web page, a file in another program, or the next slide in the presentation. Creating an action button is a two-step process. The first step is to draw the button in the slide, and the second step is to define the action that will take place using options in the Action Settings dialog box. You can customize an action button using the same techniques as customizing drawn shapes. You can also insert a hyperlink in a slide that, when clicked, will display a site on the Internet or open another presentation or file. Insert a hyperlink with the Hyperlink button on the INSERT tab.

Project

Tutorial 3.7
Inserting Action Buttons and Hyperlinks

To facilitate the running of the presentation, you decide to insert an action button at the bottom of each slide that will link to the next slide or the first slide. You also decide to insert a hyperlink to a website.

1. With **PS3-MPToronto.pptx** open, make Slide 1 active.

2. Insert an action button that, when clicked, will display the next slide. To begin, click the INSERT tab, click the Shapes button, and then click the *Action Button: Forward or Next* option (second button in the *Action Buttons* section).

3. Position the mouse pointer (displays as a crosshair) in the lower right corner of Slide 1, hold down the left mouse button, drag to create a button that is approximately one-half inch square, and then release the mouse button.

4. At the Action Settings dialog box that displays, click OK. (The default setting is *Hyperlink to Next Slide*.)

5. With the button selected, click the DRAWING TOOLS FORMAT tab and then click the *Colored Outline - Purple, Accent 6* option in the Shapes Styles group.

6. Select the current measurement in the *Shape Height* measurement box, type **0.5**, and then press Enter. Select the current measurement in the *Shape Width* measurement box, type **0.5**, and then press Enter.

7. Instead of drawing the button on each slide, you decide to copy it and then paste it in the other slides. To do this, make sure the button is selected, click the HOME tab, and then click the Copy button in the Clipboard group.

8. Make Slide 2 active and then click the Paste button in the Clipboard group. Continue pasting the button in Slides 3 through 9. (Do not paste the button on the last slide, Slide 10.)

9. Make Slide 10 active and then insert an action button that will display the first slide. To begin, click the INSERT tab, click the Shapes button, and then click *Action Button: Home* (fifth option in the *Action Buttons* section).

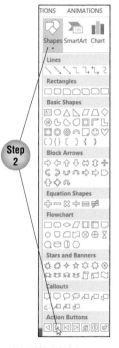

Step 2

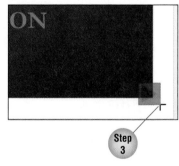

Step 3

Step 5

10 Position the mouse pointer in the lower right corner of Slide 10 and then click the left mouse button.

> When you click in the slide, a small square shape with a home icon in the center is inserted in the slide.

11 At the Action Settings dialog box that displays, click OK. (The default setting is *Hyperlink to First Slide*.)

12 With the button selected, click the DRAWING TOOLS FORMAT tab and then click the *Colored Outline - Purple, Accent 6* option in the Shapes Styles group.

13 Click in the *Shape Height* measurement box, type **0.5**, and then press Enter. Click in the *Shape Width* measurement box, type **0.5**, and then press Enter.

14 Make Slide 6 active and then create a hyperlink to the museum website. To begin, select *Royal Ontario Museum*, click the INSERT tab, and then click the Hyperlink button 🌐 in the Links group.

15 At the Insert Hyperlink dialog box, type **www.rom .on.ca** in the *Address* text box and then press Enter.

> PowerPoint automatically inserts *http://* at the beginning of the web address. The hyperlink text displays underlined and in a different color in the slide.

16 Run the presentation, beginning with Slide 1. Navigate through the slide show by clicking the action buttons. When Slide 6 (*Filming Locations*) displays, click the <u>Royal Ontario Museum</u> hyperlink.

17 After viewing the museum website, close the browser. Continue running the presentation. After viewing the presentation at least twice, press the Esc key to end the presentation.

18 Print the presentation as handouts with six slides horizontally per page.

19 Save and then close **PS3-MPToronto.pptx**.

In Brief

Insert Action Button
1. Click INSERT tab.
2. Click Shapes button.
3. Click desired action button at drop-down list.
4. Click or drag in slide to create button.
5. At Action Settings dialog box, click OK.

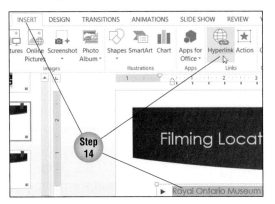

In Addition

Linking with Action Buttons

You can set an action button to link to a website during a presentation. To do this, draw an Action button. At the Action Settings dialog box, click the *Hyperlink to* option, click the down-pointing arrow at the right side of the *Hyperlink to* option box, and then click *URL* at the drop-down list. At the Hyperlink to URL dialog box, type the web address in the *URL* text box and then click OK. Click OK to close the Action Settings dialog box. Other actions you can link to using the *Hyperlink to* drop-down list include: *Next Slide, Previous Slide, First Slide, Last Slide, Last Slide Viewed, End Show, Custom Show, Slide, URL, Other PowerPoint Presentation,* and *Other File.* The Action Settings dialog box can also be used to run another program when the action button is selected, to run a macro, or to activate an embedded object.

Activity 3.8

Formatting with a Slide Master

If you use a PowerPoint design theme, you may choose to use the formatting provided by the theme or you may want to customize the formatting. If you customize formatting in a presentation, PowerPoint's slide master can be very helpful in reducing the steps needed to format slides. A presentation contains a slide master for each of the various slide layouts. To display slide masters, click the VIEW tab and then click the Slide Master button in the Master Views group. The available slide masters display in the slide thumbnails pane at the left side of the screen. Apply formatting to the desired slide masters and then click the Close Master View button in the Close group to return to the Normal view.

Project

Tutorial 3.8
Formatting with a
Slide Master

Melissa Gehring, manager at First Choice Travel, has asked you to complete a presentation on upcoming eco-tours offered by First Choice Travel. You decide to change the theme colors and fonts of the presentation, as well as insert the company's logo in the lower right corner of all slides except the title slide.

1. Open **FCTEcoTours.pptx** and then save the presentation and name it **PS3-FCTEcoTours**.

2. Click the VIEW tab and then click the Slide Master button in the Master Views group.

   Hover the mouse pointer over a slide master in the slide thumbnails pane at the left side of the screen to display a ScreenTip with information about the slide layout and the number of slides in the presentation that use the layout.

3. Click the Theme Colors button in the Background group and then click *Blue* at the drop-down gallery.

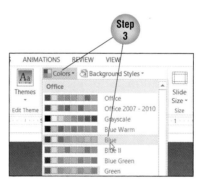

4. Click the Theme Fonts button A in the Background group, scroll down the drop-down gallery, and then click *Calibri Light-Constantia*.

5. Select the text *Click to edit Master subtitle style* in the slide in the slide pane, click the HOME tab, click the Font Color button arrow, and then click *Dark Blue* at the drop-down gallery (ninth option in the *Standard Colors* section).

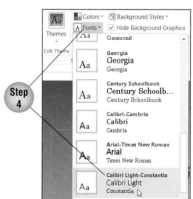

6 Click the top slide master located in the slide thumbnails pane at the left side of the screen.

7 Select the text *Click to edit Master title style*, click the HOME tab, and then click the Font Color button.

> This applies the Dark Blue font color.

8 Insert the First Choice Travel logo in the slide master (so it prints on all slides except the first one). Begin by clicking the INSERT tab and then clicking the Pictures button in the Images group.

9 Navigate to the PowerPointS3 folder on your storage medium and then double-click *FCTLogo.jpg*.

10 Make sure the logo is selected.

11 Click in the *Shape Height* measurement box, type **0.7**, and then press Enter.

12 Drag the logo to the lower right corner of the slide master as shown at the right (to the left of the current date that displays).

13 Click the SLIDE MASTER tab.

14 Click the Close Master View button in the Close group located at the right side of the SLIDE MASTER tab.

15 Save **PS3-FCTEcoTours.pptx**.

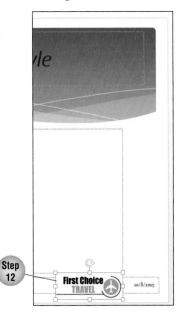

Step 12

In Addition

Applying More Than One Slide Design Theme to a Presentation

Each design theme applies specific formatting to slides. You can apply more than one design theme to slides in a presentation. To do this, select the specific slides and then choose the desired design theme. The design theme is applied only to the selected slides. If you apply more than one design theme to a presentation, multiple slide masters will display in Slide Master view.

Formatting Changes in Slide Master View

If you edit the formatting of text in a slide in Normal view, the link to the slide master is broken. Changes you make to a slide master in Slide Master view will not affect the individually formatted slide. For this reason, make formatting changes in Slide Master view before editing individual slides in a presentation.

Activity 3.9

Inserting Headers and Footers

Insert information you want to appear at the top or bottom of individual slides or on the top and bottom of individual printed notes and handout pages using options at the Header and Footer dialog box. If you want the same types of information to appear on all slides, display the Header and Footer dialog box with the Slide tab selected. With options at this dialog box, you can insert the date and time, insert the slide number, and create a footer. To insert header or footer elements you want to print on all notes or handouts, choose options at the Header and Footer dialog box with the Notes and Handouts tab selected.

Project

Melissa Gehring has asked you to insert the current date and slide number in the presentation and to create a header for notes pages.

Tutorial 3.9
Inserting Headers
and Footers

1. With **PS3-FCTEcoTours.pptx** open, insert a footer that prints at the bottom of each slide. To begin, click the INSERT tab and then click the Header & Footer button in the Text group.

Step 1

2. At the Header and Footer dialog box with the Slide tab selected, click the *Date and time* check box to insert a check mark. If necessary, click the *Update automatically* option to select it.

3. Click the *Slide number* check box to insert a check mark.

4. Click the *Footer* check box to insert a check mark and then type **First Choice Travel Eco-Tours** in the *Footer* text box.

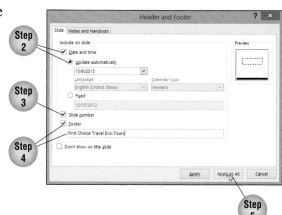

Step 2
Step 3
Step 4
Step 5

5. Click the Apply to All button.

6. Make Slide 7 active.

7. Display the notes pane by clicking the NOTES button on the Status bar.

8. Click in the notes pane and then type **Include additional costs for airfare, local transportation, and daily tours.**

Step 7

Step 8

9 Insert a header that will display on notes and handouts pages by clicking the Header & Footer button on the INSERT tab.

10 At the Header and Footer dialog box, click the Notes and Handouts tab.

11 Make sure a check mark does not display in the *Date and time* check box. If a check mark does display, click the check box to remove the check mark.

12 Click the *Header* check box to insert a check mark and then type **First Choice Travel**.

13 Click the *Footer* check box to insert a check mark and then type **Eco-Tours**.

14 Click the Apply to All button.

15 Print the presentation as handouts with nine slides horizontally per page.

16 Print Slide 7 as a notes page. To do this, click the FILE tab, click the *Print* option, click the second gallery (contains the text *9 Slides Horizontal*) in the *Settings* category, and then click *Notes Pages* in the *Print Layout* section.

17 Click in the *Slides* text box (located below the first gallery in the *Settings* category) and then type **7**.

18 Click the Print button.

19 Click the NOTES button on the Status bar to close the notes pane.

20 Save **PS3-FCTEcoTours.pptx**.

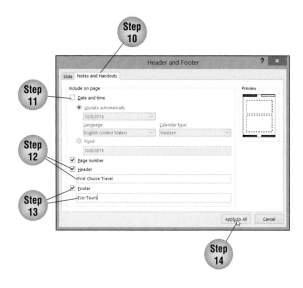

Step 10
Step 11
Step 12
Step 13
Step 14

In Brief

Insert Header/Footer on Slide
1. Click INSERT tab.
2. Click Header & Footer button.
3. At Header and Footer dialog box with Slide tab selected, choose desired options.
4. Click Apply to All button.

Insert Header/ Footer in Notes and Handouts
1. Click INSERT tab.
2. Click Header & Footer button.
3. At Header and Footer dialog box, click Notes and Handouts tab.
4. Choose desired options.
5. Click Apply to All button.

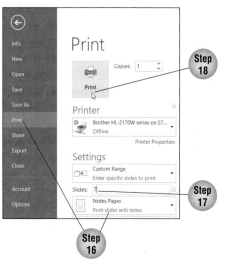

Step 18
Step 17
Step 16

In Addition

Using the Package for CD Feature

The safest way to transport a PowerPoint presentation to another computer is to use the Package for CD feature. With this feature, you can copy a presentation onto a CD or to a folder or network location and include all of the linked files and fonts, as well as the PowerPoint Viewer program in case the destination computer does not have PowerPoint installed on it. To use the Package for CD feature, click the FILE tab, click the *Export* option, click the *Package Presentation for CD* option, and then click the Package for CD button. At the Package for CD dialog box, type a name for the CD and then click the Copy to CD button.

Activity 3.10

Adding Audio and Video

Adding audio and/or video effects to a presentation will turn a slide show into a true multimedia experience for your audience. Including a variety of elements in a presentation will stimulate interest in your presentation and keep the audience motivated. You can insert an audio file or video file from a folder or from the Insert Video window.

Project

Tutorial 3.10
Adding Audio
and Video

To add interest, you decide to experiment with adding a video file and an audio file to the presentation. The slide at the end of the presentation will display the video file and play an audio file. This will allow the presenter time to answer questions from the audience while the video and audio files play.

1. With **PS3-FCTEcoTours.pptx** open, make Slide 7 active, click the INSERT tab, and then click the New Slide button.

2. Click the text *Click to add title* and then type **Let the adventure begin!**

3. Click the Insert Video button in the content placeholder (or click the Video button in the Media group on the INSERT tab and then click *Video on My PC*).

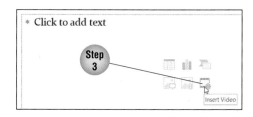

4. At the Insert Video window, click the Browse button to the right of the *From a file* option.

5. At the Insert Video dialog box, navigate to the AudioandVideo folder on the CD that accompanies this textbook and then double-click the file named *Wildlife.wmv*.

   This inserts the video file in a window in the slide with the VIDEO TOOLS FORMAT tab selected. Use options and buttons on this tab to preview the video file, change the brightness, contrast, and color of the video, apply a formatting style to the video window, and arrange and size the video in the slide.

6. Click the Play button in the Preview group (left side of VIDEO TOOLS FORMAT tab) to preview the video file.

   The video plays for approximately 30 seconds.

7. After viewing the video, click the VIDEO TOOLS PLAYBACK tab.

8. Click the up-pointing arrow at the right side of the *Fade In* measurement box in the Editing group until *01.00* displays and then click the up-pointing arrow at the right side of the *Fade Out* measurement box until *01.00* displays.

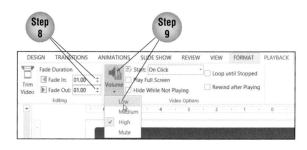

9. Click the Volume button in the Video Options group and then click *Low* at the drop-down list.

10. Click the *Loop until Stopped* check box in the Video Options group to insert a check mark.

(11) Make Slide 1 active and then run the presentation. When the slide containing the video file displays, move the mouse over the video file window and then click the Play button located at the bottom left side of the window.

(12) After viewing the video a couple of times, press the Esc key twice.

(13) You decide that you want the video window to fill the slide, start automatically when the slide displays, and play only once. To do this, make sure Slide 8 is active, click the video file window, and then click the VIDEO TOOLS PLAYBACK tab.

(14) Click the *Play Full Screen* check box in the Video Options group to insert a check mark and then click the *Loop until Stopped* check box to remove the check mark.

(15) Click the down-pointing arrow at the right side of the *Start* option box in the Video Options group and then click *Automatically* at the drop-down list.

Step 15

(16) Make Slide 1 active and then run the presentation. When the slide containing the video displays, the video will automatically begin. When the video is finished playing, press the Esc key to return to Normal view.

(17) You decide that you want music to play after the presentation. Begin by making sure Slide 8 is the active slide, clicking the INSERT tab, clicking the Audio button 🔊 in the Media group, and then clicking *Audio on My PC* at the drop-down list.

(18) At the Insert Audio dialog box, navigate to the AudioandVideo folder on the CD that accompanies this textbook and then double-click the file named *FCTAudioClip-01.mid*.

   This inserts the audio file in the slide with the AUDIO TOOLS FORMAT tab selected.

(19) If necessary, click the AUDIO TOOLS PLAYBACK tab.

(20) Click the down-pointing arrow at the right side of the *Start* option box in the Audio Options group and then click *Automatically* at the drop-down list.

(21) Click the *Hide During Show* check box in the Audio Options group to insert a check mark and then click the *Loop until Stopped* check box to insert a check mark.

(22) Make Slide 1 active and then run the presentation. When the last slide displays, watch the video, listen to the audio file for about a minute or two, and then press the Esc key to return to the Normal view.

(23) Save **PS3-FCTEcoTours.pptx**.

In Brief

Insert Video Clip
1. Click Insert Video button in placeholder.
2. Navigate to desired folder.
3. Double-click desired video clip.
OR
1. Click INSERT tab.
2. Click Video button arrow.
3. Click *Video on My PC*.
4. Navigate to desired folder.
5. Double-click desired video clip file.

Insert Audio Clip
1. Click INSERT tab.
2. Click Audio button.
3. Click *Audio on My PC*.
4. Navigate to desired folder.
5. Double-click desired audio clip file.

In Addition

Changing the Video Color

With the Color button in the Adjust group on the VIDEO TOOLS FORMAT tab, you can change the video color. If you want the video to play in black and white, click the Color button and then click the *Grayscale* option at the drop-down gallery. Click the *Sepia* option if you want the video to have an old-fashioned appearance when played.

Activity 3.11

Setting and Rehearsing Timings for a Presentation

If you want a presentation to run automatically and each slide to display for a specific number of seconds, use the Rehearse Timings feature to help set the times for slides as you practice delivering the slide show. To set times for slides, click the SLIDE SHOW tab and then click the Rehearse Timings button in the Set Up group. The first slide displays in Slide Show view and the Recording toolbar displays. Use buttons on this toolbar to specify times for each slide. Use options at the Set Up Show dialog box to control the slide show. Display this dialog box by clicking the Set Up Slide Show button in the Set Up group. Use options in the *Show type* section to specify the type of slide show you want to display. If you want the presentation to be totally automatic and run continuously until you end the show, click the *Loop continuously until 'Esc'* check box to insert a check mark. In the *Advance slides* section, the *Using timings, if present* option should be selected by default. Select *Manually* if you want to advance the slides using the mouse instead of your preset times.

Project Melissa Gehring has asked you to automate the presentation so it can be run continuously at the upcoming travel conference.

Tutorial 3.11
Setting Timings for a Presentation

1. With **PS3-FCTEcoTours.pptx** open, save the presentation with Save As and name it **PS3-FCTEcoTours-Rehearsed**.

2. Make Slide 8 active, click the audio icon to select it, and then press the Delete key. Click the video window to select it and then press the Delete key.

3. Type the following information in the content placeholder:

   * **Call today to schedule your exciting eco-tour adventure:**

     * **1-888-555-1330**

   * **Or visit our website:**

     * **www.emcp.net/fc-travel**

4. Select the content placeholder (make sure the border is a solid line) and then click the Bold button in the Font group on the HOME tab.

5. Make Slide 1 active, click the SLIDE SHOW tab, and then click the Rehearse Timings button 🖳 in the Set Up group.

   The first slide displays in Slide Show view and the Recording toolbar displays as well. Refer to Figure 3.3 for the names of the Recording toolbar buttons.

6. Wait until the time displayed for the current slide reaches four seconds and then click the Next button →.

   If you miss the time, click the Repeat button 🔄 to reset the clock back to zero for the current slide.

7. Set the following times for the remaining slides:

Slide 2: 5 seconds	Slide 6: 8 seconds
Slide 3: 5 seconds	Slide 7: 7 seconds
Slide 4: 4 seconds	Slide 8: 8 seconds
Slide 5: 6 seconds	

8 After the last slide has displayed, click Yes at the message asking if you want to keep the new slide timings.

9 Click the Slide Sorter button on the Status bar. Notice the slides display with the times listed below. The times that display may be off by one second.

> You can adjust the timings manually with options in the Timing group on the TRANSITIONS tab. See the In Addition feature below.

10 Double-click Slide 1 to change to Normal view.

11 Set up the slide show to run continuously by clicking the Set Up Slide Show button [icon] in the Set Up group on the SLIDE SHOW tab.

12 At the Set Up Show dialog box, click the *Loop continuously until 'Esc'* check box.

13 Click OK to close the dialog box.

14 Insert an audio file that will play continuously throughout the presentation. To begin, click the INSERT tab, click the Audio button in the Media group, and then click the *Audio on My PC* option.

Step 12

15 At the Insert Audio dialog box, navigate to the AudioandVideo folder on the CD that accompanies this textbook and then double-click the file named *FCTAudioClip-02.mid*.

16 If necessary, click the AUDIO TOOLS PLAYBACK tab. Click the down-pointing arrow at the right side of the *Start* option box in the Audio Options group and then click *Automatically* at the drop-down list.

17 Click the *Play Across Slides* check box in the Audio Options group to insert a check mark, click the *Loop until Stopped* check box to insert a check mark, and then click the *Hide During Show* check box to insert a check mark.

18 Drag the audio icon to the bottom center of the slide.

19 Run the presentation, beginning with Slide 1. The slide show will start and run continuously. Watch the presentation until it starts for the second time and then end the show by pressing the Esc key.

20 Print the presentation as handouts with nine slides horizontally per page.

21 Save and then close **PS3-FCTEcoTours-Rehearsed.pptx**.

FIGURE 3.3 Recording Toolbar Buttons

In Brief

Set and Rehearse Timings
1. Click SLIDE SHOW tab.
2. Click Rehearse Timings button.
3. When desired time displays, click Next button.
4. Continue until times are set for each slide.
5. Click Yes at message.

Set Up Show to Run Continuously
1. Click SLIDE SHOW tab.
2. Click Set Up Slide Show button.
3. Click *Loop continuously until 'Esc'* check box.
4. Click OK.

In Addition

Setting Times Manually

The time a slide remains on the screen during a slide show can be manually set using options in the Timing group on the TRANSITIONS tab. To set manual times for slides, click the *On Mouse Click* check box to remove the check mark and then click the *After* check box to insert a check mark. Click in the *After* text box, type the desired number of seconds you want the slide to display on the screen when running the presentation, and then press the Enter key. Click the Apply To All button to apply the time to each slide in the presentation.

Features Summary

Feature	Ribbon Tab, Group	Button	Keyboard Shortcut
action button	INSERT, Illustrations		
audio file	INSERT, Media		
Clipboard task pane	HOME, Clipboard		
draw shape	INSERT, Illustrations OR Home, Drawing		
gridlines	VIEW, Show		Shift + F9
header and footer	INSERT, Text		
hyperlink	INSERT, Links		Ctrl + K
rehearse timings	SLIDE SHOW, Set Up		
replace	HOME, Editing		Ctrl + H
table	INSERT, Tables		
text box	INSERT, Text		
video file	INSERT, Media		
WordArt	INSERT, Text		

Knowledge Check SNAP

Completion: In the space provided at the right, indicate the correct term, command, or option.

1. Display this task pane to collect and paste multiple items. _____

2. The Replace button is located in this group on the HOME tab. _____

3. Use this feature to distort or modify text and to conform text to a variety of shapes. _____

4. When you insert a shape in a slide, this tab is available for formatting the shape. _____

5. These are horizontal and vertical dashed lines that you can display on a slide. _____

6. To copy a shape, hold down this key while dragging the shape. _____

7. Use this feature for displaying columns and rows of data. _____

8. These are drawn objects that have a routine attached to them. _____

9. Create a hyperlink by clicking the Hyperlink button in this group on the INSERT tab. _____

10. When you click the Hyperlink button on the INSERT tab, this dialog box displays. _____

11. Create footer text that displays at the bottom of all slides with options at this dialog box. _____

12. Click this button in a content placeholder to insert a video file. _____
13. The Audio button is located in this group on the INSERT tab. _____
14. When the desired time displays on the Recording toolbar, click this button on the Recording toolbar to display the next slide. _____
15. Click this button on the Recording toolbar to reset the clock back to zero for the current slide. _____

Skills Review

Review 1 Formatting and Customizing a Biography Project Presentation

1. Open **MPBiography.pptx** and then save the presentation in the PowerPointEOS folder and name it **PS3-R-MPBiography**.
2. Make Slide 4 active, turn on the display of the Clipboard task pane, and then clear any contents in the task pane.
3. Select and then copy *Chris Greenbaum*.
4. Select and then copy *Camille Matsui*.
5. Select and then copy *Amy Eisman*.
6. Select and then copy *Tricia Becktold*.
7. Make Slide 5 active.
8. Position the insertion point immediately to the right of *On-Site Expenses*, press the Enter key, press the Tab key, and then click *Camille Matsui* in the Clipboard task pane.
9. Position the insertion point immediately to the right of *Benefits*, press the Enter key, press the Tab key, and then click *Chris Greenbaum* in the Clipboard task pane.
10. Position the insertion point immediately to the right of *Production*, press the Enter key, press the Tab key, and then click *Amy Eisman* in the Clipboard task pane.
11. Press the Enter key and then click *Tricia Becktold* in the Clipboard task pane.
12. Clear the contents of the Clipboard task pane and then close the task pane.
13. Make Slide 1 active and then find all occurrences of *Camille Matsui* and replace them with *Jennie Almonzo*.
14. Find all occurrences of *Tricia Becktold* and replace them with *Nick Jaffe*.
15. Make sure Slide 1 is active and then insert the file named **MPLogo.jpg**. Size and position the logo on the slide. Recolor the background of the logo to transparent color and change the brightness and contrast to *Brightness: +40% Contrast: -40%*.
16. Make Slide 2 active and then insert the name of the biography, *Silent Streets*, as WordArt. You determine the formatting and shape of the WordArt. Increase the size of the WordArt so it fills most of the slide and then horizontally and vertically center the WordArt in the slide.
17. Make Slide 6 active and then create the table shown in Figure 3.4 on page 108. Apply the Themed Style 1 - Accent 2 table style (third column, first row), select all cells in the table, and then change the font size to 24 points. Size and position the table and table columns as shown (drag the column borders to decrease the size of the columns).
18. Make Slide 7 active, create the arrows shown in Figure 3.5 on page 108, and insert the text in text boxes in the shapes as shown. Apply the Light 1 Outline, Colored Fill - Lavender, Accent 2 shape style to the shapes (third column, third row) and change the text font size to 40 points.

19. Make Slide 1 active and then draw an action button named Action Button: Forward or Next in the lower right corner of the slide. Fill the button with a color that complements the slide design. Copy the button and then paste it in Slides 2, 3, 4, 5, and 6.
20. Insert a footer that prints *Silent Streets* at the bottom center of each slide.
21. Make Slide 4 active and then insert a clip art image related to people or team. You determine the size, positioning, and coloring of the clip art.
22. Make Slide 5 active and then insert a clip art image related to money or finance. You determine the size, positioning, and coloring of the clip art.
23. Run the presentation beginning with Slide 1.
24. Print the presentation as handouts with four slides horizontally per page (the presentation will print on two pages).
25. Save and then close **PS3-R-MPBiography.pptx**.

FIGURE 3.4 Slide 6

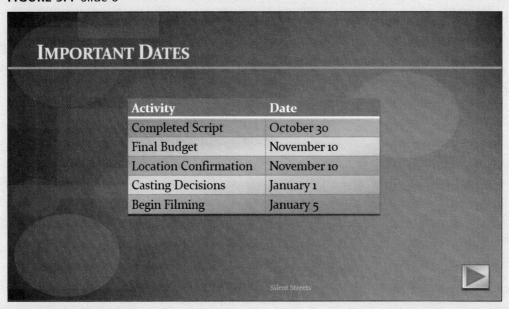

FIGURE 3.5 Slide 7

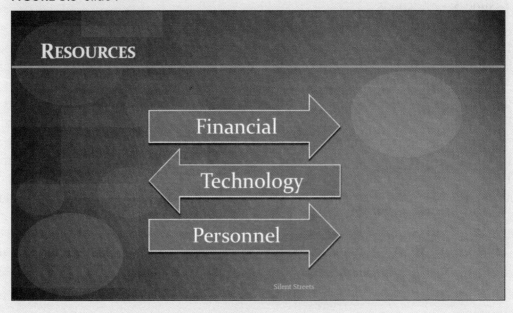

Review 2 Formatting with Slide Masters

1. Open **MPAnnualMtg.pptx** and then save the presentation in the PowerPointEOS folder and name it **PS3-R-MPAnnualMtg**.
2. Apply the Facet design theme.
3. Display the presentation in Slide Master view, click the third slide miniature in the slide thumbnails pane, and then make the following changes:
   - Apply the Slipstream theme colors.
   - Change the theme fonts to Cambria.
   - Select the text *Click to edit Master title style* and then change the font color to Blue and the font size 40 points.
   - Select the text *Click to edit Master text styles* and then change the font size to 24 points.
   - Select the text *Second level* and then change the font size to 20 points.
   - Insert the **MPLogo.jpg** file in the slide. Decrease the size of the logo so the height is approximately 0.5 inch. Drag the logo to the lower right corner of the master slide.
4. Close the Slide Master view.
5. Apply a slide transition and sound to each slide.
6. Run the presentation.
7. Print the presentation as handouts with nine slides horizontally per page.
8. Save and then close **PS3-R-MPAnnualMtg.pptx**.

Review 3 Formatting a Vacation Cruise Presentation to Run Automatically

1. Open **FCTCruise.pptx** and then save the presentation in the PowerPointEOS folder and name it **PS3-R-FCTCruise**.
2. Make Slide 1 active and then insert the **FCTLogo.jpg** file. Size and position the logo on the slide.
3. Rehearse the timings and set the following times for the slides:
   - Slide 1:   4 seconds
   - Slide 2:   8 seconds
   - Slide 3:   8 seconds
   - Slide 4:   4 seconds
   - Slide 5:   7 seconds
4. With Slide 1 active, insert the audio file named **FCTAudioClip-03.mid** (from the AudioandVideo folder on the CD that accompanies this textbook). Display the AUDIO TOOLS PLAYBACK tab, change the *Start* option to *Automatically*, insert a check mark in the *Play Across Slides* check box, the *Loop until Stopped* check box, and the *Hide During Show* check box.
5. Set up the slide show to run continuously.
6. Run the presentation and view it at least twice.
7. Print the presentation as handouts with six slides horizontally per page.
8. Save and then close **PS3-R-FCTCruise.pptx**.

Skills Assessment

Assessment 1 Formatting a Presentation for Performance Threads

1. Open **PTCostumes.pptx** and then save the presentation in the PowerPointEOS folder and name it **PS3-A1-PTCostumes**.
2. With Slide 1 the active slide, insert the file named **PTLogo.jpg**. Recolor the background to transparent color and size and position the company logo on the slide.
3. Make Slide 3 active and then insert the movie name *Ring of Roses* as WordArt. You determine the formatting, shape, size, and position of the WordArt in the slide.
4. Make Slide 5 the active slide, create a shape (you determine the shape), and then copy the shape two times (so the slide contains a total of three shapes). Insert *Research* in the first shape, *Design* in the second shape, and *Production* in the third shape. Format, size, and position the shapes in the slide.
5. Make Slide 6 the active slide and then insert the following information in a table (apply a table style and increase the size of the table to better fill the slide):

Designer	Date
Scott Bercini	June 21
Terri Cantrell	June 13
Paul Gottlieb	June 28
Tae Jeong	June 13
Rosa Levens	June 28

6. Insert the footer *Performance Threads* at the bottom of each slide.
7. Run the presentation.
8. Print the presentation as handouts with four slides horizontally per page (the presentation will print on two pages).
9. Save and then close **PS3-A1-PTCostumes.pptx**.

Assessment 2 Formatting a Presentation for First Choice Travel

1. Open **FCTSouthernTours.pptx** and then save the presentation in the PowerPointEOS folder and name it **PS3-A2-FCTSouthernTours**.
2. Make Slide 2 active and then insert *Australia* as WordArt. You determine the formatting, size, and position of the WordArt in the slide.
3. Make Slide 6 active and then insert *New Zealand* as WordArt. You determine the formatting, size, and position of the WordArt in the slide.
4. Insert a footer that prints *Southern Tours* at the bottom of each slide.
5. Rehearse the timings and determine the seconds for each slide.
6. Insert the audio file **FCTAudioClip-04.mid** (from the AudioandVideo folder on the CD) that will automatically play across all slides and loop until stopped.
7. Set up the slide show to run continuously.
8. Run the presentation and view it at least twice.
9. Print the presentation as handouts with nine slides horizontally per page.
10. Save and then close **PS3-A2-FCTSouthernTours.pptx**.

Assessment 3 Learning about Custom Shows

1. Open **PS3-A2-FCTSouthernTours.pptx** and then save the presentation in the PowerPointEOS folder and name it **PS3-A3-FCTSouthernTours**.
2. Use the Help feature and/or experiment with the Custom Slide Show button in the Start Slide Show group on the SLIDE SHOW tab to learn about custom shows.
3. Create a custom show containing Slides 1, 7, 8, and 9. (You determine the name of the show.)
4. Run the custom show.
5. Save and then close **PS3-A3-FCTSouthernTours.pptx**.

Assessment 4 Individual Challenge
Locating Information and Preparing a Presentation on Social Networking Sites

1. Using the Internet, search for social networking sites. Identify five sites that interest you (or that you currently use).
2. Using PowerPoint, create a presentation on each site (one site per slide) that includes information about the site and a hyperlink to the site. Create a title slide for the presentation that includes your name and an appropriate title. (You should have a total of six slides.) To add visual appeal to your presentation, insert at least two elements, such as WordArt, shapes, clip art images, and/or pictures.
3. Apply animation to objects in the slides.
4. Save the presentation in the PowerPointEOS folder and name it **PS3-A4-IC-SocialNetwork**.
5. Run the presentation.
6. Print the presentation as handouts with six slides horizontally per page.
7. Save and then close **PS3-A4-IC-SocialNetwork.pptx**.

Marquee Challenge

Challenge 1 Preparing a Project Schedule Presentation for Marquee Productions

1. Create the presentation shown in Figure 3.6 on page 113 with the following specifications:
   - Apply the Retrospect design theme and the blue colored variant. (You will need to click the More button in the Variants group to display the blue variant.)
   - Display the presentation in Slide Master view and then click the third slide thumbnail in the thumbnails pane. Change the font size of the master title style text to 44 points, turn on bold formatting, and then change the font color to Blue, Accent 2. Change the font size of the first level master text style to 24 points. Close the Slide Master view.
   - Delete the title placeholder in Slide 1 and then insert the **MPLogo.jpg** file. Size and position the logo as shown in the figure.
   - Center the subtitle text.
   - Insert the shape in Slide 2 using the Horizontal Scroll shape in the *Stars and Banners* section of the Shapes button drop-down list.
   - Create and format the table shown in Slide 3.

- Use the words *money* and *magnifying glass* to find the image in Slide 4 and then use the words *businesspeople* and *silhouettes* to find the image in Slide 5. If you do not have access to the clip art images shown, choose your own.
- Insert the footer on all slides (except the first slide) as shown in the figure. ***Hint: Insert a check mark in the* Don't show on title slide *check box in the Header and Footer dialog box.***

2. Save the completed presentation in the PowerPointEOS folder and name it **PS3-C1-MPProdSch**.
3. Print the presentation as a handout with all six slides on the same page.

Challenge 2 Preparing a Moroccan Tour Presentation for First Choice Travel

1. Create the presentation shown in Figure 3.7 on page 114 with these specifications:
   - Apply the Ion design theme and the orange variant color.
   - Create the WordArt text in Slide 1.
   - Insert the **FCTLogo.jpg** file in the Slide Master view so it displays on slides 3 through 6. Size and position the logo as shown in Figure 3.7.
   - Create the shape in Slide 2 using the Bevel shape located in the *Basic Shapes* section of the Shapes button drop-down list.
   - Insert the images in Slides 3 and 5, using the word *Morocco* to find the images. If you do not have access to the images shown in the figure, choose your own.
   - Create and format the table in Slide 6.
2. Save the completed presentation in the PowerPointEOS folder and name it **PS3-C2-FCTMorocco**.
3. Print the presentation as a handout with all six slides on the same page.

FIGURE 3.6 Challenge 1

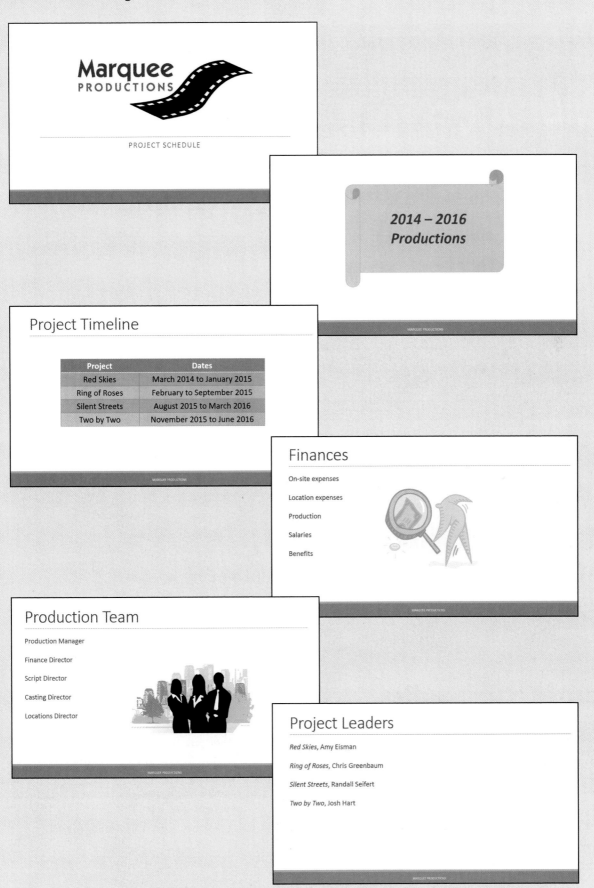

FIGURE 3.7 Challenge 2

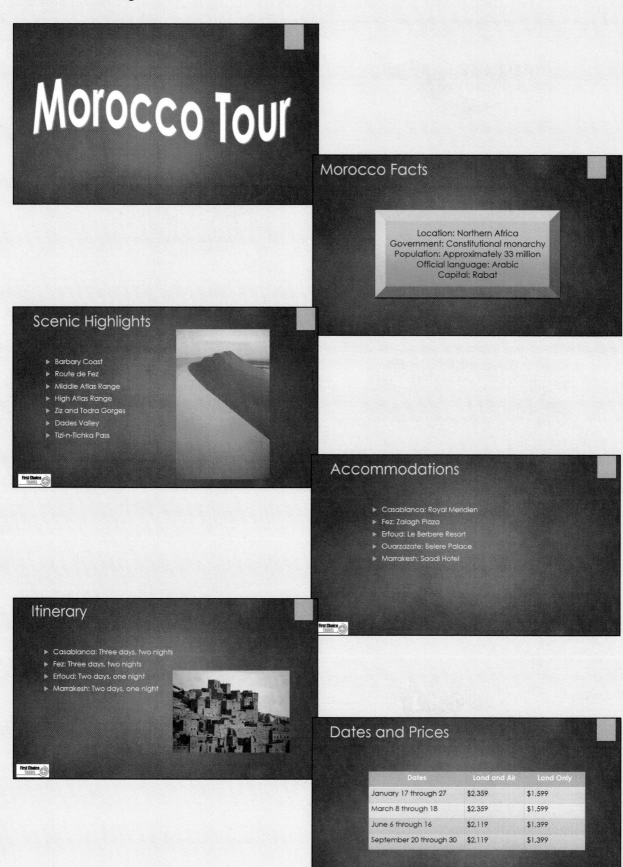

Integrating Programs
Word, Excel, and PowerPoint

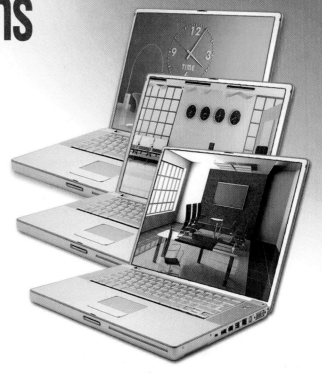

Skills

- Export a PowerPoint presentation to a Word document
- Export a Word outline document to a PowerPoint presentation
- Link an Excel chart with a Word document and a PowerPoint presentation
- Edit a linked object
- Embed a Word table in a PowerPoint presentation
- Edit an embedded object

Projects Overview

Create presentation handouts in Word for use in an annual meeting PowerPoint presentation.

Prepare a PowerPoint presentation for the Distribution Department of Worldwide Enterprises using a Word outline. Copy an Excel chart and link it to the Distribution Department meeting presentation and to a Word document and then edit the linked chart. Copy a Word table containing data on preview distribution dates, embed it in a PowerPoint slide, and then update the table.

Export a PowerPoint presentation containing information on vacation specials offered by First Choice Travel to a Word document.

Link an Excel chart containing information on department enrollments to a PowerPoint slide and then update the chart in Excel. Embed a Word table in a PowerPoint slide and then edit the table in the slide.

Model Answers for Projects

These model answers for the projects you complete in this section provide a preview of the finished projects before you begin working and also allow you to compare your own results with these models to ensure you have created the materials accurately.

Int3-NPCDivPresHandout.docx (a two-page document) is part of the project in Activity 3.1.

Slide 4

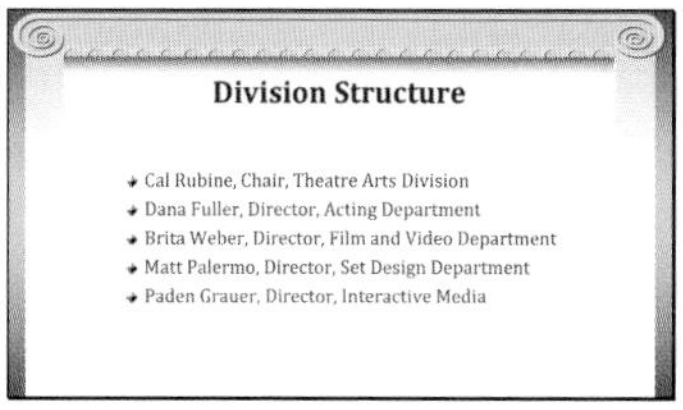

Division Structure

- Cal Rubine, Chair, Theatre Arts Division
- Dana Fuller, Director, Acting Department
- Brita Weber, Director, Film and Video Department
- Matt Palermo, Director, Set Design Department
- Paden Grauer, Director, Interactive Media

Slide 5

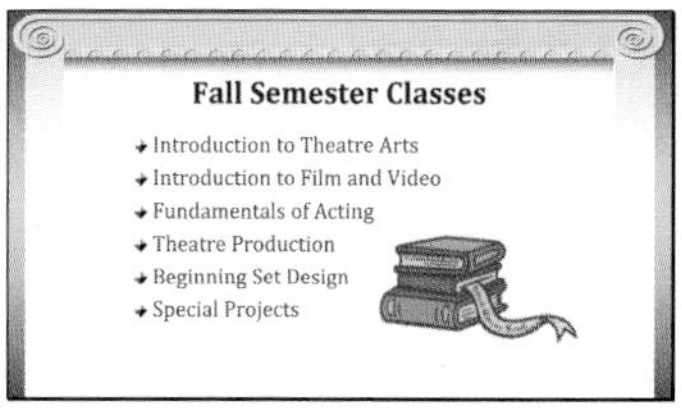

Fall Semester Classes

- Introduction to Theatre Arts
- Introduction to Film and Video
- Fundamentals of Acting
- Theatre Production
- Beginning Set Design
- Special Projects

Slide 6

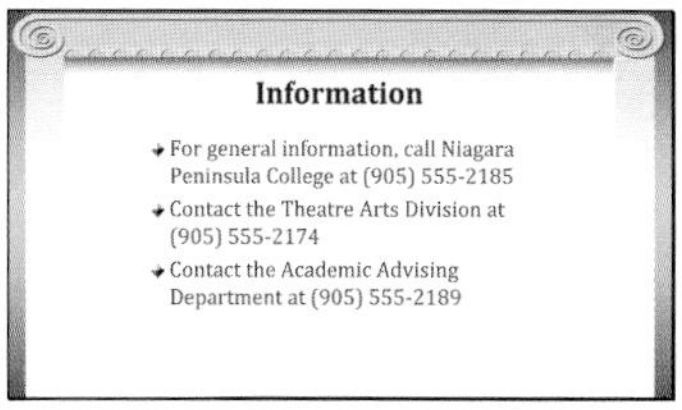

Information

- For general information, call Niagara Peninsula College at (905) 555-2185
- Contact the Theatre Arts Division at (905) 555-2174
- Contact the Academic Advising Department at (905) 555-2189

Int3-NPCDivPres.pptx is part of the project in Activity 3.1.

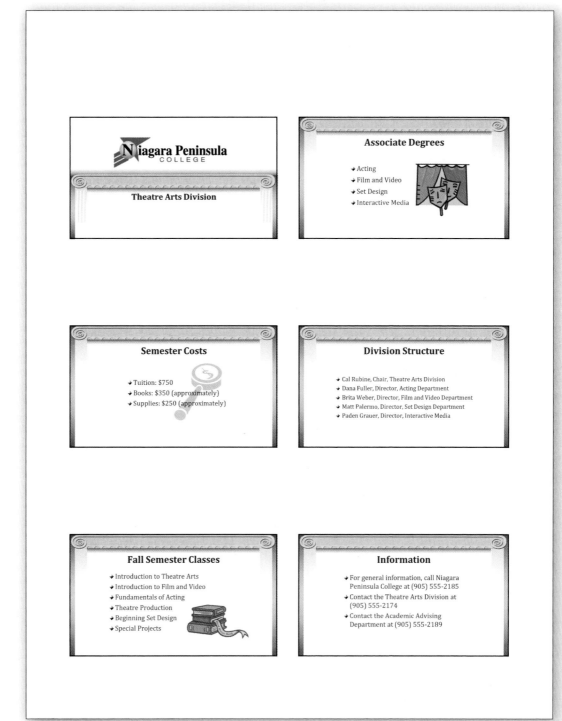

Int3-WEDistDeptMtg.pptx is the project in Activities 3.2 and 3.5 and part of the project in Activities 3.3 and 3.4.

Int3-WERevChart.xlsx is part of the project in Activities 3.3 and 3.4.

Theatre Company	Projected Revenue	Actual Revenue
Picture House	$ 95,075	$ 143,250
Cinema Plus	$ 231,452	$ 251,812
Cinema House	$ 103,460	$ 144,000
Regal Theatres	$ 69,550	$ 50,320
Reels 'R' Us	$ 95,985	$ 163,312
Movie Mania	$ 90,010	$ 85,440

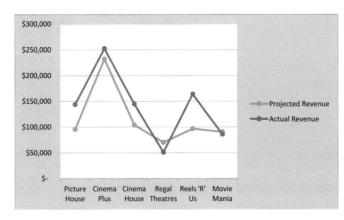

Int3-WERevDoc.docx is part of the project in Activities 3.3 and 3.4.

PRODUCT DISTRIBUTION

Projected/Actual Revenues

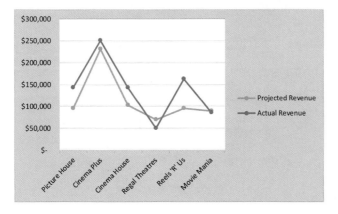

Activity 3.1

Exporting a PowerPoint Presentation to Word

You can send data in one program to another program. For example, you can send Word data to a PowerPoint presentation and data in a PowerPoint presentation to a Word document. To send presentation data to a document, click the FILE tab, click the *Export* option, click the *Create Handouts* option, and then click the Create Handouts button. At the Send to Microsoft Word dialog box that displays, specify the layout of the data in the Word document and whether you want to paste or paste link the data and then click OK. One of the advantages to sending presentation data to a Word document is that you can have greater control over the formatting of the data in Word.

Project Create a handout as a Word document that contains slides from a PowerPoint presentation on the Theatre Arts Division at Niagara Peninsula College.

1. Open PowerPoint and then open **NPCDivPres.pptx**.

2. Save the presentation and name it **Int3-NPCDivPres**.

3. Click the FILE tab, click the *Export* option, click the *Create Handouts* option, and then click the Create Handouts button.

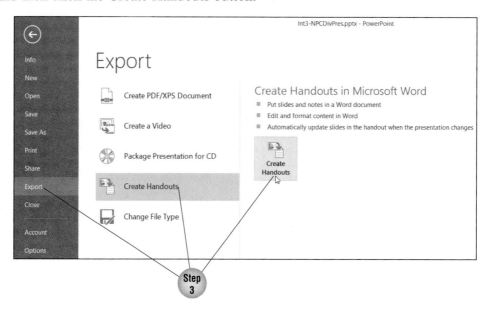

4. At the Send to Microsoft Word dialog box, click the *Blank lines next to slides* option.

5. Click the *Paste link* option located toward the bottom of the dialog box and then click OK.

6 Click the Word button on the Taskbar.

The slides display in a Word document as thumbnails followed by blank lines.

7 Save the Word document in the Integrating3 folder on your storage medium and name it **Int3-NPCDivPresHandout**.

8 Print and then close **Int3-NPCDivPresHandout.docx**.

9 Click the PowerPoint button on the Taskbar.

10 Make Slide 3 active and then change *$650* to *$750*, change *$250* to *$350*, and change *$200* to *$250*.

In Brief

Export PowerPoint Presentation to Word
1. Open presentation.
2. Click FILE tab.
3. Click *Export* option.
4. Click *Create Handouts* option.
5. Click Create Handouts button.
6. Choose desired options at Send to Microsoft Word dialog box.
7. Click OK.

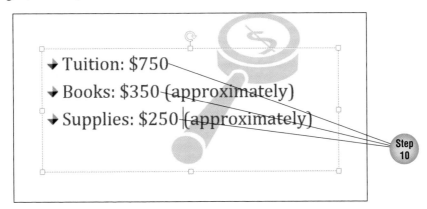

+ Tuition: $750

+ Books: $350 (approximately)

+ Supplies: $250 (approximately)

Step 10

11 Save **Int3-NPCDivPres.pptx**.

12 Click the Word button on the Taskbar and then open **Int3-NPCDivPresHandout.docx**. At the message asking if you want to update the document with the data from the linked files, click Yes.

13 Scroll through the document and notice that the dollar amounts in Slide 3 reflect the changes you made to Slide 3 in the PowerPoint presentation.

14 Save, print, and then close **Int3-NPCDivPresHandout.docx**.

15 Make PowerPoint the active program and then close **Int3-NPCDivPres.pptx**.

In Addition

Pasting and Linking Data

The *Paste* option at the Send to Microsoft Word dialog box is selected by default and is available for all of the page layout options. With this option selected, the data inserted in Word is not connected or linked to the original data in the PowerPoint presentation. If you plan to update the data in the presentation and want the data to be updated in the Word document as well, select the *Paste link* option at the Send to Microsoft Word dialog box. This option is available for all of the page layout options except the *Outline only* option.

Activity 3.2

Exporting a Word Outline to a PowerPoint Presentation

As you learned in the previous section, you can send data in one program to another program. For example, you can send Word data to a PowerPoint presentation and data in a PowerPoint presentation to a Word document. You can create text for slides in a Word outline and then export that outline to PowerPoint. PowerPoint creates new slides based on the heading styles used in the Word outline. Paragraphs formatted with a Heading 1 style become slide titles. Heading 2 text becomes first-level bulleted text, Heading 3 text becomes second-level bulleted text, and so on. If styles are not applied to outline text in Word, PowerPoint uses tabs or indents to place text on slides. To export a Word document to a PowerPoint presentation, you need to insert the Send to Microsoft PowerPoint button on the Quick Access toolbar.

Project

Prepare a presentation for the Distribution department of Worldwide Enterprises using a Word outline.

1. Make sure both Word and PowerPoint are open.

2. With Word the active program, open **WEOutline.docx**.

    Text in this document has been formatted with the Heading 1 and Heading 2 styles.

Step 3

Step 4

3. Insert a Send to Microsoft PowerPoint button on the Quick Access toolbar. Begin by clicking the Customize Quick Access Toolbar button ⬇ that displays at the right side of the Quick Access toolbar.

4. Click *More Commands* at the drop-down list.

5. Click the down-pointing arrow at the right side of the *Choose commands from* option box and then click *All Commands* at the drop-down list.

Step 5

6. Scroll down the list box that displays below the *Choose commands from* option box and then double-click *Send to Microsoft PowerPoint*.

    Items in the list box display in alphabetical order.

7. Click OK to close the Word Options dialog box.

    Notice the Send to Microsoft PowerPoint button has been added to the Quick Access toolbar.

Step 8

8. Send the outline to PowerPoint by clicking the Send to Microsoft PowerPoint button 🗗 on the Quick Access toolbar.

9. When the presentation displays on the screen, make sure Slide 1 is active. (If the presentation does not display, click the PowerPoint button on the Taskbar.)

    The presentation is created with a blank design template.

10 With Slide 1 active, change the layout by clicking the Layout button [image] in the Slides group on the HOME tab and then clicking *Title Slide* at the drop-down list.

11 Make Slide 4 active and apply the Title Only layout. Make Slide 5 active and then apply the Title Only layout. Make Slide 6 active and then apply the Title Only layout.

12 Apply a design theme by clicking the DESIGN tab, clicking the More button [image] at the right side of the Themes thumbnails, and then clicking *Retrospect* (last column, first row in the *Office* section).

13 Save the presentation and name it **Int3-WEDistDeptMtg**.

14 Close **Int3-WEDistDeptMtg.pptx**.

15 Click the Word button on the Taskbar.

16 Right-click the Send to Microsoft PowerPoint button on the Quick Access toolbar and then click the *Remove from Quick Access Toolbar* option at the shortcut menu.

17 Close **WEOutline.docx** without saving the changes.

In Brief

Insert Send to Microsoft PowerPoint Button on Quick Access Toolbar
1. Click Customize Quick Access Toolbar button at right side of Quick Access toolbar.
2. Click More Commands.
3. Click down-pointing arrow at right side of *Choose commands from* list box.
4. Click *All Commands*.
5. Scroll down *Choose commands from* option box, double-click *Send to Microsoft PowerPoint*.
6. Click OK.

Send Word Outline to PowerPoint Presentation
1. Open Word document.
2. Click Send to Microsoft PowerPoint button on Quick Access toolbar.

In Addition

Applying a Style in Word

Heading styles were already applied to the text in WEOutline.docx. If you create an outline in Word that you want to export to PowerPoint, apply styles using options in the Styles group on the HOME tab. A Word document contains a number of predesigned formats grouped into style sets. Click the DESIGN tab to display the available style sets in the Document Formatting group. Choose a style set and the styles visible in the Styles group on the HOME tab change to reflect the set. To display additional available styles, click the More button (contains a horizontal line and a down-pointing triangle) that displays at the right side of the style thumbnails. To apply a heading style, position the insertion point in the desired text, click the More button, and then click the desired style at the drop-down gallery.

Activity 3.3

Linking an Excel Chart with a Word Document and a PowerPoint Presentation

You can copy and link an object such as a table or chart to documents in other programs. For example, you can copy an Excel chart and link it to a Word document and/or a PowerPoint presentation. The advantage to copying and linking over copying and pasting is that you can edit the object in the originating program, called the *source program*, and the object is automatically updated in the linked document in the *destination program*. When an object is linked, the object exists in the source program but not as a separate object in the destination program. Since the object is located only in the source program, changes made to the object in the source program will be reflected in the destination program. An object can be linked to more than one destination program or file.

Project

In preparation for a company meeting, you will copy an Excel chart and then link it to both the Worldwide Enterprises Distribution department meeting presentation and to a Word document.

1 Make sure PowerPoint and Word are open and then open Excel.

2 Make Word the active program and then open **WERevDoc.docx**. Save the document with Save As and name it **Int3-WERevDoc**.

3 Make PowerPoint the active program, open **Int3-WEDistDeptMtg.pptx**, and then make Slide 6 active.

4 Make Excel the active program and then open **WERevChart.xlsx**. Save the workbook with Save As and name it **Int3-WERevChart**.

5 Copy and link the chart to the Word document and the PowerPoint presentation. Start by clicking once in the chart to select it.

> Make sure you select the entire chart and not a specific chart element. Try selecting the chart by clicking just inside the chart border.

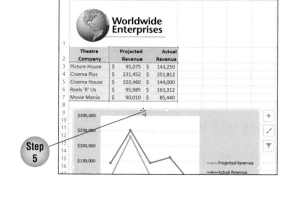

6 With the chart selected, click the Copy button in the Clipboard group on the HOME tab.

7 Click the Word button on the Taskbar.

8 Press Ctrl + End to move the insertion point to the end of the document.

9 Click the Paste button arrow and then click *Paste Special* at the drop-down list.

10 At the Paste Special dialog box, click the *Paste link* option, click the *Microsoft Excel Chart Object* option in the *As* list box, and then click OK.

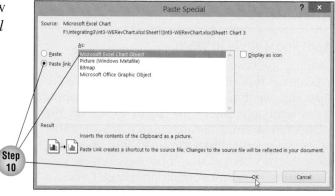

11. Select the chart and then center it by clicking the Center button in the Paragraph group on the HOME tab.

12. Save, print, and then close **Int3-WERevDoc.docx**.

13. Click the PowerPoint button on the Taskbar.

14. With Slide 6 active, make sure the HOME tab is selected, click the Paste button arrow, and then click *Paste Special* at the drop-down list.

15. At the Paste Special dialog box, click the *Paste link* option, make sure *Microsoft Excel Chart Object* is selected in the *As* list box, and then click OK.

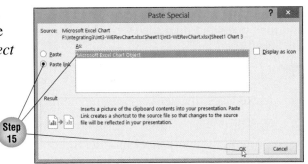

16. Increase the size of the chart so it better fills the slide and then move the chart so it is centered on the slide, as shown in Figure 3.1.

17. Click outside the chart to deselect it.

18. Save the presentation, print only Slide 6, and then close **Int3-WEDistDeptMtg.pptx**.

19. Click the Excel button on the Taskbar.

20. Click outside the chart to deselect it.

21. Save, print, and then close **Int3-WERevChart.xlsx**.

In Brief

Link Object between Programs
1. Open source program, open file containing object.
2. Select object, click Copy button.
3. Open destination program, open file into which object will be linked.
4. Click Paste button arrow, click Paste Special.
5. At Paste Special dialog box, click Paste link.
6. Click OK.

FIGURE 3.1 Step 15

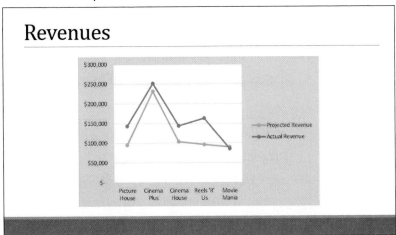

In Addition

Linking Data or an Object within a Program

In this section, you learned to link an object between programs using the Paste Special drop-down list. You can also link an object in Word using options at the Object dialog box. To do this, click the INSERT tab and then click the Object button. At the Object dialog box, click the Create from File tab. At the dialog box, type the desired file name in the *File name* text box or click the Browse button and then select the desired file from the appropriate folder. Click the *Link to file* check box to insert a check mark and then click OK.

Activity 3.4

The advantage to linking an object over copying is that editing the object in the source program will automatically update the object in the destination program(s). To edit a linked object, open the file containing the object in the source program, make the desired edits, and then save the file. The next time you open the document, workbook, or presentation in the destination program, the object will be updated.

Project

Edit the actual and projected revenue numbers in the Worldwide Enterprises Excel worksheet and then open and print the Word document and the PowerPoint presentation that contain the linked chart.

① Make sure Word, Excel, and PowerPoint are open.

② Make Excel the active program and then open **Int3-WERevChart.xlsx**.

③ You discover that one theatre company was left out of the revenues chart. Add a row to the worksheet by clicking once in cell A6 to make it active. Click the Insert button arrow in the Cells group on the HOME tab and then click *Insert Sheet Rows*.

④ Type the following data in the specified cells:

  A6: **Regal Theatres**
  B6: **69550**
  C6: **50320**

⑤ Click in cell A3.

⑥ Save, print, and close **Int3-WERevChart.xlsx** and then close Excel.

⑦ Make Word the active program and then open **Int3-WERevDoc.docx**. At the message asking if you want to update the linked file, click the Yes button.

⑧ Notice how the linked chart is automatically updated to reflect the changes you made to it in Excel.

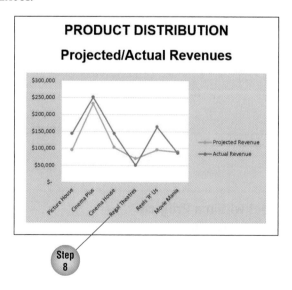

9 Save, print, and then close **Int3-WERevDoc.docx**.

10 Make PowerPoint the active program and then open **Int3-WEDistDeptMtg.pptx**.

11 At the message telling you that the presentation contains links, click the Update Links button.

12 Make Slide 6 active and then notice how the linked chart has been automatically updated to reflect the changes you made to the chart in Excel.

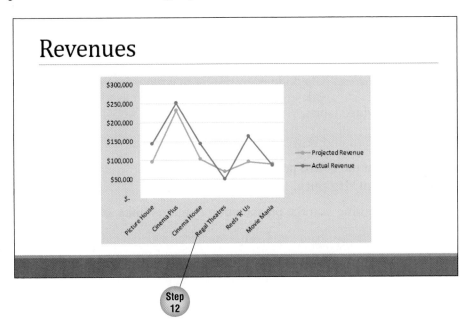

Step 12

13 Save the presentation and then print only Slide 6.

14 Close **Int3-WEDistDeptMtg.pptx**.

In Addition

Updating a Link Manually

You can choose to update a link manually in the destination program. To do this, open a Word document containing a linked object. Right-click the object, point to *Linked (type of object) Object*, and then click *Links*. At the Links dialog box, click the *Manual update* option and then click OK. With *Manual update* selected, the link will only be updated when you right-click the linked object and then click *Update Link* or when you display the Links dialog box, click the link in the list box, and then click the Update Now button.

Activity 3.5

Embedding and Editing a Word Table in a PowerPoint Presentation

You can copy and paste, copy and link, or copy and embed an object from one file into another. A *linked object* resides in the source program but not as a separate object in the destination program. An *embedded object* resides in the source program as well as in the destination program. If you make a change to an embedded object at the source program, the change will not be made to the object in the destination program. The main advantage to embedding rather than simply copying and pasting is that you can edit an embedded object in the destination program using the tools of the source program.

Project

Copy a Word table containing data on preview distribution dates for Worldwide Enterprises and then embed the table in a slide in a PowerPoint presentation. Update the distribution dates for the two embedded tables.

1. Make sure the Word and PowerPoint programs are open.

2. Make PowerPoint the active program and then open **Int3-WEDistDeptMtg.pptx**.

3. At the message telling you the presentation contains links, click the Update Links button.

4. Make Slide 4 active.

5. Make Word the active program and then open **WEPrevDistTable.docx**.

6. Click in a cell in the table and then select the table. To do this, click the TABLE TOOLS LAYOUT tab, click the Select button  in the Table group, and then click *Select Table* at the drop-down list.

7. With the table selected, click the HOME tab and then click the Copy button in the Clipboard group.

8. Click the PowerPoint button on the Taskbar.

9. With Slide 4 active, click the Paste button arrow and then click *Paste Special* at the drop-down list.

10. At the Paste Special dialog box, click *Microsoft Word Document Object* in the *As* list box and then click OK.

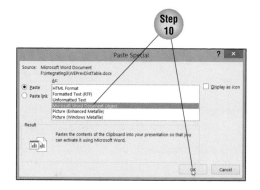

Step 10

11. With the table selected in the slide, use the sizing handles to increase the size and change the position of the table as shown in Figure 3.2.

FIGURE 3.2 Step 11

Preview Distribution

Theatre Company	Location	Date
Cinema House	Montreal, Toronto	May 18
Cinema House	Vancouver	May 11
Cinema Plus	Los Angeles, San Diego	May 4
Cinema Plus	New York, Newark	May 11
Movie Mania	Wichita	May 25
Picture House	St. Louis	May 25
Picture House	Denver	May 18
Picture House	Salt Lake City	May 25

In Brief

Embed Object
1. Open source program, open file containing object.
2. Select object, click Copy button.
3. Open destination program, open file into which object will be embedded.
4. Click Paste button arrow, *Paste Special.*
5. At Paste Special dialog box, click object in *As* list box.
6. Click OK.

Edit Embedded Object
1. Open file containing embedded object.
2. Double-click object.
3. Make edits, click outside object to deselect it.

(12) Click outside the table to deselect it.

(13) Save the presentation and then print only Slide 4.

(14) Click the Word button on the Taskbar and then close the document.

(15) Click the PowerPoint button on the Taskbar and then make Slide 5 active.

(16) Make Word the active program and then open **WEGenDistTable.docx**.

(17) Click in a cell in the table and then select the table. To do this, click the TABLE TOOLS LAYOUT tab, click the Select button in the Table group, and then click *Select Table* at the drop-down list.

(18) Click the HOME tab and then click the Copy button in the Clipboard group.

(19) Click the PowerPoint button on the Taskbar.

(20) With Slide 5 active, click the Paste button arrow and then click *Paste Special* at the drop-down list.

(21) At the Paste Special dialog box, click *Microsoft Word Document Object* in the *As* list box and then click OK.

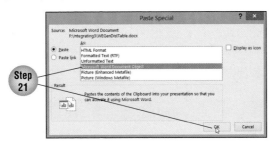

(22) Increase the size and position of the table in the slide so it displays as shown in Figure 3.3 on the next page.

(23) The distribution date to Cinema Plus in Sacramento and Oakland has been delayed until June 1. Edit the date by double-clicking the table in the slide.

> Double-clicking the table displays the Word tabs and ribbon at the top of the screen. A horizontal and vertical ruler also display around the table.

continues

24 Using the mouse, select *May 25* in the *Sacramento, Oakland* row and then type **June 1**.

25 Click outside the table to deselect it.

Clicking outside the table deselects it and removes the Word tabs.

26 Print Slide 5 of the presentation.

27 Apply a transition and sound of your choosing to all slides in the presentation and then run the presentation.

28 Save and close **Int3-WEDistDeptMtg.pptx** and then close PowerPoint.

29 Click the Word button on the Taskbar, close the document, and then close Word.

FIGURE 3.3 Step 22

General Distribution

Theater Company	Location	Date
Cinema House	Winnipeg	June 15
Cinema House	Regina, Calgary	June 8
Cinema Plus	Sacramento, Oakland	May 25
Cinema Plus	Trenton, Atlantic City	May 25
Movie Mania	Omaha, Springfield	June 15
Picture House	Dallas	June 1
Picture House	Santa Fe, Albuquerque	June 8

In Addition

Working with a Cropped Object

Some embedded or linked objects may appear cropped on the right or bottom side of the object even if enough room is available to fit the image on the page or slide. A large embedded or linked object may appear cropped because Word converts the object into a Windows metafile (.wmf), which has a maximum height and width. If the embedded or linked object exceeds this maximum size, it appears cropped. To prevent an object from appearing cropped, consider reducing the size of the data by changing formatting such as reducing the font size, column size, line spacing, and so on.

Skills Review

Review 1 Exporting a PowerPoint Presentation to Word

1. Open Word and PowerPoint.
2. With PowerPoint the active program, open **FCTVacations.pptx** and then save it in the IntegratingEOS folder and name it **Int3-R-FCTVacations**.
3. Send the PowerPoint data to Word as slides with blank lines next to them. Click the *Blank lines next to slides* option and the *Paste link* option at the Send to Microsoft Word dialog box.
4. Save the Word document in the IntegratingEOS folder and name it **Int3-R-FCTVacSpecials**.
5. Print and then close **Int3-R-FCTVacSpecials.docx**.
6. Click the PowerPoint button on the Taskbar.
7. Make Slide 4 active and then change *$950* to *$1,050*, change *$1,175* to *$1,275*, and change *$1,215* to *$1,315*.
8. Save the presentation and then print Slide 4.
9. Make Word the active program, open **Int3-R-FCTVacSpecials.docx**, and then click Yes at the question asking if you want to update the link.
10. Print only page 2 of **Int3-R-FCTVacSpecials.docx**.
11. Save and then close the document.
12. Make PowerPoint the active program and then close **Int3-R-FCTVacations.pptx**.

Review 2 Linking and Editing an Excel Chart in a PowerPoint Slide

1. Make sure PowerPoint is open and then open Excel.
2. Make PowerPoint the active program and then open **NPCEnroll.pptx**.
3. Save the presentation in the IntegratingEOS folder and name it **Int3-R-NPCEnroll**.
4. Make Slide 4 active.
5. Make Excel the active program and then open the workbook named **NPCEnrollChart.xlsx**. Save the workbook in the IntegratingEOS folder and name it **Int3-R-NPCEnrollChart**.
6. Click the chart once to select it (make sure you select the entire chart and not just a chart element) and then copy and link the chart to Slide 4 in **Int3-R-NPCEnroll.pptx**. (Be sure to use the Paste Special dialog box to link the chart.)
7. Increase the size of the chart to better fill the slide and then center the chart on the slide.
8. Click outside the chart to deselect it.
9. Save the presentation, print only Slide 4, and then close the presentation.
10. Click the Excel button on the Taskbar.
11. Click outside the chart to deselect it.
12. Save and then print **Int3-R-NPCEnrollChart.xlsx**.
13. Insert another department in the worksheet (and chart) by making cell A7 active, clicking the Insert button arrow in the Cells group on the HOME tab, and then clicking *Insert Sheet Rows* at the drop-down list. (This creates a new row 7.) Type the following text in the specified cells:
    A7: **Directing**
    B7: **18**
    C7: **32**
    D7: **25**
14. Click in cell A4.
15. Save, print, and close **Int3-R-NPCEnrollChart.xlsx** and then close Excel.
16. Click the PowerPoint button on the Taskbar and then open **Int3-R-NPCEnroll.pptx**. At the message telling you that the presentation contains links, click the Update Links button.

17. Display Slide 4 and note the change to the chart.

18. Save the presentation, print only Slide 4, and then close the presentation.

Review 3 Embedding and Editing a Word Table in a PowerPoint Slide

1. With Word and PowerPoint open, make PowerPoint the active program and then open **Int3-R-NPCEnroll.pptx**. At the message telling you that the presentation contains links, click the Update Links button.

2. Make Slide 5 active.

3. Make Word the active program and then open **NPCContacts.docx**.

4. Select the table and then copy and embed it in Slide 5 in **Int3-R-NPCEnroll.pptx**. (Make sure you use the Paste Special dialog box.)

5. With the table selected in the slide, use the sizing handles to increase the size and change the position of the table so it better fills the slide.

6. Click outside the table to deselect it and then save the presentation.

7. Double-click the table, select *Editing* in the name *Emerson Editing*, and then type **Edits**.

8. Click outside the table to deselect it.

9. Print Slide 5 of the presentation.

10. Apply a transition and sound of your choosing to all slides in the presentation.

11. Run the presentation.

12. Save and then close **Int3-R-NPCEnroll.pptx** and then close PowerPoint.

13. Close the Word document **NPCContacts.docx** and then close Word.

INDEX